Notes &
Queries

VOLUME 5

Notes & Queries

VOLUME 5

edited by

Joseph Harker

FOURTH ESTATE · *London*

First published in Great Britain in 1994 by
Fourth Estate Limited
289 Westbourne Grove
London W11 2QA

Copyright © 1994 by Guardian Newspapers Ltd

The right of Joseph Harker to be identified as the editor of
this work has been asserted by him in accordance with the
Copyright, Designs and Patents Act 1988.

A catalogue record for this book is available from the British
Library

ISBN 1–85702–266–1

Typeset by Books Unlimited (Nottm), Rainworth, NG21 0JE
Printed in Great Britain by Cox & Wyman Ltd, Reading

QUESTION: Over the past 2,500 years, some of the best brains that mankind has produced have studied the problems of philosophy. What problems of relevance to everyday life have they solved?

☐ BEFORE the 19th century, there was no science and there were no scientists, and what we would now call science was done by philosophers. Democritus contributed the atomic theory of matter; Archimedes his screw (still used in jacks and pumps as well as to propel ships and aircraft); Pascal the theory of probability; Copernicus modern astronomy; Newton the dynamics which is still universally useful in engineering; Hobbes artificial intelligence (thinking as calculation); and so on. Today, when we don't know how to set about solving a problem (when there is no established scientific method) we have to step back a pace and do philosophy – we have to think about the way we think until we can come up with a new scientific method or even a completely new science. Then we can get back to work and stop philosophising until we get stuck again. Indeed, anybody who finds himself in difficulties in work or life and stops to think about the way he is working or living, instead of pressing on in the old way, is doing philosophy.
Grahame Leman, London W3.

☐ PHILOSOPHERS are sometimes criticised for arguing amongst themselves, but artists and scientists argue amongst themselves too. Artists have brought you costume drama, scientists have brought you television, but philosophers have brought you the right to vote; the right not to be sold into slavery; the right to trial by jury and equality before the law; freedom of speech . . . Sufficiently relevant to everyday life?
Michael Hampson, Harlow, Essex.

☐ THE questioner should ask, first of all, if he/she would even be able to pose the question without the study of philosophy.
Edward Carter, Department of Artificial Intelligence, University of Edinburgh.

☐ PHILOSOPHERS do not solve problems, but create them in forms ever more difficult to solve, thus perpetuating philosophy. This is not unique; economists, sociologists and politicians behave in exactly the same way with corresponding consequences.
Professor Sir James Beament, Queens' College, Cambridge.

☐ AT THE last lecture of my moral philosophy course our professor said: 'Don't think you're no further forward. The value of studying philosophy is that you've reached a more informed state of ignorance.'
Alan Brown, Glasgow.

QUESTION: What is the purpose of sneezing, and what triggers it when it is useless? Medical works refer to my uncontrollable bouts of sneezing as non-specific allergic rhinitis, but it's difficult to imagine what it could be an allergic reaction to.

☐ NON-SPECIFIC allergic rhinitis is a nonsense term. Allergic rhinitis can only be specific, because it must be caused by an allergen. The term is implying that superficial questioning has not elicited any clear causal relationship between exposure to an allergen and the sneezing. Although it fulfils the fundamental definitions of an allergy, allergic rhinitis may not involve the type of antibody classically concerned in allergy, immunoglobulin E (IgE), and the cause or causes are often masked so that active steps have to be taken to uncover them. It may be due to house dust mites, or foods (different in different cases), but it may also be due to chemicals, mainly modern synthetic chemicals to which exposure has been increasing dramatically in the 'developed' world, especially since the Second World War. It is interesting to note that the prevalence of hay fever increased in London over a period when the pollen count actually dropped. The physiological purpose of sneezing is to free the nose of irritants, but if the nasal irritation results from the consumption of a non-tolerated food, sneezing serves no useful purpose.

D. J. Maberly and H. M. Anthony, Airedale General Hospital, Keighley, West Yorks.

QUESTION: Is it true that freemasons wear a ring on the small finger of the left hand to identify one another? If so, am I right to be worried about the large number of influential members of society who seem to sport rings on this part of their anatomy?

☐ THE fashion for wearing a 'pinky ring' on the small finger of the left hand was a popular codified way for gay men to identify one another earlier this century. There are photographs showing Oscar Wilde wearing one in the 1890s (it is prominent in Beerbohm's famous caricature of him). Ivor Novello and Noël Coward were never without one, and Jean Cocteau took to sporting one at the end of his life. The practice was by no means universal and had died out by the 1960s – perhaps to spare gay men the indignity of being mistaken for freemasons?

Adam Williams, Brighton, Sussex.

QUESTION: Why does the French president, François Mitterrand, attend Nato meetings?

☐ ALTHOUGH President de Gaulle announced in 1966 that France would withdraw from the military organisation of Nato, it remained a full member of the civil structure – where political, economic and logistical issues are discussed. France no longer participates in the work of the Nato Defence Planning Committee, and all Nato military installations in France have been transferred elsewhere. Iceland has a similar status as member solely of Nato's political structure.

Hilary Stephenson, Bedford.

QUESTION: An electrician once told me that fluorescent tubes should be arranged at angles to each other, because the polarisation of the light causes some sort of problem if they are mounted along parallel lines. What sort of problem, and why do I see them lined up on the ceiling of my local superstore?

☐ THE light from fluorescent tubes and ordinary incandescent lamps is randomly polarised – that is it has no fixed direction. Hence there can be no reason for arranging fluorescent lights in any particular pattern because of the polarisation of the light. Our eyes are in any case unable to perceive polarisation directly.
Professor Harvey Rutt, Department of Electronics, University of Southampton.

QUESTION: I am intrigued as to the origins of the word 'camp' as a description of effeminate behaviour. Can anyone enlighten me?

☐ THE expression is supposed to originate from the New York police who were alleged to have scrawled across certain detainees' files: 'Known as male prostitute' or 'Kamp'.
D. A. Fisher, Maidenhead, Berks.

☐ THE dictionary *Gay Talk* defines 'camp' as coming from a 16th-century theatrical term 'camping', meaning 'young men wearing the costume of women in a play', from the French word *campagne*, the countryside, 'where . . . mime troops entertained' in medieval times.
Anne Cunningham, Liverpool.

QUESTION: We are told we should be worrying about the increased skin cancer risks arising from ozone depletion. Given that we spend more time indoors and cover our bodies more than our primitive ancestors, shouldn't this

more than compensate for any increased ultraviolet radiation?

☐ THE dangers of ultraviolet radiation on the skin are actually made worse by spending more time indoors and covering more of our bodies than our primitive ancestors. When in hot sun, we take off bits of our clothing, often exposing untanned skin which burns in minutes. Moderate regular exposure to sun is protective as it reduces the chance of burning and cell damage. As in most things, moderation is the answer, such as a gentle, preferably complete, suntan. An additional benefit of allowing skin to be seen is that any abnormalities are immediately visible and can be treated before they become dangerous.
David Brinicombe, Ealing, London W5.

QUESTION: Does power always corrupt? Or have any despots actually been benevolent?

☐ THE answer to the first part is probably yes – at least where power means that the holder is given the opportunity to abuse it, and self-interest dictates that she/he should do so. The answer to the second part must be yes, as long as said despot is not expected to be benevolent towards everyone she/he rules. Cromwell had his supporters, for instance: those who stood to gain from the removal of feudal restrictions on commerce; from the suppression of the threat represented by the Levellers; from the crushing of independent commercial activity in Ireland – namely, the nascent English middle class. The same sort of thing might be said about Napoleon. Or even Margaret Thatcher. One group of people's 'despotism', or oppression, is usually another group's 'benevolence'. Each self-interest group used, of course, to be called a class; and difference of interests between such groups used to be called class conflict. But, as we all know, there is no such thing as class any more. The representatives of the ruling business class told us that.
Paul Burroughs, Beeston, Leeds.

QUESTION: I am very keen to stage a mummers' play. But although the major bookshops and the local library can obtain various commentaries about mummings, and Thomas Hardy outlines the plot in *Return of the Native*, an actual text remains elusive. Where can I find a copy of this ancient and traditional entertainment?

□ THE Vaughan Williams Memorial Library contains scores of mummers' play texts. Mumming (guising in Scotland) is the folk drama of villages and towns throughout the British Isles and the English-speaking world. While debate continues over origins and meaning, the most well-researched and accessible information is on the players. These range from established characters like St George, Turkish Knight and Robin Hood; to 19th- and 20th-century contemporary figures like Napoleon, Father Christmas, bikers, body builders and Nazis. It is often difficult to get hold of a play text unless your local community is involved in one. They are frequently unpublished, out of print or have a small print run. Organisations to try are ourselves; the Centre for English Cultural Tradition and Language at the University of Sheffield; and the Folklore Society at University College, London. There are also a number of individual researchers working in this field. The Library is hoping to publish a range of mummers' plays from around England in the near future. Until then the questioner can always contact us and we will be happy to supply particular texts for a small fee.

Brian Holmshaw, Vaughan Williams Memorial Library, English Folk Dance and Song Society, London NW1.

QUESTION: Who rules the bar code? Who grants, administers, controls the allocation of lines and numbers? Soon, it seems, every article on sale will carry a bar code. No doubt human beings, for convenience, will get their own. Shall I be allowed to choose my own and sign myself thus, making redundant the cumbersome signature?

☐ THE most familiar bar codes are administered by EAN International which was established in Brussels in 1977 as the then European Article Numbering Association. The now international article numbering system, or EAN as it is still known, is used in over 65 countries and administered in the UK by the Article Number Association. Each national numbering authority allocates blocks of numbers to its members, who then use these numbers (shown as bar codes) to identify their products. The bar codes contain no information; all the product details are held on a database which uses the article number as a reference. If individuals were ever bar-coded, the numbers would have to be allocated centrally so you would not be able to choose your own. Certain specific numbers associated with people – some passport numbers, for example, are already bar-coded. However, a universal and unified system for the identification of people, similar to EAN's universal and unified numbering of products, is not a prospect.
A. T. Osborne, Secretary General, Article Number Association, London WC2.

QUESTION: Why can't we buy tinned bananas?

☐ ABOUT 10 years ago, in a New Zealand supermarket, I actually bought a tin of bananas. The particular brand I encountered – which from memory was from a Pacific island – instructed the user to open the tin and upend on to a plate. We lifted the tin to reveal a freestanding mass of uniformly finger-like objects, surrounded by a sea of orange-coloured ooze. Those of us game enough to taste them agreed they tasted unnervingly un-banana, and found the dense floury texture unpleasant. We put the remainder (i.e. most of the tin) in the fridge, hoping they might taste better the next day, or the day after that. They didn't. My advice, should the questioner ever see a tin of bananas, is to walk on by.
Joy Martin-Holm, Kensal Rise, London NW6.

QUESTION: Economists and politicians tell us that it

is becoming more difficult to support the increasing
proportion of pensioners. On the other hand we are encouraged to stay healthy in order to extend our life expec-
tancy. Is this wise advice?

☐ THE introduction of VAT on heating bills should help redress the
tiresome imbalance of the ageing population.
Ian Mankin, London NW1.

**QUESTION: Considering (i) changes in the laws covering
rights of assembly and strike action; (ii) the growth of
quangos staffed by unelected Tory place men; (iii) the extent of the Official Secrets Act; and (iv) the electoral system,
is Britain now a dictatorship?**

☐ BRITAIN is described as a 'parliamentary monarchy'. In theory,
at least, elected Members of Parliament speak/act/vote on behalf
of the people of this country (their constituents). But since we do
not operate under a system of proportional representation, the
voice of the people is not always heard or heeded. MPs and civil
servants, like anybody else, can be corrupted with offers of money
or other benefits. Unfortunately, we hear about far too many in-
cidents of this kind, particularly among government ministers.
Beyond a doubt, our rights and civil liberties have been eroded so
much over the last 15 years that George Orwell would have been
spot-on had he entitled his book 1994. By European and American standards we live in a kind of police state and are at the mercy
of the establishment and bureaucrats. Our 'Freedom of Information' Act is a farce. If we had real freedom of information, there
would be no censure of the press; matters of government would
be open to public scrutiny; and we would be able to obtain details
of everything, from the exact ingredients of bangers to the names
of both defendant and plaintiff in all cases. On the other hand, a
'dictatorship' is the office of someone invested with absolute
authority, who presumably has the right to do anything he wants

within his own country without having to answer for it. Somehow, I don't think John Major could walk into the Bank of England and be given cash for his Spanish holiday, or have Mrs Thatcher shot for slagging him off. It is true that we don't have a great many liberties, but we do not live in a dictatorship.
M. Roy, Battersea, London SW.

☐ THE correct term is 'Oligator-ship'. The Oligarchs are the City, the owners of the right-wing press, directors and organisations who subscribe to Tory funds etc. They lurk beneath the surface, largely concealed from the public on whom they are preda-tory. The alligators and crocodiles are the oldest surviving relatives of the dinosaurs.
Peter Rowland, Dulwich, London SE24.

QUESTION: The human brain has approximately 1 billion cells and the Milky Way consists of a similar number of stars. Is the Milky Way likely to be sentient?

☐ IT IS not the number of items (brain cells or stars) which produce sentience, but the communication between them. In the case of a human brain possessing some 10^{12} neurons, each is estimated to receive between 100 and 1,000 inputs from other neurons giving rise to an estimated connectibility of 10^{14} to 10^{15}. Such a network has a large capacity for information-processing and obviously exhibits sentience. Large star systems, e.g. galaxies like the Milky Way, would appear to possess at best only a primitive sentience. Communication between stars is undirected, their energy (information equivalent) is radiated in all directions, not in a few as is the case with brain neural networks. In addition, inter-stellar distances are so large that, even at the speed of light, transmission is extremely slow. Although neural transmission is relatively poor at 100 metres/second, neurons are very much closer together than are stars.
David Piggins, Department of Psychology, University of Wales, Bangor.

QUESTION: In my wine bottles there appears a large lower case 'e' after the quantity, i.e. '70 cl. e' The letter appears on tomatoes from Sainsbury's but not on their tinned beans. What does it mean and why on some containers and not on others?

☐ THE 'e' is placed on packages of a weight, volume or size which is standard throughout the European Union. Standards exist for food, soaps and other products sold in more than one country. Thus, there is an 'e' on wine bottles because 75cl is standard for wine, but no 'e' on Sainsbury's tinned beans, either because there is no standard or because the tin is non-standard.
Kevin Khayat, Canterbury, Kent.

☐ MR KHAYAT is incorrect. The 'e' indicates that the measure in question is an *average* for the package concerned, rather than a *minimum*, as was the case in the UK until we adopted the European average measure system in 1979. As a result of this change, consumers now get slightly less for their money.
Simon Green, Hull, Humberside.

QUESTION: Last year when flying home from Italy I was told not to smoke my pipe in the aircraft. The stewardess told me that in the event of sudden depressurisation, the pipe would burst into flames whereas a cigarette would automatically be extinguished. Is this true?

☐ MODERN passenger aircraft are designed to supply pure oxygen when emergencies affecting cabin pressure occur. Any glowing carbonaceous material, in the presence of oxygen-enriched air, will decompose rapidly, often violently. However, I suspect that a secondary reason for prohibiting pipes and cigars relates to the fact that there are air-conditioning limitations in passenger air-craft. These systems depend on recirculated air, and excessive smoking of pipes and cigars in particular would result in a poor atmosphere in the passenger cabin.
Martin W. Kennedy (retired fireman), Dunstable, Beds.

QUESTION: The Tate Gallery apparently has a "Curator of Creative Interpretation". Does creative interpretation resemble creative accounting, and does the curator collect choice examples of it or is he free to invent his own?

☐ I AM the Curator of Interpretation at the Tate Gallery. I don't know where the 'Creative' came from – a satirical jibe by a tabloid critic perhaps? I do collect examples of good practice from other institutions, but my principal role is to write or edit the texts which the Tate produces for its general public. These include exhibition guides, such as a Picasso picture book, and free room-by-room guides, as well as the individual captions the Tate now has for every work on display in its permanent collections. I am the author of *The Tate Illustrated Companion* – 300 colour plates plus extensive commentary. I act as the Gallery's spokesman when the media get excited about piles of bricks or rice; I keep a watching brief on our visitor care generally, and am responsible for training the Tate Guides. 'Interpretations' are not invented. Our aim is to provide information about the collections that is factual. Where possible the interpretative material is based on the artist's own intentions in making the work, otherwise it is based on the most authoritative scholarship available. All major and most minor public museums and galleries nowadays have someone who performs the functions I have outlined, either under the heading of Interpretation or of Education. The increasing development of these services in recent years is the result of a new determination among museums to make their collections accessible to a wider audience, rather than remaining, as has too often been the case, the exclusive provinces of specialist curators and connoisseurs.
Simon Wilson, Tate Gallery, London SW1.

QUESTION: I am ticklish but all attempts to tickle myself are totally ineffective, why?

☐ ARTHUR Koestler, in *The Act of Creation*, explored this issue. He quotes Darwin as suggesting that the squirming is an automatic reflex to escape a hostile grip on vulnerable areas of the body not normally exposed to attack. The laughter required an additional condition – that the attack is perceived as a *mock* attempt; the laughter is a means of releasing the tension caused by fear over-ruled by intellect. Thus we do not laugh or squirm when tickling ourselves, since we do not perceive the attack attempt as real – and certainly we do not laugh when a real attack is launched at these areas.

Mark Pike, Alton, Hants.

QUESTION: I have heard that, in the early part of the First World War, the Royal Navy used sea-lions to give warning of enemy submarines in naval bases. The animals were trained to surface and bark if they heard what might be a submarine's engines. Is there any truth in this?

☐ IN 1916, the Admiralty conducted a secret series of experiments with the help of Hengler's Circus in Glasgow in which sea-lions were trained to track enemy submarines. Tests lasted for a year – first in Glasgow, later at Bala Lake in Wales, and finally in the Solent. The tests in fresh water were a success, but in the busy salt water seaway the animals were too distracted for the experiments to be adopted in active service.

Dave Harvie, Dumbarton.

QUESTION: How many sheets of A4 paper would I have to recycle to save a tree?

☐ TWO. One to write to the Mailing Preference Service requesting that they arrange to stop all unsolicited mail deliveries to your address; and the second to make an envelope for the first.

P. G. Waterson, Bishopbriggs, Glasgow.

☐ IT IS a fallacy to assume that paper is made from trees growing wild which will be spared to live out their full natural life if not used to make paper. In fact, all the trees required to make paper for use in the near future have already been planted, and will be made into paper regardless. If more paper is recycled, the price of unrecycled paper will drop in order to maintain demand. However, this reduction in price will reduce tree planting to meet anticipated future demand. So if you love trees for their own sake you should not recycle at all but on the contrary use as much unrecycled paper as possible.
Mike Scott, Chester.

☐ A SIMPLISTIC answer to this would be 15,000 sheets. This assumes that it takes between 10 and 17 trees to form the raw material for one tonne of paper, and that the weight of the paper is $80g/m^2$, standard for most printing and photocopying papers. It is true, as Mike Scott says, that most of the trees used for paper manufacture are grown for the purpose, and that the felled trees are replaced. However, the demand for paper has meant that old forests – which are more valuable for wildlife – have been replaced by managed plantations. So recycling paper does help to protect some wildlife habitats. It also has significant environmental benefits through energy savings and reducing emissions of pollutants. It is not possible to recycle paper indefinitely, as it gradually degrades in the process, so the input of some virgin fibre into the production process is necessary.
Penny Pitty, Waste Watch, London SW1.

QUESTION: An inscription at St Andrew's church at Kirson reads: 'Bleffed be the Lord God of our Fathers which hath put fuch a thing as this in the King's heart to beautify the houfe of the Lord.' Why is the letter 'S' written like an 'F' in some places and not in others?

☐ IN COMMON with other Teutonic languages, English allots two distinct sounds to the letter S. One is the soft, sibilant sound, whilst the other is harder and equates to a 'Z'. Until about 200 years ago, English, like German, used two symbols to represent these sounds: the 'long S' at the beginning or medial position of a word, and the normal form of S at the end, as for example in words like 'mifs', 'fuccefs'. German retains a special character, the 'eszett' for the double S. As long ago as 1749, Joseph Ames, in his *Typographical Antiquities*, discarded the long form, but it was not until after John Bell had turned to the exclusive use of the short S in his Shakespeare of 1785 that the long S began to be generally abandoned. By 1820, most printers, who by then had changed their type founts from 'old style' to 'modern' (which only had the short S) had completely abandoned the use of the long forms. There was, however, a revival during the middle of the 19th century when the Chiswick Press restored the use of Caslon's old face roman which still retained its 18th-century long S and its various combinations. The traditional use of two forms of S persisted until the early years of this century in everyday handwriting.

Dr D. Nuttall, National Printing Heritage Trust, Dodleston, Cheshire.

QUESTION: I used blackcurrants, which I had frozen last year, to make jam. To my surprise I found that it was full of little stones, similar to cherry stones, inside some of the currants. Have these stones developed as a result of being in the freezer too long or is there another explanation?

☐ I FREEZE blackcurrants too, and I also freeze sloes to keep my supply of sloe gin going. A large blackcurrant and a small sloe are indistinguishable in bags in the freezer. I made a blackcurrant crumble using two bags of apparently identical fruit from my freezer. When we ate it we found some had small stones in just as the questioner described. It was delicious. I wonder if the questioner has ever picked and frozen sloes, as well as blackcurrants?

Maureen Lyon, Middle Handley, Derbyshire.

QUESTION: Who invented the traffic cone and where were they first used?

☐ AT SOME point in the Devonian period (approximately 350 million years ago) it is thought that a decisive event occurred in the evolution of the cone: the first cones began to adapt to life on land, while those that remained in the sea were to become the ancestors of the modern buoy. It is difficult to state with any certainty when Man first made use of cones, but it seems that the earliest record we have is to be found in the New Testament, which tells of St Paul experiencing a diversion on the road to Damascus. It is worth mentioning that although Britain might appear to support a healthy cone population, the circular-based species is threatened with extinction. Such cones tend to topple over in high winds, and are then crushed beneath the wheels of passing cars. Happily, Britain at last appears to be waking up to its responsibilities towards its cone population, and large areas of our motorways have been designated as protected breeding grounds. Last week I saw a small colony of circular-based cones grazing on a sectioned-off lane of the M25 whose bases had been artificially weighted in order that they might survive our maritime climate. Also, excitingly, now that the Channel Tunnel has opened up the possibility of land migration, we may one day witness the appearance in Southern England of the French green cone, hitherto unseen on our roads.
W. Huntley, Barnet, Herts.

QUESTION: Can anyone tell me why, in a lot of promotional competitions, there is a note saying 'No Purchase Necessary' when, in fact, you have to purchase the product to enter the competition?

☐ PROMOTIONS which state 'No Purchase Necessary' are not competitions in the eyes of the law – they can be entered free of charge or, if the participant chooses, by buying the product.

Competitions, to be legal, have to be skill-based and, often, entrants have to write slogans. But they don't attract mass entry because most people find them difficult. Promotions based on chance rather than skill can have up to 10 times the entry level of the traditional skill-based competition. However, the Lotteries and Amusement Act 1976 prohibits 'lotteries', which are paid-for games of chance. Therefore, to avoid falling foul of this, people are offered a 'no purchase' way of participating. Usually this will involve being able to write in on a plain piece of paper to enter the draw or, in the case of the current crop of popular instant-win promotions ('Is there a car in this can?'), involve people writing in and teams in handling houses opening real products. These operations are all supervised by independent witnesses. Of course, these promotions work because most people prefer the convenience of buying the product, to see instantly if they have won. The industry has a strict code of practice to ensure that all who enter, whether they buy a pack or send off their name and address, will have an equal chance of winning.

Graham Griffiths, Promotional Campaigns Ltd, Keston, Kent.

QUESTION: 1992 1p and 2p coins are strongly attracted by a magnet. Coins minted in previous years are not. Why?

☐ THE specification of these coins was changed in 1992 to copper-plated steel, and it is the steel core which gives them their magnetic properties. Prior to 1992 they were made from an alloy of copper, zinc and tin. The decision to change the specification was taken because it was becoming more expensive to manufacture the coins in their traditional material than their respective face values.

Linda Viner, Royal Mint, Pontyclun, Mid-Glamorgan.

QUESTION: All skyscrapers will eventually have to be demolished. The standard method uses explosives. How

will this be achieved without damage, where they stand one next to the other in places such as Manhattan?

☐ THE assertion that all skyscrapers will have to be demolished is contentious. Skyscrapers can be, and have been, strengthened (e.g. the Tour Maine Montparnasse in Paris) or stiffened (e.g. the Hancock Tower in Boston). The second assertion – that the standard method involves the use of explosives – has been true for the demolition of large panel pre-cast concrete and reinforced-concrete frame tower blocks used in 1960s housing. Most of the Manhattan skyscrapers, however, are steel-framed with masonry, concrete panel or glass cladding. Demolition, or rather dismantling, of such structures might be difficult and expensive, but could proceed without any use of explosives. I would anticipate that dismantling would reverse the erection sequence, more or less. Cranes would be required at roof level – possibly delivered by helicopter. Cladding of the building would be removed, storey by storey, permitting dismantling of the steel skeleton by flame-cutting, sawing or simply loosening bolts.
Graeme Orr, Edinburgh.

QUESTION: Which is the world's only true religion and how do we know?

☐ ANY faith claiming to be 'The world's only true religion' is, ipso facto, not a true religion.
Rev Walter Gill, Hartlepool, Cleveland.

☐ BAHA'U'LLAH, founder of the Baha'i faith, the latest of the world's major religions, taught that there is truth in all the faiths. He said that each represents a staging post in the spiritualisation of mankind, as we advance towards a mature global society. Baha'i scripture states that God has revealed Truth progressively through the ages, according to mankind's spiritual capacity and the social needs of the time. This was through a succession of divine Teachers – Abraham, Moses, Jesus and Mohammad are

those most familiar to the West. Baha'u'llah, whose name means 'The Glory of God', is believed by followers of the Baha'i faith, to be the latest in this line of succession – though not the last, as Divine Revelation is continuous.
Mrs S. M. Brice, Bromley, Kent.

☐ SUPPOSE that the Divine Being, reading the question, appeared everywhere in the sky and answered the question. Would even that do? I expect the Vatican would take several hundred years to authenticate (or not) the word of God; the Church of England would immediately become embroiled in a debate as to whether the answer was consistent with the admission of women as priests; Sinn Fein would ask for further clarification; and John Major would claim that, while God's appearance clearly suggested that recovery was on the way, we should not place too much faith in a single divine revelation.
Bill Allen, Oxshott, Surrey.

QUESTION: Vehicle registration plates in this country have to display characters on a white background at the front of a vehicle and on an orange background at the rear. What possible purpose is served by this distinction?

☐ SO YOU can tell whether you have just been, or are about to be, run over.
David Reed, London NW3.

☐ THE surface of the modern 'reflective' number plate is composed of numerous glass beads which bend and emit the light falling on them from the headlights of following cars. The Construction and Use Regulations, issued by the Transport Secretary under the provisions of the Road Traffic Act, prohibit the showing of a white light to the rear of any moving vehicle other than for the purposes of reversing. A white 'reflective' number plate is deemed to 'show' a white light and, therefore, obviously cannot be used on the rear of a vehicle.

N. F. Taylor, Birmingham.

QUESTION: Why is it that to make the poor work harder you pay them less, but to make the rich work harder you pay them more?

☐ IF THE working man earns enough to satisfy his needs from 30 hours' labour he will be tempted to down tools and slope off for the day. But if his wages are only half that amount he will be forced to work twice as long, to the greater profit of his employer. This theory was certainly foremost in the minds of the early agrarian capitalists. And in the colonies, where the local population had no need to work for the white man in order to survive, taxation was used to force them to work for money. The rich don't have to work. Their earnings derive from their control of production and distribution, so they naturally arrange for the distribution of wealth to be in their own favour. The idea that they work in order to earn their income is a fairy story put around in order to protect themselves from revolutionary ideas, and to reassure themselves of the legitimacy of their wealth. For this reason, many high earners find it necessary to work excessively long hours, instead of making the most of the advantages providence has granted them.

Jonathan Morton, London W11.

☐ IT IS down to orthodox economics and religion. The Bible makes clear that 'Unto him that hath shall it be given, from him that hath not shall it be taken away, even that that he hath'. The idea is to ensure the poor enter heaven, through the eye of the needle, while the rich are kept out (being compensated for their exclusion in the here and now). But since the powers that be clearly do not believe in tomorrow, and certainly not Sunday, it is time for the old policies to be ditched and for the meek to inherit the earth.

R. A. Leeson, Broxbourne, Herts.

QUESTION: If you were run over by a hovercraft would you be seriously injured?

☐ SPEAKING as one to whom this has happened, I can relate that the experience is fairly unremarkable. One is aware of the passing of the flexible bow skirt over one's body; there follows a period of comparative calm as the hovercraft passes overhead; and then the stern skirt brushes over. The cushion pressure inside the skirt of a small commercial hovercraft is low, usually less than 3 ounces per square inch above atmosphere (the pressure inside a car tyre is typically more than 200 times higher than this). This low-pressure air is enough to support the 'hard' structure of the hovercraft about 18 inches above the ground. The skirt which contains this 'cushion' of air, usually made of flexible rubber, is designed to conform to uneven surfaces and allows the craft to negotiate obstacles without harming them. A previous employer of mine who built small hovercraft used routinely to run employees over to demonstrate the principle to potential clients. I should add that the experience is not particularly enjoyable, since the bottom of a hovercraft is one of the wettest and muddiest places I know.
Russ Bagley, Griffin Hovercraft, Southampton.

QUESTION: The term 'duck-billed platypus' suggests that there are other breeds. Could anyone supply me with the names and, if not, why was it given such a misleading name?

☐ THE platypus belongs, along with the spiny anteater or *echidna*, to a small group of mammals called the *Monotremata*. The name means 'single-holed' and refers to the fact that these animals have only a single orifice for both excretion and reproduction. The description 'duck-billed' (*ornithohynchus*) is inaccurate, but has its origins in the 19th century and the confusion among naturalists as to how to classify an animal which seemed to possess both bird-like and mammalian characteristics (the monotremes lay eggs but

also feed their young from mammary glands). The 'bill', which is covered in soft skin, is in fact a delicate sensory organ, precisely adapted to a life spent foraging in shallow rivers. The anteater's snout might be different in shape but has the same structure and function and must be the result of a similar evolutionary development.
Michael Hutton, London SE5.

QUESTION: If a supermarket chain opens a new site does it – on balance – add to the wealth of the area or drain wealth from it?

☐ IN A small community, money spent in locally-owned shops is circulated around that community on other goods and services in those shops. Large supermarkets prefer to bring in standardised goods and return the majority of turnover to headquarters. This leads to the closure of local shops, with reduction of choice and local jobs only partially offset by the creation of fewer new jobs, often part-time, at the new supermarket. There will be an increase in lorry and car usage, contributing to hidden costs of pollution and traffic congestion, and destruction of green field sites and/or housing.
R. A. Plant, London SW19.

QUESTION: Are levels of literacy and numeracy now lower than they were 50 years ago?

☐ IN 1902, local authorities were empowered to provide secondary education, but it was restricted to those who could pay or to the approximately 25 per cent who were awarded a 'scholarship' based on an examination consisting of a composition and an arithmetic test. Primary schools were judged by the number of grammar school places awarded and the curriculum in most was geared to getting children through this examination. The tendency now is to compare the pupils in comprehensive schools with those in grammar schools, ignoring the 75 per cent who did not 'pass the scholarship'. Of course, the method of selection used had a low validity, and some of that majority were able to improve their education later. But most were employed in work which, however important, did not require the literacy and the knowledge of mathematics demanded today.

Norman Brindley, Senior Lecturer in the History of Education (retd), St Albans, Herts.

☐ WE ARE reminded of the telling remark made by Eric Bolton, Professor at the University of London Institute of Education and former Chief HMI, at the launch of the National Literacy Trust. There are, he said, just as many illiterates now as there ever were. The difference now is that all the illiterates can read and write.

Drs Barry Stierer and Brian Street, Brighton, Sussex.

QUESTION: In Trafalgar Square is an empty plinth sited at the top left-hand corner. Was there ever an intended statue for that place – if so, why is it still unoccupied? If not, any suggestions as to which person would be suitable to place on it now?

☐ THIS plinth was originally intended for a statue of a great British statesman and politician renowned for his honest, moral rectitude and adherence to the principles of public service. That's why it's still empty.

Roy Twitchin, Southgate, London N14.

☐ THE area covered by Trafalgar Square today was formerly the open courtyard of the Great Mews serving Whitehall Palace. By the early 19th century the Mews was no longer used by the Royal Household, and the redevelopment of the site was under investigation. The square was virtually clear of buildings by 1830, but the name Trafalgar Square is first recorded in about 1835, some

30 years after Nelson's death. Following the first meeting of the Nelson Memorial Committee in 1838, William Railton's design for the memorial was selected and work started in 1839 with completion in 1852. Sir Edmund Landseer's lions did not arrive until 1867. No statue was planned for the north-west corner of Trafalgar Square; indeed, the mounted statue of George IV in the north-east corner was only placed there 'temporarily' in 1843, its intended location being on top of Marble Arch. Of the other statues, Napier was erected in 1856 and Havelock in 1861. A statue of General Gordon was erected between the two fountains in 1888, but was moved to the Embankment Gardens in 1943 to make way for a Lancaster bomber during 'Wings for Victory' week! Should a statue be erected on the vacant plinth, from an aesthetic point of view, a mounted figure matching that of George IV would be preferable. May we therefore suggest a statue of Wellington, thus completing the trio of leaders who led Britain to victory over Napoleon?
M. Sargeant, London SW1.

☐ THE plinth is to support a statue of the next King of England, when it will be known as the Plinth of Wales.
Gerry Rutter, Merryoaks, Durham.

QUESTION: How do we know the correct way to pronounce a dead language?

☐ WE ASK a ghost writer.
David Leah, Liskeard, Cornwall.

☐ OLD languages don't die. They just fade into new languages (at least most of them do.) While the entire sound system of an ancient language rarely survives intact, fragments can usually be found scattered around its various daughter languages. For example, many traits of Latin pronunciation are directly observable in Italian, French, Spanish and Romanian. The job of the linguistic historian is to try to piece these various bits together. The most tried and tested technique is comparative reconstruction, which focuses on the systematic sound correspondences that emerge when we compare the same words in different sister languages. Where this exercise turns up different sounds, it is usually possible to trace them back to a common historical source. For example, many English words beginning with 't' correspond to words beginning with 'ts' (spelt z) in the sister language German; compare English *ten*, *to*, *time* with German *zehn*, *zu*, *Zeit*. On the basis of this and many similar correspondences, we can reconstruct a common Germanic parent language in which the older sound in this particular instance is the knowledge that each type of sound change takes place in one direction only. On the strength of what happens in many other languages, we know that 't' at the beginning of a word can turn into 'ts' but not vice versa. The more widely we cast our comparative net, the further we can reach back into the mists of time. The 't' of early Germanic itself derives from an even older 'd' – contrast English *two* and *tooth* with, say, Italian *due* and *dente*. Ultimately we arrive at the sound system of an ancient Indo-European tongue, the common ancestor of languages as apparently diverse as English, French, Russian, Irish, Greek and Urdu.

John Harris, Department of Phonetics and Linguistics, University College, London.

QUESTION: If identity cards are the best way to reduce social security fraud and will save money, what is the best way to combat tax evasion/avoidance – and which would save more money?

☐ THE maximum estimated loss to the Treasury via social security fraud is between £500 million and £1 billion, out of a £79 billion annual budget. The cost of introducing an identity card system would be around £150 million, for social security claimants alone. The government has refused to provide any figures at all for the probable scale of loss via tax evasion, or to give details of the

commonest methods of avoidance and evasion. In 1985 and in 1986 the Inland Revenue's attempts to study the problem were blocked by Treasury ministers. The commonest form of tax evasion or avoidance is the placing of the ownership of UK assets such as shares in companies, and land, in trusts abroad – mostly in tax havens. In 1988 the Inland Revenue unofficially calculated that £10 billion had been lost to the Revenue that year as a result. In any year since then the loss has been somewhere between £5 billion and £10 billion, or £140 billion since 1980 – three times the current Public Sector Borrowing deficit. The best way to halt this loss is to treat the tax havens as domestic territories for tax purposes, as the Americans do, and to impose a buyers' premium on the purchase of domestic assets in foreign ownership, as some countries do. A recent report showed that 37 Tory MPs are advisers, consultants or partners in companies which give active advice on tax avoidance via offshore tax havens.
Kevin Cahill, London WC1.

QUESTION: In the late 1960s, some aggrieved citizens on the Isle of Dogs tried to declare independence from the rest of Britain. Can anyone remember what this was about? Could such an attempt ever be a feasible revolutionary act?

□ THIS took place in March 1970, when Islanders barricaded the (then) single road which led on and off the Isle of Dogs. People stood on the bridges, refusing to allow road traffic across and preventing the bridges being raised to allow ships to enter the docks system on the island. It was therefore probably the only demonstration in London which stopped all traffic on land and water at the same time! The purpose of the UDI was to bring attention to the Islanders' demands for better social conditions in the area which, after years of campaigning, petitions, deputations, demonstrations, and marches, to the town hall, the GLC County Hall, and numerous government departments, had got nowhere. It was decided that we should 'declare our independence from the rest of London and press for separate borough status'. Our argument was based on the fact that our next-door neighbour, the City of London, had been given this right under the 1965 London Borough Act. Since the Isle of Dogs and the City are, roughly, the same size in area, we reckoned we had good grounds – particularly as the Isle of Dogs, (then) with its active docks bringing wealth into Britain, produced most of the money which the City spent! I led the Isle of Dogs UDI and was dubbed by the media at the time as 'President Ted of the Isle of Dogs'. We did not, of course, succeed in gaining independence. But we did get our complaints into the media spotlight. And some tangible improvements were made in the area: a new secondary school; housing schemes; and improved public transport. Sadly, despite a government so-called Regeneration Programme which has spent public money in the order of £1 million per week, every week for the past 11 years, it still appears that the wealth that is generated here is still being spent by the City. And social conditions on the Isle of Dogs are as poor now as they were in the 1960s. Perhaps the Isle of Dogs will close the bridges one more time.

Ted Jones, ex-President of the Isle of Dogs, London E14.

QUESTION: What makes my knees crack?

☐ YOU don't know Tonya Harding, do you?
Stuart Newstead, Oxford.

☐ THERE are three sources of noise from a joint – arthritis, tendon flick or gas bubbles. The knee, like many other joints in the body, consists of a fluid-filled bag containing smooth bony surfaces covered in a thin layer of cartilage. The fluid acts as a lubricant, and movement is powered by surrounding muscles operating through tendons attached to the next bone. If the knee is arthritic, then the surfaces of the bones become roughened, and may grate as they move, creating noise and pain. In a non-arthritic knee, the tendons pulling around move past the outer part of the knee, often under considerable tension. If they catch on any small part of the bones, they may flick past it as the movement continues, creating a distinct 'snap'. Although this does happen in the knee, it is a lot commoner in the ankle. Many people can make a snap with their ankles at will. The most likely cause is the phenomenon of gas-bubble formation. Any gas normally carried in the bloodstream will also be found in the normal fluid of the joint. These gases come out of solution more readily when the pressure on the fluid reduces. These bubbles occur all over the body in divers who depressurise too quickly, causing the 'bends'. In the knee, if the joint is moved to its extreme the curved bone surfaces can lever away from each other, stretching the surrounding ligaments and reducing the internal pressure considerably. At the new low pressure, gas bubbles can form quite readily although, unlike the bends, these are harmless. The gas bubbles expand, allowing the joint to expand with a 'snap'. On return to a more relaxed position, the gas bubble will redissolve over a few minutes, and the knee won't crack again during that time.

Dr Steve Seddon, Newcastle-under-Lyme, Staffs.

QUESTION: Are bacteria animals or plants? How do we know?

☐ BY ANCIENT reckoning, bacteria are plants. By modern criteria, they are neither animals nor plants, but monera. Until the 1960s, organisms were placed in the animal kingdom if they were irritable, mobile and heterotrophic, and in the plant kingdom if they did not have the characteristics of animals. With the advent of electron microscopy and molecular biology, the ancient categories have been revised. All recent taxonomies recognise at least four kingdoms: monera (which are organisms without cell nuclei), animals, plants and fungi. Monera have cell walls of mucoprotein, plants have cell walls of cellulose, fungi have cell walls of chitin, and animals have no cell walls.

Donald Rooum, London SW2.

QUESTION: Who changed the name of Richard to Dick? Why?

☐ THIS came about, first, through the very common shortening of names – for example, Will for William, Sim for Simon, Gib for Gilbert, and Wat for Walter. These short forms were then subjected to rhyming process. Some examples are: William – Bill; Robert – Hob, Bob; Roger – Hodge; Molly – Polly. Dick is one of the earliest to be mentioned in records, in 1220. During the 13th to 15th centuries, it is probable that the majority of peasants were called these short and rhyming forms. Such names resembled the Old English names which had been generally used before the Norman Conquest. Because these forms were usually for the peasants, they gave rise to use as common nouns, such as: jack/dick – man/fellow; hodge – country labourer.
Ann Addison, Nuneaton, Warwicks.

QUESTION: During the Second World War, a German-language newspaper, *Die Zeitung*, was on sale in the Welsh village where I was evacuated. Why, and what happened to it?

☐ DIE *Zeitung* was conceived in the summer of 1940, at the time of the Battle of Britain, and first published on 12 March 1941. From 2 January 1942, a 12-page weekly replaced the original four-page daily newspaper. The last edition appeared on 1 June 1945. *Die Zeitung* was created by and for German-speaking refugees, but boycotted by some socialists in exile until late in 1944. It saw itself as the only free, independent German-language newspaper in Europe and perceived Britain, in the light of Germany's invasion of its neighbouring territories, as the last free haven in Europe. The newspaper was given the approval of the British government. In what it published in its political, economic and cultural sections, *Die Zeitung* opposed Hitler in every way it deemed possible. The editors were soon encouraged to distribute the newspaper abroad. The success of the subsequent 'overseas edition' is reflected in its own transformation from an eight-page fortnightly newspaper into a 12-page weekly. In June 1945, with Hitler's Germany defeated, *Die Zeitung* declared that it had reached its goal and ceased publication. The editors felt that the tasks facing journalists in post-war Germany should be tackled by a different newspaper. *Die Zeitung* had always been regarded as a war-time initiative. A full set of the British *Zeitung* is available for consultation in the National Library of Scotland in Edinburgh. Despite the paper shortages facing the country, the government of the day permitted several foreign-language newspapers to be printed in London – a situation eventually challenged in Parliament in June 1943.

Dr Donal McLaughlin, Department of Languages, Heriot-Watt University, Edinburgh.

QUESTION: Printed on the labels of many compact discs are initials such as BIEM/STEMRA or BIEM/MCPS. To what do they refer?

☐ THESE initials can be found on all formats of recorded music, such as records, cassettes, compact discs and other derivatives. They refer to the collection societies who license the mechanical reproduction of copyright music on behalf of composers and publishers. For example, MCPS (the Mechanical-Copyright Protection Society Ltd) is a British society, STEMRA is Dutch, GEMA is German, etc. When the initials are printed on labels of records/cassettes/compact discs, it implies that the manufacturer has been granted a licence to reproduce recordings of specific compositions and has paid or has agreed to pay the appropriate royalty to the society for subsequent distribution to the individual publishers and composers.

Paul Mooney, Managing Director, Ardent Music, Co Durham.

QUESTION: I sometimes find myself humming a song

from a 1950s children's TV programme: 'Billy Bean built
a machine to see what it would do/He built it out of sticks
and stones and nuts and bolts and glue.' Who was Billy
Bean and did the director, producer or Billy himself go on
to achieve greater things?

☐ YOO HOO the cuckoo on 'Billy Bean and his Funny Machine'
was the protégé of a Mr Ivan Owen, who later went on to have a
hand in the booming success of Basil Brush. He discovered Basil
in 1964 in an act called 'The Three Scampies', and the two have
been hand in glove since. Posterity does not record the fates of
either Yoo Hoo or Basil's other two scampy co-stars – no one else
has lifted a finger for them in years.
*Ian Potter, National Museum of Photography, Film & Television,
Bradford.*

☐ BILLY Bean Was a puppet who named his invention the Funny
Machine because 'it did the funniest things you've seen'. The machine was operated by Lester, Bean's unseen assistant, with whom
he communicated by means of a speaking tube of nautical design.
The chief function of the Funny Machine appeared to be the
generation of images on to its screen, 'the funny old Cartoonera-
tor'. The song bothers me also, largely because I cannot remember
how it continues.
Bill White, Chesham, Bucks.

QUESTION: Why can't someone design a urinal that does
not splash back?

☐ IS THE questioner bragging or complaining?
Alan Thornton, Bolton, Lancs.

☐ NATURE has provided the ultimate in non-splash urinals, in the
form of privet and other small leafed hedges.
Tim Hogan, Welwyn Garden City, Herts.

☐ A SPLASH-free urinal was patented before the end of the last

century. It is only with today's compact urinals that the problem has become widespread! A Horwich, Lancashire, company manufactured and marketed splash-free urinals from about 1895 until at least the outbreak of the First World War. The secret was to get the angle exactly right – based on the idea that, assuming the height of an average man to be 5 feet 6 inches, the critical angle could be guaranteed by equipping the urinal with a target to aim at! That target, a small bee (Latin: *Apis*!) was printed on to the stone under the glaze, and at least one example has been in constant use ever since in Wigan, with no obvious signs of wear! For small boys, however, the bee proved to be too high up.
John Hannavy, Wigan, Lancs.

QUESTION: When *Mein Kampf* is borrowed from the local library, who benefits from the Public Lending Right fee?

☐ ONLY authors who have registered with the Public Lending Right office qualify for payments for loans of their books from public libraries. Like Agatha Christie and Enid Blyton, Hitler died before the PLR scheme got off the ground in the early 1980s, and therefore does not qualify. Had he been alive today he could have applied to register *Mein Kampf*, as the UK has a reciprocal arrangement with Germany. PLR registration is also open to editors and translators – they qualify for 20 and 30 per cent PLR shares respectively. So if a new edition of *Mein Kampf* is published, an eligible editor or translator may apply for payments from that edition. The remainder goes back into the PLR fund for distribution to other authors.
Jim Parker, Registrar of PLR, Stockton-on-Tees, Cleveland.

QUESTION: I once read in an article that electricity could be delivered to houses without wires, but that the idea was rejected because of the difficulty of charging consumers. How would this system have worked?

☐ BY ELECTROMAGNETIC induction: a changing electric current

through a conductor produces a changing magnetic field around the conductor; when this field passes through a second conductor, a current is induced. This effect is used in transformers. A practical example over a large area is the induction loop for hearing-aids in cinema and theatres. Disadvantages are that appreciable power would be wasted, and the power consumed by individual receivers could not be measured, and therefore charged for, by the power-supplier.

Alan Hassell, Lymington, Hants.

QUESTION: It often seems to me that the ears of older people are larger than when they were younger. Do ears continue to grow when other parts of the body have ceased to do so? Are there other bits which pursue an independent line in this way?

☐ EARS can sometimes appear to become larger with age and this is also true of noses, but whether the changes are due to continued growth or simply to a loss of elasticity, for example, is rather difficult to prove. However, the lens of the eye is the one body organ where it has been established beyond doubt that new cells are continually added to the existing structures, so that it grows and increases in weight throughout life. The growth of the lens is, in fact, so constant that its weight is routinely used as a means of accurately determining the age of any animal that has died in the wild. In humans, a dramatic decrease in the rate of growth of the lens is a sure sign of impending cataract.

Dr George Duncan, School of Biological Sciences, University of East Anglia.

QUESTION: Does a symphony orchestra actually take its time/tempo from the conductor? Or does he just wave his arms about, more or less in time with the music, for effect?

☐ A CONDUCTOR'S job is to free the players so that they can play.

He has to set the tempo, communicate how he wants the piece to go, stimulate, unite and, above all, inspire. How much time-beating he needs to do, as distinct from how much he actually does, varies with the complexity of the piece. A first-rate orchestra needs very little. Occasional indications at awkward or crucial points are enough, and help to keep the players alert. Sir Thomas Beecham, the story goes, said that after a rehearsal he knew what the members of the orchestra were going to do but they didn't know what he was going to do, so they were on their toes and gave a great performance. Even amateur orchestras need a time-beat far less than they and their conductors imagine. Players require anticipatory impulses; in a way, the conductor has to keep giving permission to make sounds. The conductor has to be an inspired personality. Furtwängler, apparently, could change the sound of an orchestra he was to conduct simply by entering the room. Conductors often indulge in acting, sometimes for the effect on the audience, sometimes in order to communicate with the orchestra. Players will play well for someone they respect. I remember a concert given by a stony-faced Philharmonia doing the absolute minimum for a conductor they clearly held in low esteem. The ideal situation is when a rapport exists between players and conductor such that the music seems to be playing itself. The players play in freedom, and the conductor can wave his arms about – or, like Dorati, just stand still and listen.
Keith Harrison, Cheltenham, Glos.

QUESTION: We have an earthenware bottle that states: 'To buy, sell or use this bottle is illegal.' It is labelled 'PICKUP, Leeds, Bradford & Manchester' and dated 1921. What did it contain and what was the point in making it?

☐ THE bottle had probably contained strong ginger beer, which was very popular in Yorkshire. The empty container was supposed to be returned to the supplier so that it could be refilled and resold, as the bottles were expensive to produce. However, they were

greatly prized as extremely efficient hot-water bottles. My father invented a small gadget to prevent the cork becoming accidentally dislodged. Eventually the manufacturer changed to selling the ginger beer in special glass bottles because the return rate of the earthenware containers was so low as to be uneconomic.
Doreen Pickles, Halifax, West Yorkshire.

QUESTION: Do giraffes take special precautions during thunderstorms?

☐ No. THEY mate freely whatever the weather.
Arthur Wren, Guildford, Surrey.

☐ GIRAFFES have no need to take evasive action. Survival traits plus natural selection have resulted in the perfect solution to a potential problem. When a high potential differential (voltage) is applied across an air-filled gap, lines of force supporting a force field exist across the gap. Given dry air and perfect conditions such as exist between parallel flat surfaces, the lines of force are parallel and the force field is symmetrical. However, if the force field is distorted and the lines of force congested, then the potential gradient across the gap is modified and breakdown (flashover) is more likely to occur. Breakdown will be initiated across the region of maximum electric stress introduced by field distortion. The highest appendage of a giraffe consists of two upright stalks with rounded globular-like ends which provide the perfect interface surface for minimising localised electric stress during thunderstorms. They act as the antithesis of a lightning conductor in that they ensure that any electrical breakdown will occur elsewhere. Breakdown will be to the nearest point of maximum electric stress even if that point is much nearer to the ground than the giraffe's head. This also explains why rhinoceroses instinctively steer well clear of giraffes during stormy weather.
R. W. Pearson, Leicester.

QUESTION: Why do so few English placenames start with the letter J? If J is an unlucky letter for places, why is it not for personal names?

☐ MOST English placenames are of Anglo-Saxon origin but J (along with K, Q, V and Z) does not figure in the Old English alphabet: the letters were introduced after the Norman invasion of the 11th century. Although many French elements are to be found in English placenames, it is no great surprise that non-native initial letters are not strongly represented. The one exception is K, which replaced Anglo-Saxon C in certain cases where the hard pronunciation was indicated.
Alan Clarke, Redland, Bristol.

QUESTION: With a £19 million overdraft, the Conservative Party must surely be at risk of being declared bankrupt. If the party's creditors foreclosed, what implications would this have for the government? Is there any hope of this happening?

☐ MEMBERS of Parliament are (in theory, at least) elected as individuals, not as representatives of an organisation. In the short term, the bankruptcy of the party would have no more effect on the position of an MP than the closure of any other club to which he or she belonged. If John Major could continue to rely on the support of like-minded MPs, his government could remain in power until the next election. Indeed, the absence of a party organisation would be an incentive to put off the election for as long as possible and would also be a powerful force for loyalty among MPs wishing to be re-elected. Of course, once the election came along, the Conservatives would have no money to fight it. A lack of resources and image of financial mismanagement would almost certainly lead to defeat. For this reason it is most unlikely that the government's friends in business and the City will ever allow the party to bankrupt itself. The show will go on.
Paul Ferguson Cowan, South Shields, Tyne and Wear.

QUESTION: Who first 'lost his bottle'?

☐ SHAKESPEARE wrote about lager louts in the early 17th century in *The Tempest*, Act IV, Scene 1. After a drunken and fruitless chase across wild marshland led by the 'monster' Caliban, the bedraggled Trinculo bemoans the fact that he and Stephano have sunk so low as 'to lose our bottles in the pool'. Stephano agrees – 'There is not only disgrace and dishonour in that, monster, but an infinite loss.'
Colin Morley, Totteridge, London N20.

☐ THE 'bottle' is, in full, the Cockney rhyming slang 'bottle and glass'. The 'loss' refers to the control of the anal sphincter in moments of great danger or stress. From this, we can deduce that Adam was the first to experience this unpleasant occurrence, when called to account in the Garden of Eden.
Joseph Cramp, Clayhall, Essex.

QUESTION: Why do dead batteries appear to be self-regenerating if left for a while? The power only lasts a short time but it is noticeable.

☐ A BATTERY comprises two parts: the electrolyte and the electrodes. The electrolyte is the chemical mixture which fills the bulk of the battery. It will be either a liquid (as in a car battery) or a pasty solid (torch batteries). There are two electrodes, made of different materials, and they make the connection with the external circuit via the + and – terminals. An electric current flows when chemical reactions involving the electrolyte take place on the surface of the electrodes. The electrolyte is gradually consumed, and products of the chemical reaction build up in the electrolyte near the electrodes. The build-up of products makes it harder for unreacted electrolyte to gain access to the surface of the electrodes, hence the voltage drops. Slowly, as a result of the natural movement of their particles, the products of the reaction will diffuse

away from the electrodes. Thus, the reaction can take place much as before, and the voltage rises again. But it is only a temporary respite, as the products will soon build up again, and eventually there will be nowhere free of products to which they can diffuse. This also explains why power can sometimes be restored temporarily to a battery by putting it in an oven: the particles diffuse away more quickly at a higher temperature. It is, however, extremely dangerous as toxic gases can be produced, and the battery could explode. Incidentally, we should be talking about an (electrical) cell, rather than a battery. It only becomes a battery if two or more cells are joined together. A 1.5 volt 'battery' should thus be called a cell, but 3, 4.5, 6 and 9 volt batteries are properly named, as they contain 2, 3, 4 or 6 cells joined together.
Dr Peter Borrows, Epping, Essex.

QUESTION: What is the accuracy of the Pools Panel in predicting the results of postponed football matches?

☐ THE Pools Panel, in making its decisions, takes into account such 'match factors' as: home and away records of the respective teams in the current season; the records for meetings of the two teams over the past five seasons; the effects of changes in team membership and injury records; known play patterns and set-piece plays; and the relative 'strictness' of the referee. A televised experiment in 1973 recorded the Panel's deliberations for the postponed Newcastle United vs Chelsea match. It predicted a home win, with a privately agreed result of 2–1 or 3–1. The match was eventually played 10 days later and, as part of the experiment, the Panel was reconvened prior to the game to see if its prediction remained the same. It predicted a score draw on this occasion, based on publicity which had just broken over the alleged extra-marital affair of a Newcastle full-back, and on the earlier broadcast of its own prediction. The result was 1-0 to Newcastle.
Gary Walker, London N17.

☐ TEN years ago, I analysed the success rate of the Pools Panel in the 1981–82 season. It convened five times and invented 182 results. When the matches were played, the hit rate was about 39 per cent. But its performance on draws was much weaker: the success rate for home wins was 49 per cent; away wins, 46; 0–0 draws, 0; score draws, 23. The Panel's accuracy also deteriorated lower down the league: Division 1 predictions were 43 per cent accurate; Division 2, 41; Division 3, 35; Division 4, 20. On its best Saturday, the Pools experts would have amassed 14 points. Presumably they wouldn't have let it change their lives.
David Guest, London N5.

QUESTION: If person A is unrequitedly in love with person B, does person B have any moral obligation or duties towards A?

☐ THE notion that one can 'fall in love' with someone who does not reciprocate the feeling is a latter-day fallacy. Love has very little to do with erotic attraction, and nothing at all to do with the often urgent need to pacify one's own feelings of loneliness or insufficiency. Sounds to me like person A is projecting a supposed solution to their own neurosis on to person B. Person B has a duty I hope we all recognise – to look after others and ourselves, and to use the force of our personalities in a productive and compassionate way. Failing the above, dysfunctional relationships of dependency may be curtailed by the use of extreme physical violence.
Simon Phillips, London W9.

☐ A SIMILAR problem was considered by Spinoza in the 17th century in his *Ethics*. Spinoza came to the conclusion that a man who loves God cannot expect God to love him in return. In the following century the great German poet and thinker Goethe advanced the argument and succinctly wrote: 'I love you, why should that be any concern of yours!' If an attempt is made at a definition of love, perhaps one of the best that we can come up with is: unconditional positive regard. If this definition be accepted, then it is easily seen that the notion of B having any obligations or duties towards A involves a contradiction in terms. Kant considered that feelings of affection cannot be demanded of us as a duty. Kant also believed strongly in the autonomy of human personality. I am sure that Kant would also support the view that the question must be answered in the negative.

Douglas N. Passant, Chingford, London E4.

☐ LOVE, in effect, is an emotional contract between two people. Person B would have no moral obligation – unless, by word or deed, he/she accepted the contract.

Simon Vogel, Harlow, Essex.

QUESTION: A recent television advert suggests that it is possible to fit the entire world's population on to the Isle of Wight. How true is this statement?

☐ THE Isle of Wight has an area of 381 square kilometres. It is possible to squeeze about 10 average British adults into one square metre, and thus 3.81 billion of them on to the island. The world's population, at present, is in the order of 5.56 billion. If (i) the average person requires only 90 per cent of the space required by the average Briton; (ii) 12 per cent of the population, being aged four or less, requires no space at all; and (iii) a further 20 per cent, aged between 5 and 14, require only half the amount of space occupied by adults, the potential capacity of the Isle of Wight increases to 5.34 billion. Hence, the original question can only be accurately answered after detailed analysis of the demographic and anthropometric make-up of the world's population.

Geoffrey Taunton, Portsmouth, Hants.

☐ IT IS highly unlikely, because of the limited running of the Red Funnel Steamers and the other none-too-frequent ferries. The first few million to arrive would have eaten everything available, probably have blocked the sewerage systems, and would

undoubtedly have died before the last visitors had even gained an entry visa.
Richard Trim, Narborough, Leics.

QUESTION: Why does Parliament enjoy three weeks' holiday at Christmas, when the general public gets only three days?

☐ THE Members of Parliament need three weeks at Christmas if they are to take full advantage of the 15 free travel warrants they are allowed each year. These can be used for themselves and their spouses and offspring up to the age of 18, to travel anywhere in the world, over land, sea or by air.
Bill Punt, Lydney, Glos.

☐ BILL Punt is wrong. MPs' travel warrants, like those for their spouses and children, can only be used to the nearest train or air terminus to their constituency. I can travel between Wigan, Liverpool or Preston and Westminster by rail, or between Manchester and the London airports by air. And that is it. If our warrants really allowed us to travel anywhere in the world I would still be hankering after visits to friends in New Zealand and Australia.
Colin Pickthall MP, West Lancashire.

QUESTION: Is there a book in the public domain which details who owns all the land in the UK?

☐ NO. IN theory no such book could be written because there is no compulsory registration of land ownership in England and Wales. The mandatory registration of *transactions* in land in England and Wales commenced in 1925 and was completed in 1990, but this has left up to 50 per cent of all the acreage of the two countries outside the official land registry. The Scottish land registry, known as Sassines, is much more complete, however. A guide to *Who Owns Scotland*, by John MacEwen, was published in the

1970s. It has been out of print for 10 years. The *Guardian*'s Richard Norton-Taylor wrote a book, *Whose Land Is It Anyway*, which identified a number of large estates. Orion will be publishing a book, compiled by myself, in 1995. It will identify the groups and individuals who own about 95 per cent of the island. The first 'book' on the land ownership in England was the Domesday Book, completed in 1086, which was probably no more than 15 per cent accurate. It was used by William the Conqueror as a device to 'fix' the conquest by parcelling out the ownership of England amongst his barons. There was an attempted second Domesday in 1874 when the Earl of Derby, through the House of Lords, ordered a survey to prove that the aristocracy did not own most of the UK. The research proved that it did, indeed, own 66 per cent of the country, and publication plans were quickly shelved.
Kevin Cahill, London WC1.

QUESTION: I see that my Alpen with 'no added sugar' contains malt extract (a sugar), and that my 'sugar free' Orbit chewing gum lists glucose syrup (also a sugar) as one of its ingredients. How can food manufacturers get away with it?

☐ THE answer is in the word 'added'. All products with naturally contained sugar are not included, as they are not added to by the manufacturers.
Michael O'Sullivan, Clifton, Bristol.

QUESTION: Is there any evidence to suggest that the Soviet Union ever contemplated the possibility of making a military assault on Western Europe?

☐ ACCORDING to secret documents seized from the military archives of the former East Germany, the Warsaw Pact planned a

modernised version of Hitler's Blitzkrieg against the West, using spearheads of tanks and tactical nuclear weapons. These documents, covering the period from the 1960s to the mid-1980s, were made public in March 1993. They convinced German military planners and historians that the Soviet bloc not only seriously considered an assault, but also had achieved a far higher level of readiness than western intelligence had assumed. The Warsaw Pact intended to push forward on five fronts to reach the French border in 13–15 days, according to the documents. Having conquered West Germany and the Low Countries, Soviet-bloc forces would then push through France to reach the Spanish border and the Atlantic coast within 30–35 days. A training exercise in 1980 developed a strategy for supporting the advance of the first front with 840 tactical nuclear weapons (targeted on Schleswig-Holstein, East Lower Saxony, North Hessen and East Bavaria). Warsaw Pact exercises were offensive and rarely practised defence against a Nato attack, as this was regarded as unlikely by the East's military planners. Soviet-bloc planning for a military offensive against the West was so detailed and advanced that the communists had already made street signs for western cities, printed cash for their occupation government, and built equipment to run eastern trains on western tracks. Furthermore, an estimated 8,000 medals ready for an offensive against the West were discovered in the former East German defence ministry headquarters. This secret decoration for bravery was known as the Blücher Order, after the Prussian field marshal who helped Wellington to defeat Napoleon at Waterloo.
Tony Martin, Nunhead, London SE15.

☐ AS IS usual in anti-Soviet stories, Tony Martin does not enable us to check the authenticity of his sources (which in any case should be Soviet, not German, to hold any water). My fascination with this question began when we re-armed Germany in 1951, to the great dismay of our former ally – Germany being a power that had twice been our mortal enemy and which had spread death, destruction and genocide across Europe and Russia on an

unprecedented scale. In my compulsive quest for information, I failed to find one piece of cast-iron, irrefutable evidence that the Soviet Union could have contemplated such a step. They lost 20 million, plus countless wounded, which must have left cruel mental scars on the surviving population. Material destruction was on a scale unimaginable, even to those of us who remember the bombing of our cities. The Soviet Union was striving to prove the superiority of a planned economy. One can hardly imagine them being diverted into military gambles. Mr Martin could not quote a single Russian leader from Lenin onwards who ever nursed such an idea. The reverse is true: the West did contemplate an assault on the Soviet Union, from John Foster Dulles and his 'Roll back Communism' through to Reagan's 'Star Wars' which, it was hoped, would allow a successful first strike. As stated by A. J. P. Taylor in *The Russian War* (1978): 'The greatest crime of the Soviet Union in western eyes is to have no capitalists and no landlords.' Now that these are being reinstated we can be buddies. Incidentally, they have been running through-trains from Moscow to Ostend and return for many years. They simply crane up the coaches and change the bogies at the frontier.
John L. Beasley, Penzance, Cornwall.

QUESTION: I am unable to work out the coding system used in the numbers, in TV programme listings, for the automatic setting of video recorders. Will somebody please explain the system?

☐ I ALWAYS thought the code stated the number of times a programme had been rerun.
N. Rossi, London N22.

QUESTION: How relevant is the Old Testament to Christianity?

☐ THE question should be: how relevant is Christianity to the so-called 'Old Testament'? The first Christians regarded themselves as a group within Judaism. There were many such groups at the time and it has been one of the great tragedies of the world that the two faiths separated. There are many different points of view (theologies) in both the Old and the New Testament. The 'Old' is saying that God created a beautiful world but this has been thrown into a state of chaos because humanity has gone its own way. Those who could, have grasped power and run things according to their own arrogance instead of in the manner of God's love. God intends to restore order. The prophet, seeing the arrogance of one world power, was inspired to say: 'Bright morning star, how you have fallen from heaven, thrown to earth, prostrate among the nations . . . You thought to yourself . . . I shall make myself like the Most High!' (Isaiah 14: 12–14). Psalm 2 puts it in this way: 'Why are the nations in turmoil? Why do the peoples hatch their futile plots?' Jesus saw his role as being to restore the divine order and set people free from the chaos that had been caused. For him, the evil was much more than the arrogance of human rulers. They were only the slaves of Satan, who was making a concerted attack on God's world. For this reason, his mission begins by rebuffing Satan (Luke 4: 1–13) and the climax comes after his disciples have carried out a successful mission, which shows that Satan is no longer in control. Quoting from Isaiah 14, he exclaims: 'I saw Satan fall, like lightning, from Heaven' (Luke 10: 18). Tradition records that the promise of Psalm 2 was fulfilled in his Baptism (Luke 3: 22). The Gospel is that the principalities and powers have been shackled (Ephesians 1: 20–23). *Rev John B. Geyer, Dundee Congregational Church.*

□ THE Old Testament has continued to influence Christianity in many ways. It has shaped its understanding of human nature (the story of the Garden of Eden); it has supplied language for its devotion (the Psalms); it has seemed to legitimate its wars (the book of Joshua); it has provided its utopian visions (swords into ploughshares). Perhaps its greatest relevance today is that it deals with the concerns of society in a way that the New Testament,

through the circumstances of its origin, does not. Without the concern for justice which pervades the prophets, the law codes and the wisdom literature, Christianity would be tempted to confine its attention to personal religion and the inner life of the church. Christians are increasingly aware that they are not the sole heirs of the Old Testament. The tendency to refer to it as the Hebrew Bible testifies to that. Perhaps the most fruitful approach to dialogue would be for Jews, Christians and Muslims to get behind their traditional readings of this Bible and study it afresh together.
Rev Roger Tomes, Manchester.

QUESTION: What is the science of cooking, from raw mixture, home-made Christmas puddings? Our traditional family recipe says: 'Steam for 6 to 10 hours, then reheat for at least 2.' Why?

☐ WHEN families were larger than is usual nowadays, small Christmas puddings were useless. Steaming is a slow process as the temperature never rises above 100°C and it also generates a damp atmosphere as the steam condenses again to water. This long, slow, wet cooking would not be tolerated on Christmas Day, so the puddings were cooked from raw beforehand and just reheated on The Day. Their size meant it took 2 hours to reheat through to the middle. Puddings, cakes and mincemeat were also prepared in advance, from October onwards, to spread the cost and the labour of the Feast of Christmas.
Gwen Baker, Wolverhampton.

QUESTION: Why do most financial years start in April? If this has something to do with the onset of summer, does this put southern hemisphere budgeting at any disadvantage?

☐ UNTIL 1752, the civil year in England began on 25 March, the feast of the Annunciation, or Lady Day (nine months before

Christmas). Thus, for example, the day after 24 March 1648 was 25 March 1649, and the financial year began 25 March. In 1752 the British calendar (which still largely followed the calendar introduced by Julius Caesar in 44 BC) was reformed to bring it in line with the Gregorian calendar, introduced by Pope Gregory in Europe in the 1580s. The reform here had two aspects. First, by 1752 our calendar was out of synch with the Gregorian by 10 days, so 10 days (4th–13th) were chopped out of September in that year; the resulting riots used the slogan "Give us back our 11 days" because people subtracted the 3rd from the 14th instead of counting the gap. Secondly, the start of the civil year was shifted to 1 January *except* for the financial year. The beginning of that was shifted (no doubt because of pressure from employers of agricultural labourers, who contracted to work for a year at a time) to the date that would have been 25 March under the old calendar, which was 6 April. And there it has stayed, even though, on a pedantic interpretation of the old calendar, it should have been shifted by a further day in 1800 and 1900. The present government's shifting this year of the budget from the spring to the autumn breaks part of the link with this tradition, and may in time lead to the British financial year being redefined to coincide with the calendar year.

Greg Brooks, Reading, Berks.

QUESTION: Will the earth ever stop spinning? If so, when?

☐ USUALLY about five hours after one has stopped drinking. Adopting a horizontal position may help.
Tim Goodwin, London NW6.

☐ THE moon's gravitational attraction on the earth causes the well-known phenomenon of tides. Because of friction between tidal waters and shallow sea floors and continental margins, a net tidal force (torque) pushes against the rotation of the earth. The sun exerts a similar but smaller force. The result is a gradual increase in the length of the earth's day of about one second every 60,000 years. At the same time, the bulges of tidal water exert torques on the moon which push it out further from the earth, where its orbital period will be longer. Eventually, the earth should slow until it rotates only once per month, so that the earth and moon would become tidally locked and each would keep the same face pointed towards the other body. Calculations show that the spin period and month would then be about 47 of our present days in length. The same calculations imply that this should take 50 billion years to occur. Long before this prediction comes to pass, however, other events will intervene. In less than 5 billion years, as the sun consumes its finite supply of hydrogen, it will gradually increase in luminosity to the point where the seas will boil due to the increase in earth's surface temperature. Without liquid water, the tidal friction will cease to be important. Life on earth will be extinct. Not long afterwards, cosmically speaking, the sun will swell up into a red giant star, possibly engulfing the earth in its atmosphere, and vaporising it. So, although the earth is gradually slowing at present, the only thing that will bring the spin to a stop is its eventual vaporisation by the sun, billions of years from now.

M. M. Dworetsky, Department of Physics and Astronomy, University College, London.

QUESTION: When a television is left on standby, does it use as much electricity as when the picture is showing?

☐ NOT at all. A Panasonic 21-inch television, for example, uses just over 2 watts of power on standby mode. The television will only use 20 units per year in this state, costing around £1.50 per year (other televisions can cost up to £8). This is a nominal sum compared to the £84 it would cost to leave a television on all year (1150 units).

Joe Walton, Lee, London SE12.

QUESTION: We are led by the Gospels to understand that Christ and his disciples lived and dressed simply – so what gave rise to the tradition of magnificent palaces and gorgeous vestments, and when did it start?

☐ THROUGHOUT the New Testament period and beyond, the Christian Church continued to meet in dwelling-houses or modest buildings privately owned. When, in the 4th century AD, the Emperor Constantine accepted the legal existence of the Church throughout the Empire, it was officially able to own property and to receive legacies. From this time onwards, some great palaces and basilicas were given to the Church by wealthy benefactors, whose names and portraits have survived within the buildings themselves. Certain bishops were admitted to the Imperial court, and they dressed accordingly. Many of the vestments worn today by ecclesiastical dignitaries resemble the court fashions of the Late Roman and Byzantine periods. There have been attempts within the various branches of the Church to re-establish the practice of poverty – notably that of St Francis of Assisi, when he founded the Franciscan order in the 13th century. Even at a High Mass in St Peter's, Rome, the Pontiff discards his extra adornments and approaches the altar in simple garments, such as Jesus would have worn in his earthly life.

J. M. Frayn, Kingston-on-Thames, Surrey.

QUESTION: New regulations a few years ago permitted all the plumbing equipment in dwellings to run straight off the mains, instead of from storage tanks within the dwelling. The freezing-cold water entering warm, steamy bathrooms naturally generates massive condensation from pipes and cisterns. Whom are we supposed to sue for the cost of replacing rotten floorboards: the architect, the builder, the Department of the Environment, the EC or the person who wrote the new regulations? Who was (s)he in any case?

☐ THE requirement for a cold-water storage cistern in the home arose from the need to store a sufficient supply of water in areas of poor or fluctuating pressure, and from the desire to break the water supply on entry to the house in order to prevent bacteria from sanitary appliances returning through the pipes to contaminate the public supply. This was a major 19th-century concern in cities such as London and Liverpool, which enforced rigid regulations. Many areas of the country did not have regulations requiring the storage cistern, and so have always had a direct supply to the appliances, as have most foreign countries. With (arguable) improvements in water pressure and treatment, and contamination from the toilet prevented by its own cistern, the regulated areas were allowed to be brought into line with the rest of the country. Direct systems are now generally fitted in the interests of cheapness.

Michael Brown, Liverpool.

☐ PLUMBING directly connected to the mains gives homes a much higher water pressure, which is particularly good for showers. A large amount of loft space is freed because there is no need for each household to have a reservoir. There is less pipework, and less risk of water damage (if the cold water tank leaks you are in big trouble). A mains-based system can also be switched off at one stopcock, and all cold-water taps can provide drinking water, whereas households with cold-water tanks are advised to take drinking water from the rising main connection only – usually the kitchen sink tap. The questioner thinks that cold water from the loft tank will be significantly warmer than that from the mains, but this is unlikely given that the cold water tank in a modern insulated house is little warmer than outside. A large tank of water requires a lot of heat to raise its temperature significantly. His condensation problems are most likely to be the fault of a badly ventilated (and perhaps cold) bathroom. An extractor fan should solve this. My previous house (with tank) had bad bathroom condensation; my new house (with tank, fan and double glazing) does not.

Roger Saunders, Abingdon, Oxon.

QUESTION: Why is the control area of an aircraft called the cockpit?

□ A COCKPIT was a small dugout circle enclosed by wooden rails and used for cock fighting, a popular 17th-century sport. Similar structures came to be called a cockpit by analogy: for example, the Cockpit Theatre, which would often feature bloody scenes on its confined stage. Later, the back part of the orlop deck of a man-o'-war became known as the cockpit. It was narrow and deep, with wooden railings, and there was another connection with blood – during battle, wounded sailors were transferred to it. This opened up new meanings for cockpit linked to travel, while retaining the idea of a confined space. In some ship designs the cockpit was also used for navigation. Travel in narrow, deep spaces was a feature of early aircraft. And the language of flying picked up many terms from seafaring – aeronautics, knots, navigation. So the 'cockpit' was borrowed to refer to the confined space in the fuselage for crew and passengers. Later it was specialised to mean the pilot's area.
Doug Gowan, Hornsey, London N8.

QUESTION: Please can any of your readers explain how the manufacturers of tinned mandarins manage to get the individual segments clean of pith and the membrane skin they are wrapped in?

□ IN MARMALADE factories and mandarin-canning enterprises all over the world, an essential member of staff is the comedian to take the pith out of the oranges.
Ms J. E. Howard, Bedford.

QUESTION: When did the England cricket team consist of 11 players born in England, and who were they?

□ FOR the third Test between England and Australia played at

Edgbaston, Birmingham, on 6–11 July 1989, the England players (with place of birth) were as follows: Gooch – Leytonstone; Curtis – Chislehurst; Gower (capt) – Tunbridge Wells; Tavare – Orpington; Barnett – Stoke-on-Trent; Botham – Heswall; Russell – Stroud; Embury – Peckham; Fraser – Billinge; Dilley – Dartford; Jarvis – Redcar. The game, badly disrupted by rain, ended in a draw. Man of the match was the Australian batsman D. M. Jones who, in his first innings, was dismissed when caught by a substitute fielder, I. Folley – also born in England (Burnley). England made three changes to their team for the fourth Test in Manchester, including the selection of Smith (Durban, South Africa). Australia won the six-match series by four tests to nil.
Richard Rose, Orton, Northants.

☐ THE inclusion of non-English-born players is by no means a modern trend. The England team of 1931 contained two Indians (Duleepsinhji and Jardine), a Peruvian (Freddie Brown), a Scot (Peebles) and an Australian ('Gubby' Allen). But this was only to be expected, given that the chairman of the selectors was a West Indian, 'Plum' Warner. In recent years, one might have thought Colin Cowdrey or Ted Dexter would have put a stop to such unpatriotic goings-on – but they're foreigners as well.
Steve Pittaro, Langport, Somerset.

QUESTION: Why did Britain and France, having guaranteed Poland's frontiers, not declare war on the Soviet Union on 17 September 1939, when the Soviets invaded eastern Poland?

☐ SINCE they were already at war with Germany, it would have been a daft move. But, additionally, the 'Agreement of Mutual Assistance' signed London, 25 August 1939, didn't require it. Article 1 of the agreement stated: 'Should one of the Contracting Parties become engaged in hostilities with a European Power in consequence of aggression by the latter against that Contracting

Party, the other Contracting Party will at once give the Contracting Party engaged in hostilities all the support and assistance in its power.' Item 1(a) of the Secret Protocol that accompanied the agreement stated: 'By the expression "a European Power" employed in the Agreement is to be understood Germany.'
Peter R. Brooke, Aberdeen.

QUESTION: Why is it that I seem unable to buy a simple Geiger counter as a toy, as I can a metal detector? Is there some regulation which prohibits their sale, to prevent the public from discovering radiation hot spots?

☐ I HAVE one built from a kit sold by Maplin Electronics. The current price is £105, so it may not qualify as a toy. Its sensitivity is rather low. To get a big enough count to detect small changes in background radiation will take hours or days, so you also need a separate electronic counter. It really isn't going to detect small amounts of radioactivity in food either. However, if Hinkley Point blows up, it should provide plenty of warning of immediately dangerous radiation. At one time, people used to buy Geiger counters in the hope of finding a uranium mine and getting rich. Now we know better. That's probably why they aren't common any more.
Steve Hayes, Swansea.

QUESTION: In words such as pheasant, phoney, morphine and sapphire, why is the sound 'f' represented by 'ph'? These words do not all derive from the Greek.

☐ IN ANCIENT Greek, the sound indicated by the Greek-letter equivalent of *ph* was originally a kind of P. This had evolved into an F-sound by the time Greek-derived roots such as *morph-*, *graph-* and *phon-* were being borrowed by other languages. While the *ph* in *pheasant, morphine and sapphire* is historically accurate, its extension to non-Greek words such as *phew*, *caliph* and *bumph* is an etymological aberration. (The origins of *phoney* are obscure.)

The sound F is voiceless. The reason *ph* in the name *Stephen* is pronounced as a V, the voiced counterpart of F, is due to a sound change which took place in Old English, when F turned into V in the middle of words. The change is now extinct, but relics of it survive in pairs such as *wife–wives*, *leaf–leaves* and *loaf–loaves*. Greek forms which were borrowed before this time, including *Stephen*, got caught up in the change as much as native words. However, subsequent borrowings and coinings, such as *graphic* and *telephone*, arrived too late to be affected by it. The word *nephew*, with its variant V and F pronunciations, is something of an oddity. The form with V follows the Old English pattern. The F variant is a relatively recent innovation, probably influenced by the *ph*-spelling, which in this word is unetymological. A generalised version of the F-to-V change affected other fricative sounds (usually written as *s* or *th*), although this is not consistently reflected in the spelling. For example, we find voiceless S in the noun *house* but a voiced Z-sound in the plural *houses*. Similarly, compare the voiceless version of *th* in, say, *path* and *bath* with the voiced version of the sound in *paths* and *baths*.

John Harris, Department of Phonetics and Linguistics, University College, London.

QUESTION: Why is it called corpsing when actors lose control and start laughing?

☐ BECAUSE when an actor loses control and starts laughing, he 'kills' the performance.
Jo Montagu, Chiswick, London W4.

☐ THE origin of the expression corpsing was coined many years ago after a production of *Hamlet*. In the final scene, Fortinbras plus Ambassadors enter to a scene of littered bodies all over the stage. Unfortunately, and rather untimely, the elastic in Fortinbras' breeches gave way – much to the delight of the then writhing bodies. Thus corpsing has come to mean laughing on stage at an inappropriate time.
Corinne Corre, Finchley, London N3.

☐ To CORPSE – to reduce someone to a state of uncontrollable laughter – derives, of course, from the Keystone Corpse, who often had this effect on people.
Michael Trollope, Bishampton, Worcs.

QUESTION: According to encyclopaedias, the rhinoceros has roamed the earth for 70 million years. If dinosaurs became extinct about 60 million years ago, why did the rhinoceros survive?

☐ It is probably simplistic to assume that dinosaurs (there were more than 100 families of them) died out suddenly 65 million years ago, destroyed by asteroids or meteorites. The most likely explanation is a gradual decline brought about by climatic change, which mammals like the ancestors of the rhino were able to exploit to their advantage. Mammals evolved from mammal-like reptiles between 250 and 200 million years ago, so dinosaurs and mammals co-existed over a period of nearly 200 million years. In this time, many dinosaur families – the anchisaurids, brachiosaurids, diplocids etc, simply died out. So mammals, birds, reptiles and amphibians are dinosaurs that have adapted to changing conditions. The evolution of the rhinoceros may provide part of the answer to this evolutionary conundrum. The rhinos of Africa and the tapirs of South America are related: their common ancestor was possibly *Indricotherium* from Asia, which was 18 feet high at the shoulder and weighed 32 tons. It died out in the Miocene period. Later in the Miocene, the horned rhino evolved: sub-species included the Woolly rhinoceros and the *Brontotherium*. These latter were ecologically replaced by the giant rhinos of the late Oligocene, about 35 million years ago.
Robert Turpin, Peverell, Plymouth, Devon.

☐ Both the question and Robert Turpin's answer are in error. Rhinoceroses have certainly not 'roamed the earth for 70 million years'. Ancestral rhinoceroses have been found in deposits of late Eocene age (about 40 million years old), while the dinosaurs died out 65 million years ago at the end of the Cretaceous period. Therefore a gap of about 20 million years separates the dinosaurs from the line of mammals that gave rise to the rhinos of today. Rhinos and tapirs are closely related, but *Indricotherium* was not the 'common ancestor' of the two groups. *Indricotherium* was in fact an early offshoot of the lineage that gave rise to modern rhinos. Also, the woolly rhino (*Coelodonta*) could not have been ecologically replaced by the '. . . rhinos of the Oligocene', as the Woolly rhino lived during the Pleistocene, 21 million years after the end of the Oligocene! Although dinosaurs were on the decline before they finally became extinct, we cannot, at present (if ever), assign this to a single cause. The world's climate was changing at the end of the Cretaceous period, and there is good evidence of an asteroid impact 65 million years ago. However, the relative importance of these factors (and other environmental and biological changes occurring at the same time) is a matter of great contention. Finally, the following statement: 'So mammals, birds, reptiles and amphibians are dinosaurs that have adapted to changing conditions,' is just not true. The dinosaurs were a distinct group of animals. It is thought that some small carnivorous dinosaurs are ancestral to birds, but living mammals and amphibians are only distantly related to the dinosaurs. In fact it is thought that dinosaurs are more closely related to birds than to living 'reptiles' (turtles, lizards and snakes, and crocodiles).

Paul M. Barrett, Department of Earth Sciences, University of Cambridge.

QUESTION: In the board game Monopoly, as in real life, the players as 'landowners' are free to exploit the other players as 'tenants'. The wealth gap widens rapidly and the losers starve. How should the rules of Monopoly be revised to reflect landowners' responsibilities to the community?

□ MONOPOLY beautifully illustrates the inability of the free market to sustain itself. Inequalities soon emerge and are rapidly amplified

by chance and skill through the market mechanism – until the game eventually comes to a stop when all the money and most of the assets end up in the hands of one player. It is only the 'social' – i.e. non-market income received by each player on passing 'GO' – that keeps the game going long enough to be worth playing. The free market is no better than any other perpetual motion contraption. It requires an external source of demand to drive it. If you want to model the welfare state, you could impose a progressive tax on rents to go to the Community Chest, and you could increase the 'social income' received by players. In short, 'Tax and Spend', the ultimate anathema of the free market believers. But you would then face the possibility of an endless game!
Ralph Herdan, Stockport, Cheshire.

□ THE game of Monopoly is based on an older game, the Landlord's Game, devised in the United States in the 1890s and intended by its inventor, Elizabeth Webb, as propaganda against slum landlordism. In the 1970s a small US manufacturer produced a game called Anti-Monopoly in which the aim was to break up, rather than create, large capitalist enterprises – but was promptly sued for breach of copyright by Parker Brothers, the US manufacturers of Monopoly. A new edition of this game has appeared recently, so the dispute seems to have been resolved.
Roger Sandell, Richmond, Surrey.

□ WHEN any player amasses more than £100,000 in cash, he should give half to the Conservative Party and go directly to Cyprus. His remaining property should be sold and a pension fund should be established for the other players after 10 per cent has been deducted for the Royal Train.
Rev Dr Bernard E. Jones, Fulwood, Lancs.

QUESTION: I was told that there are three words in the English language ending in 'shion'. The first two were 'fashion' and 'cushion'. Can anyone tell me what the third word is?

☐ THERE are more than three, according to the Chambers Dictionary. Apart from hyphenated forms – air-cushion, leaf-cushion, king's-cushion, lady's-cushion and parrot-fashion – there are also two derivative forms, refashion and pincushion, which are not hyphenated. However, the questioner is probably referring to fushion, a Scots version of foison, meaning plenty or strength.
Dorothy Harrison, Peverell, Plymouth, Devon.

☐ THE word is hushion, a Scots dialect word for a footless stocking (also spelt 'hoshan'). The Oxford English Dictionary also lists parishion (meaning the same as 'parishioner'); but the word never really settled down to any definite spelling before being dropped from use in the 16th century. (Source: *Questions of English*, Oxford University Press, 1994.)
Nina Dobner, Oxford University Press.

QUESTION: Why do red peppers cost more than green peppers?

☐ RED peppers are ripened green peppers. The high cost of the former reflects the additional cost of delaying harvesting and marketing until the immature green-skinned pepper matures to a sweeter red-skinned pepper.
Philip Roberts, Preston, Lancs.

QUESTION: During the 20th century, has there ever been an instance of a petition having any effect on decisions of policy and/or law?

☐ THE RSPCA is regularly lobbied by individuals and by other organisations to organise or take part in petitions on a huge range of animal-related issues. Individuals get hugely enthusiastic about the logistics of petitions but they have very little clue as to their purpose. Petitions are a valuable campaigning tool in the political or opinion-forming process but they are not an end in themselves. Whereas they can be dismissed or quietly absorbed by those they are aimed at, the process of collecting signatures will have given hundreds of thousands of opportunities for drawing attention to the issue, and for giving out further information on it. Those involved in gaining signatures also become more committed, better informed and better able to argue their case. The direct effect on decisions is therefore hard to assess, as the petition tactic is merely part of a much bigger political process. I believe that when Sir Keith Joseph, as Education Secretary, was questioned as to precisely how many representations he had received which had caused him to turn the spotlight on political influences in schools, he admitted that there had only been two letters. Conversely in 1991 we became involved in a worldwide anti-bullfighting petition; when we presented our part of the petition of more than two million signatures to the Spanish Embassy, the press attaché commented to the effect: 'So? What about your fox hunting?'

Jerry Lloyd, director of public relations, RSPCA, Horsham, West Sussex.

QUESTION: Taking the earth's orbit of the sun to be horizontal, where will I have to go to be 'on top of the world' at the very start of the next century?

☐ LET us assume that we stand with our heads upwards. The earth's equator is inclined to the ecliptic, and the angle of inclination is equal to the angular distance of the Arctic Circle from the North Pole. Thus the point on the earth which is 'on top of the world' is always on the Arctic Circle. The start of the century will be at midnight on 31 December/1 January 2001. We can assume that the century will start at the first place where the local mean time will be midnight. This will be defined by the place where one day ends and the next starts – the international dateline. So the location of the place 'at the top of the world' is the crossing point of the dateline and Arctic Circle. In 2001 this will be, approximately, at latitude 23° 26′ N and longitude 168° 58′ W. This is in the Chukchi Sea, about 90′ N of the Diomede Islands. Unfortunately, nobody sets their clocks to this time, and so it is only a theoretically correct solution. We could take the start of the century as being when the first country will celebrate the start of the new century. This will be Tonga which is 13 hours ahead of GMT. The top of the world at midnight Tonga time, will be at longitude 165° E, about 40 kilometres from Devil Mountain in Alaska where the local time will be 2 a.m. on 31 December. Or we could take it that the century begins when the date is 2001 January 1. This occurs at midnight on the prime meridian, in which case the top of the world will be on that meridian and the time will be midnight GMT, which is when we will all be celebrating anyway (except those who mistakenly think that the century begins in the year 2000!)

Dr Peter Andrews, Royal Greenwich Observatory, Cambridge.

☐ I AM sorry to have to contradict a member of the Royal Greenwich Observatory, but it is impossible to be 'on top of the world' at local midnight on New Year's Day. Both the 'top of the world' and the midnight line move around the world as it rotates but at slightly different rates. They are about 170 degrees apart on New Year's Day. The point defined as the 'top' of the world by the questioner is the axis of the ecliptic, and always lies on the Arctic Circle, as Dr Andrews says (which is 66½° N, not 23½°). Along with all other celestial phenomena, it completes a circuit every 23 hours and 56 minutes, thereby gaining on the midnight line by a little less than one degree of longitude per day, and lapping it once a year, on Midsummer's Day, which is therefore the only date anyone can be on top of the world at midnight. We have defined the 'top of the world' to be the point at which an observer sees the plane containing the orbit of the earth as horizontal. The sun must therefore be in a plane horizontal to the

observer and on the horizon. The 'top of the world' point at any given instant is therefore one of the two points where the day/night terminator crosses the Arctic Circle. From the winter solstice to the summer solstice it is the point of sunrise; for the other half of the year it is sunset. Sunrise on the Arctic Circle on New Year's Day (only 11 days after the Winter Solstice) is at about 11.15 a.m. local time, and it is at this time, rather than midnight, that you would be on top of the world. The first point in the world to enter any new day is Tonga (13 hours ahead of GMT). At midnight Tonga time on New Year's Day the 'top' point is on the Arctic Circle. However, it is not on Tonga's longitude of 165° W (which would put it in Alaska) but about 4° E of the Greenwich Meridian, 250 miles off the coast of Norway. Astronomers, aviators and others who need a worldwide measure of time use the time known as 'Universal', or 'Zulu' time – better known to us as GMT. At midnight GMT on New Year's Day, the 'top of the world' lies on the Arctic Circle at about 169° E, in eastern Siberia, 2317 local time (sunset on the Antarctic Circle) on New Year's night.
T. G. E. Lidbetter, Surrey.

QUESTION: What is the female equivalent of a misogynist?

☐ A MISTEROGYNIST.
R. Sumner, Manchester.

☐ THE word is 'misandrist' – one who hates men. Strictly speaking, neither misogynist nor misandrist specifies the gender of the person who hates: you should be able to be both female and to hate women.
Clare Passingham, Headington, Oxford.

QUESTION: Why does the surface above an underground nuclear test sink, to form a crater, without any material appearing to be blown out of the hole? Air-to-ground

filming of such tests appears to show that an implosion, rather than explosion, takes place. What has happened to the missing soil?

□ UNDERGROUND testing of atomic bombs contains the explosion and radiation. For this reason the depth to which the bomb is buried varies from 5–600 feet to 2–3,000 feet, depending on the size of the bomb. When the bomb is detonated, the temperature of the blast is around 100 million degrees centigrade and the pressure many millions of atmospheres. This has the effect of melting the surrounding rock and blowing it up into a huge underground bubble several hundred feet in diameter. Shortly after the explosion, the temperature and pressure drop, leaving a void into which the overlying rock collapses. This is manifested on the surface as a crater.
Chris Waller, Yate, Bristol.

QUESTION: Are there any recorded instances of surgeons performing operations on themselves?

□ YES, although DIY operations aren't limited to surgeons. With the full permission of a hospital in Colorado, Dr George Balderston removed his own appendix – in the hospital's surgical theatre he sat down, anaesthetised himself, opened up his abdomen, snipped and closed the wound with clamps and stitches unaided within an hour (reported 21 March 1978, London Evening News). For unqualified DIY operations, however: Poppy Faldmo, 21, of Salt Lake City, took out her own tonsils because she didn't have medical insurance to cover the £700 hospital bill. She spent hours every day in front of a mirror, removing the inflamed tonsils a little at a time with nail scissors and a modelling knife, using a toothache gel as an anaesthetic. Doctors say she did a perfect job (*Daily Mirror*, 9 February 1993). The case of a man who performed his own ad hoc castration and then went to a hospital for a professional

opinion is reported in the *AMA Journal* for May 1974. Thanks to
the *Fortean Times* for supplying me with the relevant facts.
Stephen A. Graham, Carlisle, Cumbria.

□ AS A dental surgeon I have, on two occasions, extracted an offending tooth from my own mouth.
H. H. Reeves, London SW11.

**QUESTION: Is it true that one of the slum houses described
in Frederick Engels's *Condition of the Working Class in
England* in 1845 is still occupied?**

□ I SEARCHED for the last of Engels's back-to-backs in Manchester
in the early 1960s. All I could find was a terrace parallel and east
of Oxford Road, at right angles to the river. They were used by
small businesses. However, there were residential back-to-backs
being used near the Regent Street/York Road area of Leeds, certainly until the mid-1970s. With 1.5 million homes unfit for
human habitation in Britain today, the numbers of slum houses
have not changed much since 1848.
Franklin Medhurst, Greystone, Stockton on Tees.

**QUESTION: If someone were to undergo a DNA profile test
soon after receiving a substantial blood transfusion, would
the results reveal part of the blood donor's profile? If so,
how long would this last, and would it have implications
for the test's use in criminal cases?**

□ THE issue of possible genetic contamination of blood samples
has been around long before 'DNA profiling'. In practice there are
several reasons why the contamination may not be detected or
may not be relevant to the 'DNA profile'. Transfused blood carries
DNA only in white blood cells, since red cells lose their nucleus
which contains the DNA during their maturation in the bone
marrow. Even after a substantial transfusion, the amount of DNA

introduced is much less than might be expected. Blood for transfusion is usually stored for days or weeks before it is transfused into
a patient, and during storage the white cells will adhere to blood
bags or will die and disintegrate, leaving only fragments of DNA.
Following a transfusion, a patient's own blood greatly dilutes the
donor white cells and the immune system eliminates them – probably within hours – again reducing the likelihood of contaminating DNA in a blood sample. There are several methods of
establishing a 'DNA profile' and some depend on the use of the
Polymerase Chain Reaction which amplifies a specific DNA sequence up to a million times. Using such techniques it would be
possible to identify contaminating DNA, as there would be
measurable inconsistency. In 'DNA profile' methods not using
DNA amplification, however, it is unlikely that contaminating
DNA from blood transfusions would be revealed. Contamination
of a blood sample with non-self DNA is a potential problem that
all laboratories using 'DNA profile' techniques must be continually
on the watch for. DNA contamination can arise apart from blood
transfusions: for example, it is known that women may carry
tissue cells derived from their children many years after giving
birth; and organ transplant recipients can become 'infected' with
cells migrating from donor organs, especially into the skin – this
may be part of the process of successfully accepting the foreign
organ. In a criminal case, contaminating DNA would be identified.
As well as this, anyone who had received a blood transfusion would
have the procedure carefully documented in medical notes, as
would the donor of that blood, allowing the possibility of a check.
*Philip Dyer (Tissue Typing Laboratory) and Rob Elles (Molecular
Genetics Laboratory), St Mary's Hospital, Manchester.*

QUESTION: Bottle banks are springing up in every car
park throughout the country. What percentage of bottles
are now made using recycled glass? Does recycling save
money?

☐ IN 1992 the average glass bottle manufactured in the UK

contained 26 per cent recycled glass. In 1993 that figure was around 30 per cent. Green bottles manufactured in this country contain at least 60 per cent, and sometimes as much as 90 per cent, recycled glass. Recycling glass saves both raw material and energy consumption: using one tonne of cullet (recycled glass) in the furnace saves 1.2 tonnes of raw materials and 30 gallons (150 litres) of oil. Glass recycling also saves landfill space and, therefore, reduces waste disposal costs.
Alison Morris, British Glass, Sheffield.

QUESTION: What problems might I incur if I shot down a model aircraft flying about 100 feet above my land?

☐ TRYING to avoid falling shrapnel.
P. C. Mitchell, Failsworth, Manchester.

☐ VIOLATION of another's airspace is trespass, not a crime. In the absence of any criminal offence by the plane's operator – which would permit reasonable force to be used to prevent the continuation of the crime – the action contemplated could give rise to a charge of causing criminal damage. If it were the intention not to return the plane, once shot down, to its owner, a charge of theft would also lie. Even if it were intended to return the plane to its owner, if the damage to it was such as to cause it to have lost all its value, then a charge of theft might still lie. The possession and use of a weapon might also incur liability under the Firearms Act 1968. The appropriate remedy for trespass is a civil action for damages, or to seek an injunction restraining the plane's operator from violating another's airspace, or for causing a nuisance.
Robert Lynn, lecturer, Cardiff Law School.

QUESTION: What are the large ugly square boxes that are appearing on the side of red pillar-boxes?

☐ THEY are drop boxes put there for second/third bag(s) for postmen or women to collect during their delivery round. This allows additional mail to be delivered by one postman/woman without exceeding the agreed weight limit. The boxes are not always sited at the side of pillar boxes, but are sometimes free-standing.
S. J. Doncaster, postwoman, Bideford, Devon.

QUESTION: Why are psychiatrists given the name 'shrink'?

☐ IT'S short for 'headshrink' or 'headshrinker' and comes from the United States. According to the OED the first substantiated use was in 1966.
Peter Barnes (editor, Shrink Rap, *Grafton Books), Milton Keynes, Bucks.*

QUESTION: What is, or was, Queen Anne's Bounty?

☐ QUEEN Anne's Bounty was a fund established by Queen Anne in 1704 for the relief of the poorer clergy, many of whom had incomes of less than £50 per annum at that time. It was created from tithes formerly given to the Pope but annexed by Henry VIII. The fund was increased by Parliament a century later but merged with the Ecclesiastical Commission in 1948.
Malcolm McDougall, Hampton Wick, Kingston upon Thames.

QUESTION: Is Lady Thatcher a patron of any charity and, if so, which?

☐ SHE is a patron of the Elizabeth Garrett Anderson Hospital Appeal Trust, which perhaps explains why that hospital still exists, whereas the South London Hospital for Women, for example, is long gone.
Tony Black, Otford, Kent.

QUESTION: Who was the last person to be beheaded in this country? Was an official decision made to stop the practice?

☐ SIMON, Lord Lovat, was the last person beheaded in England (9 April 1747). Beheading is said to have been introduced into England by William the Conqueror in the 11th century and the punishment was usually reserved for offenders of high rank. (The ancient Greeks and Romans regarded it as a more honourable form of execution too.) The fourth Earl Ferrers was hanged after a petition (1760) to be beheaded was refused. In 1814 the King of England was empowered by royal warrant to substitute hanging as the ordinary method of executing criminals. Yet beheading remained part of the common law method of dealing with treason as late as 1820: traitors had their heads cut off by a masked man after they were hanged.
Tony Martin, Nunhead, London SE15.

QUESTION: What does 'Twenty-twenty vision' mean and what is the measurement scheme it comes from?

☐ THERE are several methods for the measurement and recording of vision, but all are based on the angular subtense at the eye of the smallest object (typically a letter) that can be resolved. In the UK and US it is customary to use Snellen's notation, where Vision equals the actual distance from the test chart divided by the distance at which smallest letters read subtend an angle of 5 minutes. The testing distance employed in the UK is usually 6 metres (a 3-metre consulting room with a plane mirror), and below each row on the test chart is printed the distance at which the letters would subtend 5 minutes of arc. Once a person has read as far down the chart as he/she can, the vision is recorded in a fractional form. For example, if only the large letter at the top of the chart can be resolved, the vision is recorded as 6/60. A vision of 6/6 (six-six) is taken as a good standard of vision, although many people perform better than this. As a comparison, the characters on a standard British car number plate, at a distance of 54 metres, would be almost the same angular size as a 6/6 letter. In the US the testing distance is usually 20 feet, so a vision of 20/20 is equivalent to 6/6. Thus a person with 'twenty-twenty' vision is considered to have good eyesight.

Dr Eve Pascal, Vision Sciences Department, Glasgow Caledonian University.

QUESTION: What is the origin and derivation of the word 'wimp'?

☐ THE Wymps were characters in children's books a century ago by Evelyn Sharp, who liked playing jokes but tended to cry if anyone got their own back. In *Arrowsmith* (1925), Sinclair Lewis wrote of 'Wimpish young men'.

Ivor Solomons, Norwich.

☐ ALTHOUGH the Oxford English Dictionary suggests that it may have originally been US slang, Webster's believes it originated in the UK. In 1917 the phrase 'go wimping' was Oxford University slang for a male on the look-out for females for sexual gratification. By the 1920s, 'wimp' had modified to denote a woman or a girl. The word may be an abbreviated corruption of 'women', or it may be derived from 'whimper'. The Oxford English Dictionary invites us to compare it with the English dialect word 'wimp', meaning (of a dog) to whine.

Maxine Simmons, Enfield, Middlesex.

QUESTION: 'No hawkers, no circulars', says the sign outside some older houses. If I put one up saying 'No circulars, no free newspapers', what legal force would it have?

☐ IF YOU have a front gate, a path and a letterbox, you give implied permission (a licence) to anyone including the postman to come on to your property and deliver items through your letterbox – otherwise they would be trespassing. If you put up a sign saying, 'no circulars, no free newspapers', you revoke that licence, and any such persons would then be trespassing. In fact they would commit two forms of trespass: first, coming on to your property; and secondly, leaving undesired goods. If you are not present when the trespass occurs, then all you can do is require whoever left the circular or newspaper to remove it. If they fail to do so the law says you are entitled to keep it! The only way to prevent further intrusions would be to obtain an injunction – not a realistic proposition as you have to be able to identify the offending party. If you are present when such trespass occurs you may ask the person to leave, along with the offending material; give the trespasser enough time to do so peacefully; and then use reasonable force to eject the trespasser. But you can do this to any unwelcome visitor, whether you have a sign or not. The only effect of a sign is that you should have fewer unwelcome visitors.

Kevin J. Cowen, Kidderminster, Worcs.

□ IN MY case such a sign has proved to be the perfect deterrent to the unwanted delivery of free newspapers. We have not had one since putting up the sign four years ago.

D. Metcalf, Wigginton, Herts.

QUESTION: Why was it decided that 999 should be the telephone number of the emergency services in Britain? Who made this momentous decision, and when?

□ THE emergency code had to be easily remembered, and standard across the country. To work in London, a three-digit code was much to be preferred and, to be usable on the figure-only dials used in most places, the code needed to be a real number. A letter code like 'TIMe' and 'ENGineer' – perhaps 'HELp' – was never in with a chance. 000 was out – 0 was the code for the operator, and the whole point of this was to provide a by-pass for emergency calls, ensuring an immediate answer. In the end, 999 was pretty much forced on the designers. Callers had to be able to dial the code with as much ease in a payphone as on any other line, and this meant being able to do so without needing to insert any coins. The Button A/B payphone was such that the dial was useless until the correct local call fee had been prepaid. The digit 0 was an exception, and could be dialled straight away, without coins, to raise the operator. It was relatively simple task to modify things to extend coin-free dialling to the next dial number, namely 9. Hence 999. The service was introduced in London in July 1937. It is convenient to assume that the person who made this decision was a faceless civil servant in the Post Office engineering department. However, matters of such public interest rarely went ahead without the authority of the responsible minister – the Postmaster General – and so it is much fairer to say that the ultimate decision was made by a politician.

Neil Johannessen, Manager, BT Museum, London EC4.

QUESTION: What became of the Terra Nova, Scott's ship on his disastrous polar expedition?

☐ THE *Terra Nova* was built in 1884 as a whaling ship, but became better known as a polar expedition ship. She served with the Jackson-Harmsworth expedition of 1894–7, as relief ship for Scott's *Discovery* expedition in 1903, and returned to the Antarctic with Scott's 1910–1913 expedition. She was repurchased by her previous owners, Bowring Brothers Ltd, in 1913 and from 1914 to 1942 was based in Nova Scotia. She served in the seasonal Newfoundland seal fishery during the months of March and April, but was generally laid up for the rest of the year. During the First World War she also made some coastal trading voyages with cargoes from Canada's Maritime Provinces to St John's, Newfoundland, and at least one voyage to Cardiff, with pitprops. In 1942 she was chartered to carry supplies for US bases in Greenland. On Sunday 12 September that year, while on passage from Greenland to Newfoundland, she developed a bad leak and

at 1920 hours transmitted an SOS message. This was answered
by the US coast guard cutter *Atak* which, by daybreak next day,
had picked up the crew of 24 men from the *Terra Nova*, by now
sinking and burning. The master of the *Terra Nova* was the last
man to board the *Atak*, which then ensured her sinking with 23
rounds of 3-inch gun fire. Her approximate last position was 60°
30′ N 46° 30′ W, off the south-western coast of Greenland.
*Iain MacKenzie, Maritime Information Centre, Greenwich, London
SE10.*

QUESTION: Some time ago Alistair Cooke mentioned in
his 'Letter from America' that before the end of the century,
the UK had to repay the US for war loans made during the
1939–45 war. Have these loans been repaid and, if not,
how much do we owe and when is repayment due?

☐ THIRTY billion dollars-worth of ships, tanks, guns and planes
were supplied, under Lend Lease and free of charge, to the British
Commonwealth. In exchange, Britain paid for the subsistence of
US servicemen stationed in the UK and the building of bases in
Britain, Australia and India – estimated at $7.6 billion. Britain's
repayment of loans to the US had nothing to do with Lend Lease
during the Second World War. On 6 December 1945, Attlee's
Labour government requested two loans from the Americans to
pay for post-war development, including the cost of the National
Health Service. According to HM Treasury figures, the total sum
outstanding at 31 March 1993 was $1.357 billion. On 31 Decem-
ber each year, Britain makes two payments, one on each loan. The
payments made on 31 December 1992 totalled $115 million prin-
cipal, $22.5 million interest.
Tony Martin, Nunhead, London SE15.

☐ TONY Martin says that 'Attlee's Labour government requested
two loans from the US to pay for post-war development, including
the National Health Service'. This accusation, that the US was
financing Labour's welfare state, was widely believed, especially

in America, then and later. It is totally false. The money was borrowed to cover the UK's balance-of-payments deficit, not domestic spending. And this deficit was mainly caused by the UK's continuing high overseas military spending, at a time when America was vigorously cutting back its own.
Peter Stephenson, London NW3.

QUESTION: What was the original 'red herring'?

□ A RED herring is a smoked herring, or kipper. Its figurative sense derives from the use of kippers as a decoy to draw hounds off a scent. The earliest mention of red herrings recorded in OED is from a cook-book dated 1430, but the *locus classicus* for all scholars of the kipper is that neglected masterpiece, Nashe's Lenten Stuffe, published in 1599. Subtitled *The Prayse of the Red Herring*, this was the last known work by the Elizabethan pamphleteer Thomas Nashe. It is a eulogy of the herring fishermen of Great Yarmouth, where Nashe lived while in exile from London; and of the kipper itself, the 'stuffe' which fed him during this lean period. The figurative sense of the red herring is implicit throughout the book, as a series of rhapsodic tangents or diversions from his theme.
Charles Nicholl, Lower Breinton, Herefordshire.

□ CHARLES Nicholl is seriously in error when he defines a red herring as 'a smoked herring or kipper'. The kipper is very much with us; the red herring is something of an endangered species. The herring is gutted and opened out flat before smoking to produce a kipper, while the red herring is smoked for far longer periods and retains its uncut fishy form.
C. H. Read, Bradwell, Norfolk.

QUESTION: How did the English court system come to have a 12-person jury?

□ THE first clause of the Assize of Clarendon in 1166 stated '. . .

declarations shall be made for every county and for every hundred by twelve of the more competent men of a hundred'. This is the first recorded statute requiring a jury of 12 in a court of law, but juries had already been in existence for some time – jurors had been widely used during the Domesday Inquest of 1086 to swear to the extent of landholding before the Domesday Commissioners. It has to be understood that juries at this time were not present to decide on a verdict but were in fact attestors or witnesses. In the royal courts they appeared before the judges to swear that a certain crime had been committed and that the prisoner on trial had been the person who committed that crime. Similar procedures had been current in Anglo-Saxon law and the Norman Conquest had introduced ideas that had been common under Carolingian law in France. It was the Norman kings of England, however, who refined the process and formulated the 12-man jury as an alternative to trial by combat or trial by ordeal: trial by jury became common practice from about 1200. Juries of eight or nine were quite common in the Domesday Inquest, and later Grand Juries could be much larger, but the figure of 12 decided upon for the Anglo-Norman jury seems to rest on a practice common to areas of Lincolnshire around the year 1000 when 'twelve leading thanes of the wapentake' swore they would neither protect the guilty nor accuse the innocent. Other than that, one can only say that 12 has always been a significant mystical number – 12 months, 12 signs of the zodiac, 12 apostles, the duodecimal system devised by the Babylonians, etc.

Colin Pilkington, Burscough, Lancs.

QUESTION: Is evolution a theory still waiting to be proved by the discovery of 'missing links'?

☐ No. EVOLUTION is known to happen; there are sequences of 'links' without missing bits. Moreover, we can see evolution happening. The best-known example is a type of moth in which, originally, most individuals were pale and camouflaged against the bark of birch trees. There were always a few darker individuals. When industrial pollution stained the trees, white moths were easily seen and picked off by birds but dark ones were now well-camouflaged. The population evolved from being predominantly white to being predominantly dark. If the questioner was referring more specifically to human evolution, then we scientists must be more careful. Although there are fossils showing parts of the evolutionary pathway, and although there is other evidence (we share something like 98 per cent of our genetic code with chimpanzees), we cannot prove scientifically that humans evolved from something non-human. A belief in evolution is the only known scientific way of making sense of the evidence but it would be arrogant and unscientific of us to state human evolution as a fact.

Dr Peter Cotgreave, Department of Zoology, Oxford.

☐ LIKE all good scientific theories, this theory is framed in such a way as to be eminently falsifiable: the discovery of the bones of a horse or baboon in the same geological stratum as the remains of a dinosaur, for example, would comprehensively demolish it. Despite this, no such contrary evidence has been found and all that we have learnt from genetics and molecular biology, two sciences unknown to Charles Darwin, has supported the theory – though there is still room for debate about the details (is natural selection the only driving force? is the rate of evolutionary change constant?). Use of the words 'missing link' suggests a fundamental misconception of what the theory states. Evolution cannot be likened to simple linear process, like a ladder with distinct rungs that have to be slotted in in a particular sequence. A better model would be a continuously branching tree. From this we can see that our nearest biological relatives, the primates, are all as far along their particular branches of the tree as we are along ours and our relationship to them, from the close to the not-so-close, can be shown directly. The theory does not require a 'link' at some notional man–ape boundary.

Michael Hutton, Camberwell, London SE5.

QUESTION: The symbol of Christianity in the early centuries was the fish. When did this change to a cross bearing the figure of Christ and why?

☐ WHEN the early Christians were persecuted they used the arcane, coded symbol of the Fish. Its Greek translation *Ixthus* was an acronym for *Iesus Xristos, Theou Uios, Soter*, meaning Jesus Christ, Son of God, Saviour. Later, when Christianity was expediently combined with the Almighty Apollo and Mithras cults to form the official Roman religion, it became safe to display the crucifix openly, although the Emperor Constantine in AD 312, allegedly seeing the conquering sign XP (Chi Ro) in the sky was obviously still reading in Greek, not Latin. The fact that the Greek Chi, for Christ, coincidentally was an 'X' helped to associate it with the Cross.
Benedict Sandham, Mannamead, Plymouth, Devon.

QUESTION: Just what is so good about bees' knees?

☐ 'IT'S da bee's knees' is mock-Italian (probably from US vaudeville usage) for 'It's the business' – in other words, the very thing, just what you/we need. It gave rise to many parody forms, especially with 'cat': it's the cat's meow/whiskers/pyjamas and so on. According to Wentworth and Flexner, in *Dictionary of American Slang*, such phrases were archaic by the early 1950s.
Liyi Tan and John Brunner, South Petherton, Somerset.

☐ I ALWAYS understood it to be a short form of 'The Bs and Es' – the significant initial letters of 'Be-alls and End-alls' of whatever subject might be under discussion.
Enid Braddock, Horbury, Wakefield.

QUESTION: Duracell batteries sell at shocking prices in the shops but for very much less in street markets. The

batteries look identical, except for the packaging. Are they actually the same product? And will they be subject to the new VAT charge on 'fuel'?

☐ THE cheap Duracell batteries bought in street markets are almost certainly imported from Belgium and are the standard zinc-carbon type, not the alkaline 'high power' version marketed by Duracell in the UK. They are identifiable by the blister packaging which tells the purchaser the country of origin. The company chooses to market the different versions under the same brandname in similar packaging throughout the world. This causes an increase in the practice known as parallel trading: a distributor buys stock in one country where prices are low and transfers them to a high-priced country, thereby making a profit. In most cases this only benefits consumers as the quality is uniform, but in the case of Duracell a lower quality version is being purchased. It does seem that market-stall vendors of batteries are either ignorant or less scrupulous than the questioner expects. Unfortunately it is unlikely to be a high priority for trading standards officers, given the other calls on their time. And by the way, we already pay VAT on batteries.
P. Stern, Warwick Business School, Coventry.

QUESTION: Where do you draw the line?

☐ PLIMSOLL got it right. If you ignore him, you're sunk.
David J. Nicolle, Bexley, Kent.

☐ YOU draw the line – or you used to draw the line – in the prize ring in the days of alfresco prize-fighting. A line was scratched in the turf for each of the fighters to 'toe the line' at the beginning of each round. Fighters were not allowed to 'overstep the mark'. Fights were fought to a finish and, if a fighter was unable to toe the line because he did not feel 'up to scratch' he lost the contest.
Harry Humphreys, Lytham St Annes, Lancs.

QUESTION: Does anyone know where the phrase 'the world's oldest profession' to describe prostitution originates? Is it *really*?

□ THERE is a similar phrase in the morality play *The Fall of Righteousness* (circa 1340). Cain, having been exiled, is wandering in the wilderness when he is visited by Lilith, an agent of Satan. Her function is to explain to him the nature of the post-Fall society he is to encounter and, during her description of this world of sin, she claims: 'Whoredom is the original business of woman.' This should probably be taken less as a statement of fact than as an example of medieval misogyny.
Alwyn W. Turner, London NW5.

□ A GARDENER, an architect and a politician were discussing which is the oldest profession. 'Horticulture,' said the gardener. 'Who made the Garden of Eden?' 'No,' said the architect. 'It must be architecture, for God created the Earth and the Heavens out of Chaos.' 'Yes,' said the politician, 'but who created the Chaos?'
Anna R. Cooper, Bournemouth.

□ OF COURSE prostitution is not the world's oldest profession. For 90 per cent of our history, humans have lived as hunter-gatherers, and I have encountered no instance of prostitution in societies organised in this manner. Prostitution is better seen as a recent aberration in human history – though one could argue the same for professionalisation. Midwifery is really the world's oldest profession. Shamanism probably runs it a close second; occasionally the two are combined.
Roxana Waterson, Singapore.

QUESTION: How do I know whether my pain threshold is low or high?

□ IF YOU can only tolerate listening to Margaret Thatcher, Michael

Howard or Peter Lilley for up to five minutes you have a low pain threshold. Up to 10 minutes is a high pain threshold, and more than 10 minutes probably means you don't feel pain at all.
David Way, Leamington Spa, Warwicks.

QUESTION: 'Political correctness' is a term of derision applied by the smug, inconsiderate and reactionary to the language and ideology of the charitable, considerate and liberal. Does this process occur in reverse? If so, what is it called?

☐ IF POLITICAL correctness is a term objected to by those who have already made up their minds as to who is right or wrong, as your correspondent clearly has, then the opposite is 'being open-minded'.
David Simmons, Middx.

☐ POLITICAL correctness is an oxymoron: liberal ideology is another. The term is thus of necessity used ironically; you do not change attitudes by changing the terminology. Perhaps, like Margaret Thatcher, the questioner is ironically challenged.
Jacqueline Castles, London W2.

☐ POLITICALLY Conservative.
David Ilderton, Birmingham.

☐ POLITICAL correctness comprises the dying echoes of a phenomenon widely seen in the 1960s and '70s, called political consciousness. This was a belief that the root of most individuals' problems lies in the economic and political structures of society, which should therefore be changed. However, in the closing of the political universe that took place in the 1980s, a new approach developed, called PC, which teaches that the root of most individuals' problems lies in other individuals, who should therefore be changed. As to the existence of 'reverse PC', it is doubtful that the

'reactionary and inconsiderate' have time for such indulgences. They are far more profitably occupied maintaining the bases of their political and economic power, the education and social services and employment systems, etc, and leave the practice of the politics of form to others.
Andrew James, Newport, Gwent.

QUESTION: Why did it take 35 years to knit together the discoveries of moving film and recorded sound?

□ THE simple answer is it didn't. In 1893 Edison demonstrated his 'kinetophonograph', a combination of his moving-picture peepshow machine and his phonograph. In 1896, in France, the Pathé Company used the newly-invented gramophone discs to add sound to some of their films. In the following years there were many similar attempts with such names as the Vivaphone and the Cinéphone. In 1910 the Edison Company produced a whole series of short films featuring opera and vaudeville performers with the sound recorded on phonograph cylinders. Two technical problems, however, delayed the widespread introduction of the 'talkies'. First, the difficulty of accurately synchronising the sound with the pictures and, second, the inability to produce sound of sufficient volume to fill a large-size hall. Both were finally solved in the early 1920s, mainly by the efforts of Lee De Forest, who devised a practical method of recording the sound on the film itself and also invented the valve, thus making possible the building of sound amplifiers. That it took Hollywood several more years to take up the idea is another story.
Graham Murray, Gravesend, Kent.

QUESTION: It has been possible for several years to produce cars that use non-toxic and non-pollutive fuels such as water. Why has nobody done so?

□ WATER is not a fuel but the non-toxic by-product of burning

hydrogen. The question should really have been: why do we not use hydrogen to fuel cars? The writer may have been confused by the fact that hydrogen can be extracted from water and reused. There is obviously an energy cost here which would be greater than the benefit gained, although some battery-powered cars have been designed which do this, I believe. Incidentally, batteries have to be recharged using electricity generated in power stations, which, in most cases, are not non-polluting.
Catherine Dack, Fleckney, Leics.

QUESTION: What function is served by the disproportionate deliciousness of unhealthy foods, such as chocolate, compared with that of healthy ones such as oats?

☐ TASTE is a rule of thumb used to assess the quality of food: if it tastes good, eat it. Those lucky enough to possess '20/20' taste would enjoy a perfectly balanced diet, were it not for the manipulative nature of most foods. Oats are healthy but, like many foods, have a long tradition of trying to escape being eaten. Naturally they are prudent with their palatability. Not so the flesh of fruit, which is both healthy and tasty, especially when compared to any seeds it may contain. Predators discard the latter and the plant achieves its aim – seed dispersal. Chocolate is designed to be tasty enough to outweigh its adverse effects on health; it hijacks our rule of thumb. But such a hijack can only be temporary, natural selection will see to that. To improve the taste of a chocolate bar could mean instant financial returns, but a manufacturer wishing to corner the market for, say, the next 10,000 years had better start thinking nutrition.
Geoff Morgan, Consultant in Environmental Strategy, Mold, Clwyd.

QUESTION: Is it true that the voice behind Captain Scarlet is Cary Grant? And who is the voice of the Mysterons?

☐ THE voice of Captain Scarlet is not that of Cary Grant. It is the

voice of my brother, Francis Matthews. At the time Gerry
Anderson was planning the series he heard Francis on a radio chat
show 'doing' a Cary Grant voice as a joke. Anderson liked the
trans-Atlantic flavour of the voice and asked Francis to 'be'
Captain Scarlet.
Maura Collard, Caterham, Surrey.

☐ THE sinister, booming tones of the unseen Mysterons were created by the aptly-named Donald Gray, who was also responsible
for the voice of arch-villain Captain Black. Donald Gray was also
behind the paternal tones of Colonel White. Captain Grey, however, was voiced by Elsie Tanner's screen husband, Paul Maxwell.
Bob Richardson, BBC TV, London W12.

**QUESTION: Why did the Church of England recognise the
title 'Saint' when the Catholic Church is responsible for
canonisation?**

☐ THE term 'Saint' is properly applied to any man or woman,
now dead, who when alive was a witness to the Faith of Jesus
Christ. Many Christian churches use the stories of such people as
a means to encourage the present generation of the faithful – and
often, as in the Church of England, places of worship are dedicated to God in the name of a saint. It was only around 1200 AD
that the Vatican established a formal procedure for canonisation
– before then the recognition of particular individuals as worthy
of the status of saints was entirely a matter of local veneration. The
protestant reformers particularly objected to the way in which, in
the late medieval church, the (largely legendary) stories of the
saints had supplanted the regular reading of the Bible in many
services. Hence, although the Church of England preserves the
traditions of the saints, only those whose stories are told in scripture have a fixed place in the calendar of readings for daily services.
Tom Hennell, Withington, Manchester.

QUESTION: What is the origin of the term 'Third World'?

☐ I HAVE always thought the term originates from the car insurance industry. In a car accident, the innocent victim is called the third party. Thus 'Third World' refers to the idea that it is an innocent victim of a collision between the capitalist First World and the communist Second World.
John Anderton, Weaverham, Cheshire.

☐ THE term comes from the 'original' world (i.e. the Middle East, Mediterranean Europe, Mainland Europe, British Isles) being termed the 'Old World' when the 'New World' (i.e. the Americas) was settled by Europeans. This left the rest of the world (i.e. Africa, Asia etc) which was renamed the 'Third World' in the latter part of this century.
David A. Dix, Newcastle under Lyme, Staffs.

☐ I DISAGREE with Mr Dix's explanation. The term is a translation from the French *Tiers-Monde* created by the late economist and demograph, Alfred Sauvy. Modelled after the *Tiers-État* of the pre-1789 era (meaning those who weren't aristocrats or church members), the *Tiers-Monde* was applied to those countries who weren't part of the western world (which the English renamed the First World) nor the communist world. The term had a wide success because, just as the *Tiers-État* was the power behind the French Revolution, the third world could become a new revolutionary actor. Since these times, a new term, the *Quart-Monde* (Fourth World) has appeared in France, and it comprises all those who are poor in rich countries (unemployed, tramps, etc).
Xavier Leroy, Johannesburg, South Africa.

☐ YOUR correspondent Xavier Leroy has the right translation of Third World as coming from the French *Tiers-Monde*. However, I think he misunderstands the actual English meaning of it. *Tiers* means third in the sense of 'the fraction one-third', not in the sense of 'third in a sequence'. Thus, by inference, *le tiers monde* means the third of the world which does not enjoy the same standard of

living as the remaining two-thirds. There are thus no First or
Second worlds.
D. R. Allum, Towcester, Northants.

**QUESTION: Is it possible to have a dream which is suffi-
ciently frightening as to cause a heart attack, and for the
dreamer to die without waking?**

☐ YES, according to Drs Kartz and Melles of the San Diego School
of Medicine, who conducted a study of physically healthy young
Asian men who suffered from night terrors in the 1980s. 'What
distinguishes night terrors from severe nightmares is that victims
begin to shout in their sleep, toss and turn violently. Within less
than a minute their heart rate shoots up uncontrollably, sometimes fatally, often in men with no previous sign of heart disease.
If they survive the attack they remember having violent nightmares. This phenomenon seems to be associated with deep depression and usually affects refugees or immigrants, but as the
young men become more established in their adopted countries
the incidence of night terror decreases.'
Jacqueline Castles, London W2.

**QUESTION: In 1973 our local paper carried an advertise-
ment for a 'Patagonian bursting rabbit – one burst only'.
What is it and why did it burst?**

☐ ACCORDING to my copy of *Bert Fegg's Nasty Book for Boys and
Girls*, published in 1974 by Eyre Methuen and reputedly the responsibility of Terry Jones and Michael Palin, the Patagonian
Bursting Rabbit is but one of many interesting animals inhabiting
The Wonderful World of Nature. It is described thus: 'This extremely dangerous rodent eats up to six times its own weight in
food, refuse and old copies of *The Watchtower*. It then lies in wait
for its prey, disguised as the comparatively harmless Patagonian

Shoe-Cleaning Rat and, upon contact with the victim's shoe, explodes with the force of 20lbs of TNT, covering the victim in an unpleasant mixture of pre-digested food and evangelical magazines.' Other little-known creatures include, the Limping Fish from South Dakota, the Bengali Bomber Ant, and the much-feared West Bromley Fighting Haddock.

Maggy Holland, Lindale-in-Furness, Cumbria.

QUESTION: If the skin and underlying muscles are constantly renewing themselves, why is it that tattoos remain visible for a lifetime?

□ THE tattooist's needle introduces carbon or coloured salts of mercury and cobalt through the outer layer of the skin (the epidermis) into the deeper layer, the dermis. Particles of these pigments are then taken up by scavenging cells in the dermis called histiocytes, which are unable to break down the pigments, but simply 'contain' them. The cell layers of the epidermis grow constantly outwards and are shed, but the pigments are not lost because they are below this level. The 'connective tissue' cells of the dermis (including the histiocytes) are also continually replaced throughout life, but are more slowly turned over 'from within', so that when one pigment-containing histiocyte dies, the pigment is simply taken up by a new histiocyte at the same site. Therefore the pigment particles remain in the same area of the dermis, permanently. As a result, you get your money's worth from the tattooist in terms of longevity; but unfortunately, would need full-thickness skin removal surgery to get rid of your tattoo, should you later find youself with a different girlfriend.

Dr C. R. Peirce, Isle of Wight.

QUESTION: What happened to the non-iron shirt?

□ THE non-iron shirt is still around, although it is not called non-iron any more but a polyester/cotton shirt. If you cannot afford a

washing machine, these shirts can be hand-washed, hung on hangers to drip-dry. Then when they are dry, the wearer's body heat eliminates any surplus creases in about 10 minutes. This was the theory behind non-iron shirts. Now, when technology is more advanced, poly/cotton shirts, washed in an automatic washing machine and promptly put in a tumbler dryer, can be said to be 'non-iron' as creases can magically disappear if only six shirts or less are washed or dryed together.
Ena Reid, Suffolk.

☐ I RECOLLECT that the description 'non-iron' was quite literal – any attempt made to iron one and the shirt promptly melted.
John Gayton, Cambridge.

QUESTION: Why are Automobile Association offices called Fanum House?

☐ WHEN the AA was founded in 1905, car ownership was restricted to the wealthy, who conducted much of their day-to-day correspondence by telegraph. The fledgling AA needed a telegraphic address. Thus, a great deal of correspondence was addressed to 'AA, Fanum, London' and it seemed natural to name our first headquarters building in Leicester Square Fanum House. As the AA developed, regional offices were given the same name. Fanum is the Greek word for temple and in *This Motoring*, Stenson Cooke's romantic account of the early days of the AA, he writes that he imagined the organisation becoming a 'temple of motoring'. A rather more prosaic explanation of his choice is that the AA's first office was in the offices of a solicitor in Temple Bar, Fleet Street. Fanum is still in use as a call sign for AA road service vehicles, and as the name of several AA buildings. At the beginning of 1994, however, our national headquarters moved from Fanum House in Basingstoke across town to a new office block named after the Duke of Norfolk, a former AA President.
Michael Passmore, AA Archivist, Fanum House, Basingstoke.

QUESTION: The British and US Americans conventionally write dates in a different order. As both nations spring from the same culture, why this difference, and were they the same at any time since North America was colonised?

☐ IT IS historical because the written word developed with newspapers and the date in the 17th century was conventionally written 'month first'. This style was used in *The Times* (1788) and the Manchester *Guardian* (1855) and is still used to this day. The first issue of the *Observer* was dated 4 December 1791 but this paper changed to 'number first' style about 20 years ago. It is likely that American newspapers, particularly since Independence (1776), followed the same style and they are less willing to change anything slightly historical as we seem to. The change to 'number first' is probably more due to the numeric styling of the date which we use but calculators designed for the (bigger) American market follow the International standard of year, month and date (e.g. 94-10-08), for October 8.
Jack Griffiths, Ferring, West Sussex.

QUESTION: Who was the man with the gong in the 'Yes/no interlude' on Michael Miles's 'Take Your Pick'?

☐ BOB Danvers-Walker – also known as the voice on numerous cinema newsreels in the 1950s.
Richard Spender, Sidcup, Kent.

☐ THE answer is Alec Dane. Dane was not his real name but was adopted because of his Danish nationality and difficult-to-pronounce (to an English audience) surname. He died some years ago.
Andrew Miles (son of the late Michael Miles), Teddington, Middx.

QUESTION: Why are almost all stringed instruments

designed so that the fretboards or equivalent are manipulated with the left hand, while the more articulate right hand merely moves a bow or plucks the strings?

☐ THE earliest string instruments were simple forms of harp, with a stretched string or strings attached to a bowed piece of wood and/or a sounding board or box. The left hand would have been used simply to support the instrument while the right (or stronger) did the active job of playing the strings. On instruments with few strings it would have been a simple matter for the left hand occasionally to stop a string to stretch it or shorten the vibrating length to produce extra notes. This led to the development of fingerboards and fretboards and to increasing work opportunities for the left hand; it must have been a combination of respect for tradition and force of habit that stopped the instruments being turned around by players. In support of the traditional method, I should say that the right hand (or left if you're left-handed) is better at rhythmic precision and expressive variations in volume and tone, which would apply to the control of a bow as well as to plucking or strumming. Also, I might add that in flamenco guitar, for example, the right hand has at least as interesting a job as the left.
Jon Riley, London W5.

☐ THE questioner obviously has never tried to bow a violin. The excruciating sounds produced by the tyro violinist are partly the result of poor intonation by the fingers of the left hand but far more the product of an inarticulately-manipulated bow. A good, expressive tone on the fiddle is produced by both hands in partnership, of which the right, bowing hand, is the senior. (The right wrist and arm are crucial too.)
Kevin Adams, Castlethorpe, Bucks.

QUESTION: What is the Bilderberg Group? Who can become members, and does it do anything useful?

☐ THE Bilderberg Group was founded in 1954, an outgrowth of various right-wing and anti-communist organisations, such as the

American Committee for a United Europe. The main figure behind its formation was an enigmatic Polish philanthropist and 'political philosopher', Joseph Retinger. The group has connections with the CIA, the OSS, the Trilateral Commission, the Council for Foreign Relations, and other shadowy organisations. They first met in the Hotel Bilderberg in Oosterbeek, Netherlands. To this day no one knows if Bilderberg is their real name or not, since they go to any lengths to avoid publicity and membership is also highly secret. The minutes of the group's first meeting recorded that one of their primary interests was in 'evolving an international order' which would 'look beyond the present crisis', and this goal of creating one world government still seems to be their main driving force today. In 1989, they are alleged to have plotted the political assassination of Margaret Thatcher, because of 'her refusal to yield British Sovereignty to the European Superstate that is due to emerge in 1992.' The alleged list of attendees at the annual bash in 1991, held in Baden-Baden, included Queen Beatrix of the Netherlands, Karl Otto Pohl, then president of Deutsche Bundesbank, Katharine Graham, chair of the *Washington Post*, David Rockefeller, Lord Carrington and Governor Bill Clinton of Arkansas.

Grahame Gardner, Glasgow.

QUESTION: Why is Great Britain referred to as the United Kingdom, when it has been headed by a Queen for the last 40 years?

□ KING in the word kingdom means ruler or head of state. Queen is in reality king, except when the she is the king's consort. In an Act of Parliament about 1700, Queen Anne is called king. In the register of Mayfield in Sussex can be found: '29 March 1602. At two of ye clock in the morning died that famous Prince... Queene Elizabeth.'

Ivor Solomons, Norwich.

QUESTION: According to the Reader's Digest *Atlas of the World*, the Big Bang theory postulates that the universe expanded from the size of an atomic nucleus, at time zero, to a sphere of radius 10 billion miles within one-millionth of a second. As this represents an average velocity of 10 million billion miles per second, how does this square with a supposed absolute maximum velocity of 186,000 miles per second?

□ EINSTEIN'S theory of Special Relativity is the fundamental explanation for the behaviour of matter at very high speeds – matter approaching the speed of light, 300 million metres per second. Einstein derived an equation known as a velocity transformation, to measure the velocity of a moving object from the frame of reference or inertial frame of an independent observer. Resultant values for high speed matter have been verified experimentally and also can be used to derive strange results such as the slowing down of time and length contraction at very high speeds. The important point, however, is that by using these equations an upper limit of the speed of light cannot be exceeded or the mathematics becomes meaningless. The results are valid only when measured from the inertial frame of an observer for which the speed of light is a maximum and an inertial frame cannot exist outside the universe. There is therefore no absolute value for the speed of expansion of the universe, only that which can be measured from within, which would be almost at the value of the speed of light.
Kevin Mulhall, Richmond.

□ KEVIN Mulhall has confused Einstein's two theories of relativity. The special theory says that nothing can travel through space faster than light, and this is confirmed by experiments. The general theory says (among other things) that the universe is expanding because space itself is expanding. In the early stages of this universal expansion, the space between the particles of matter in the universe was stretching 'faster than light', but the special

theory was not violated, because no material particle was moving through space at these speeds. Think of the raisins in a loaf of raisin bread being carried apart as the dough rises, but not moving through the dough.
Dr John Gribbin, East Sussex.

QUESTION: If the wealth of all British citizens were taken and shared out equally among the population, how much would everybody have?

☐ BETWEEN £25,000 and £30,000 per person; total net personal wealth is between two and a half and three times Gross Domestic Product.
Donald Roy, London SW15

☐ DONALD Roy's estimate is too low. The total marketable wealth (that is, excluding pension rights) in 1991 was £1,694 billion, and there were 44.5 million adults, according to Inland Revenue Statistics 1993 (HMSO). So the figure two years ago was £38,064; since then house prices have fallen a little, and the value of houses accounts for nearly two-thirds of the total; shares and gilts have risen a lot, but only account for one-tenth of total wealth. I would guess that the figure has not changed much. And the actual distribution of wealth? The average wealth of the richest 1 per cent of adults is about £700,000 each, 105 times as much as the average for the poorer half of the population, which is about £6,500 each.
John Rentoul (author, The Rich Get Richer*), London E3.*

QUESTION: Where do the terms left-wing and right-wing come from?

☐ THE political terms 'right' and 'left' date from the early days of the French Revolution, and derive from the seating arrangements

in the National Assembly in 1789. In the Estates General in May, the Nobility sat in the place of honour on the right-hand side of the Chair. In the Constituent Assembly in July, the supporters of the Old Regime also sat on the right-hand side of the Chair, and their opponents therefore sat on the left-hand side, with the moderates in between. The result is described by Thomas Carlyle in *The French Revolution* (1837): 'Rudiments of Methods disclose themselves; rudiments of Parties. There is a Right Side (Côté Droit) a Left Side (Côté Gauche); – sitting on M. le President's right hand, or on his left: the Côté Droit conservative; the Côté Gauche destructive. Intermediate is Anglomaniac Constitutional-ism, or Two-Chamber Royalism.' This pattern has continued in French and other assemblies, especially those with a circular or semi-circular hall. Left and right 'sides' later became left and right 'wings', as the image of seats in a hall was replaced by one of units in a battle, and conventional political terminology was fixed for ever. In the English Parliament, the government sat on the right-hand side of the Chair but it continued to do so whether its politics were 'Left' or 'Right'. This pattern has continued in assemblies copied from the British model, especially those with two sides facing each other in a rectangular hall.
Nicolas Walter, London N1.

☐ THE terms come from the physical make-up of the Parliament in post-revolutionary France. The revolutionaries sat on the left side of the house (denoted by the colour red), the bourgeoisie sat in the centre (denoted by white) and the royalists sat on the right (denoted by blue) – a make-up which can be recognised in the design of the French flag.
Ann Moody, London SW6.

☐ THERE is no connection between the layout of the seats in the French Assembly and the development of the red, white and blue tricolour, as suggested by Ann Moody. It's true that red was asso-ciated with the left and a red flag hung outside the Jacobin Club, and that white was the colour of the monarchists (it was the livery colour of the Bourbons). There is also a case to be made for identifying the colour with the three Estates. But the development of the *Tricolore* was completely coincidental, and was based on colours originating in the municipal arms of Paris, combined with the Bourbon white. In any case the *Tricolore* was established well before the 'post-revolutionary Parliament'. The cockade was officially adopted on 31 July 1789, and the tricolour flag on 24 October 1790, but the first revolutionary assembly did not open until 1791.

William Crampton, Director of the Flag Institute.

☐ USE of the terms 'left' and 'right' in fact pre-dates the French Revolution by over a century. They were used in the 1680s by the Societies United in Correspondence ('Convanters'). The Societies used them in the opposite sense to ours, Right being extremists and Left moderates. In the late 19th century the American and French revolutions and the first English working-class political organisations were influenced by the tradition handed down from the Societies of the 17th century. It is probable that the French Assembly adopted the phrase from this tradition, and in it the extremists sat on the right and the moderates on the left. But when the chairman called on a speaker he called him from his right or left hand, with the result that the meaning of the words reversed.

C. Wason, Bridgwater, Somerset.

QUESTION: Why does Britain's road system have so many roundabouts? If they are such a good thing, why are they not so common in other countries?

☐ HOLLAND used to have many roundabouts. The problem in Holland and most continental countries is that traffic from the right has right of way (that would be from the left in Britain) unless one of the roads has an indicated priority. In the case of roundabouts this leads to congestion: traffic entering the roundabout comes from the right and has right of way, which fills the

roundabout but does not clear it. As a consequence, most Dutch roundabouts have been abolished. The British system works because traffic from the left does not have right of way and because traffic on a roundabout always has priority over the traffic approaching it.
Thomas Van den Bergh, Tunbridge Wells, Kent.

☐ THE reason for having so many roundabouts in Britain is that our transport planning has been dominated by engineers obsessed with increasing the 'capacity' of the road system. Most other countries long realised that such features are major interruptions and extremely dangerous for the vulnerable road user such as cyclists. Large sums of money are now being spent fitting signals. Ironically, as well as improving safety, these also improve traffic flow, as the free-for-all at roundabouts in peak hours has now become a source of congestion in its own right.
Don Mathew, Consultant on Transport and the Environment, Lowestoft, Suffolk.

QUESTION: A friend recently told me that the term for a group of ravens is 'an unkindness'. What's the origin, and are there any other similarly bizarre names for groups of animals?

☐ THE origin of the term is presumably related to an old (now obsolete) sense of the word 'unkindness', meaning 'unnatural conduct'; the raven was traditionally regarded as a bird of evil omen and mysterious or unnatural conduct. The word as used for a flock of ravens dates from the mid-15th century, and is included in a list of 'proper terms' in the *Book of St Albans* (1486). Other group terms include: 'a hastiness of cooks', 'an observance of hermits', 'a shrewdness of apes', 'a cloud of flies', 'a blush of boys', 'a piteousness of doves', 'a desert of lapwing' and 'a bevy of ladies'.
Judy Pearsall, associate editor, Oxford English Dictionaries, Oxford University Press.

☐ JUDY Pearsall defines an 'observance' as the group name for hermits. Surely a group of hermits constitutes a contradiction in terms?
Greg Mackay, Rome, Italy.

☐ THE collective term for our financial advisers must be 'a wunch of bankers'.
David Lambert, Harlow, Essex.

☐ NO ONE has yet mentioned James Lipton's *An Exaltation of Larks*, which includes not only this but a comprehensive catalogue of collectives. Some of the other ornithological ones are delightful: a charm of finches; an ostentation of peacocks. Others are racy, humorous, sardonic or serendipitous, like: a wince of dentists; a piddle of puppies; a stampede of philatelists.
(Mrs) Else Pickvance, Northfield, Birmingham.

☐ How about 'A Morbidity of Majors' included in the Groups of a Kind listed in the 1990 Penguin edition of the *Quickway Crossword Dictionary*?
Tom Egan, Eglwyswrw, Dyfed.

☐ I WAS once told by college lecturers that the collective noun for a group of college principals was 'a lack'.
Ian Lucraft, Sheffield.

☐ MY RESEARCH has elicited the following: sac – a group of gastroenterologists; colony – a large group; bellyfull – a large group in a small room; appendix – a splinter group; rumbling appendix – a noisy splinter group; burst appendix – a splintered splinter group; abdomination – a group of splinter groups; eructation – the hot air generated by an abdomination.
John Hazlehurst, Cumbria.

QUESTION: Are there any places left unexplored on earth?

☐ ONLY a very tiny proportion of the ocean floor has been visited

by man, and the oceans cover most (71 per cent) of the earth's surface.
Paul Redfern, London W10.

QUESTION: 'Early music' in the catalogues dates from the Middle Ages. Is there nothing earlier? Did the Greeks and Romans, for example, write musical scores? If so, what happened to them?

□ EVIDENCE of ancient music abounds – ancient Egyptian wall paintings depict harp playing as early as the 10th century BC. A horn similar to those used in fox hunting was buried with Tutankhamun and it can still be played. In spite of this, it is impossible to reconstruct the music which was played on it. As for the Greeks, there are numerous references in surviving texts, such as those written by Aristoxenes of Tarentum, Claudius Ptolemy and Aristide Quintilian. These tell us about music in the same way that a newspaper music critic might review a new record. It is equivalent to future generations trying to reconstruct a symphony from the *Guardian*'s music critic. There is even less hard information about Roman music, although the fact that the Roman Catholic Church is the direct descendant of the Roman Empire gives us some clues. The earliest surviving western music is liturgical. The Gregorian Chant, named after Pope Gregory I (540–604), is a musical link with Antiquity. As for the Classical scores, the ancients did have a notation but only fragments have survived. These are too short to give any clue as to how ancient music sounded.
Peter Stockhill, Middlesbrough, Cleveland.

QUESTION: Why does 'bastard' as a term of abuse apply only to men?

□ BASTARD as a term of abuse can be traced back to the figure of the illegitimate malcontent of Elizabethan and Jacobean drama and culture (e.g. Edmund in *King Lear*, Don John in *Much Ado About Nothing*). This type, enviously plotting the downfall of his legitimate siblings and peers, is necessarily male as it is the male illegitimate child who most obviously challenges and is excluded from the ruling power structures and lines of inheritance. Typical characteristics are deviousness, unscrupulousness, ambition and a complete contempt for the rules and codes of society. Although there are many more positive images of bastards in European culture, where he becomes self-made hero rather than Machiavellian schemer, the male bastard is still seen to inherit his parents' subversive sexual energy, to be untrammelled by society's rules, and this feeds into the half-hostile, half-admiring meanings of 'bastard' today.

Jenny Bourne Taylor, London N8.

□ THE term bastard is an indirect insult to women as it implies that 'your mother is a slut'.

Lucia Asnaghi, London NW2.

QUESTION: How do you organise a piss-up in a brewery?

□ THE only good piss-up is a disorganised piss-up.

A. Jameson, Belfast.

QUESTION: Why did ancient Roman soldiers wear their swords on the right-hand side of their bodies? Were they all left-handed?

□ THE sword most commonly used by Roman legionaries was the *gladius hispaniensis*, so called because it was a Spanish native weapon adopted by the Romans. This was a short sword, about 50cm in length, which hung from a belt on the right thigh. I recall seeing a demonstration by an expert on Roman weaponry who drew a replica *gladius* from its sheath with his right hand in only a split second using a 'cocked wrist' action. The shield would be held in the left hand covering the body. The right hand would need to be unencumbered in order that the legionary could first throw his *pilum* (a kind of javelin) before engaging with the sword. With the sword on the right thigh, it can be drawn without losing the body protection of the shield. If the sword were on the left, the shield would have to be moved away from the body in order to complete the move.

(Dr) John Pamment Salvatore, Archaeological Field Unit, Royal Albert Memorial Museum, Exeter.

□ THEY looked more sinister that way.
Harry Turnbull, West End, Southampton.

QUESTION: Looking at a teapot on a shop shelf, how can I tell whether it will pour without spluttering, dribbling, splashing or overshooting the cup?

□ THE narrowest point of the spout should be at the tip, which is why a metal teapot usually pours well. If you look down the spout and it becomes narrower further down than at the end, as is the case in many cheap teapots, it will not pour a good stream of tea.
Colin Kirkham, Colby, Isle of Man.

QUESTION: The dictionary defines a merkin as 'a hair-piece for the pubic region'. When were merkins worn, by whom and why?

□ I HAVE heard of two instances of pubic wigs being used. In one case a pre-war striptease artiste in the United States was arrested and charged with stripping completely naked, which at that time was illegal. She was found not guilty because she was, in fact, wearing a G-string made of monkey fur which simulated pubic hair. Monkey-fur G-strings became common in American bur-lesque shows. There was a short story called 'Wigs' published just

after the war which told of the prostitutes of Milan being forcibly depilated in the pubic region because of an epidemic of crab lice and of the GIs stationed there not going with women who had been so treated for fear of infection. In consequence the women took to wearing pubic wigs in order to carry on their trade.
Jascha Pruchidnik, Woodford Green, Essex.

□ IN MY work as a stage designer I read during research that boy actors, in the days when they played women's parts, would wear a merkin to cover their genitals so that in bawdy scenes they could expose themselves as women.
Rodney Ford, Norton, Sheffield.

QUESTION: Why are the primary colours of transmitted light red, blue and green, when the primary colours of pigments are red, blue and yellow?

□ COLOUR perception is the eye's reaction to a narrow band of electromagnetic radiation. Green and yellow occur at roughly the mid-point of this range. Primary colours are so-called because other colours can be obtained by mixing them. Apart from blue and red at the ends of the scale, a third colour, green or yellow from the mid-range, is required. Two forms of mixing are involved here – subtractive in reflected light and additive in transmitted light. In pigments mixed on a palette, colour is generated by subtracting (absorbing) all but a narrow range of wavelengths from the white light that strikes the surface. The wavelength of the reflected light then lies between that of the colours used in the mixture. Subtraction in a mixture of blue (wavelength 450 nanometres) and yellow (610nm) gives green at 510nm, while a mixture of yellow and red (750nm) yields orange at 680nm. Green (blue plus yellow) added to red gives brown, not yellow. Accordingly, for colour generated by reflection from pigments the primaries are blue, yellow and red, as can be shown by mixing water colours, for example. In additive or optical mixing, the light

reflected by two or more differently coloured surfaces is blended
at the retina of the eye; this gives a quite different impression of
colour from that of the components. For this mixing, the coloured
points must be so closely spaced that the eye cannot resolve them.
For example, a film of small, coloured particles deposited on glass
will transmit rays of different wavelength that are mixed when
they reach the eye. Yellow is then obtained by blending red and
green light at the retina. This can be verified by inspecting the
screen of a colour TV with a magnifying glass. Areas that seem
yellow at a distance will be revealed to be made up of tiny blobs
of red and green colour. White areas contain blue, green and red
dots.
Allan Brown, West Lulworth, Dorset.

QUESTION: Is there anything that will rid the breath of the smell of garlic?

☐ PARSLEY, when a green leaf is chewed, has a remarkable deodorising effect upon garlicky smells and this virtue is strongest in
the curled variety. The herb was used medicinally by the Greeks
but was first used for deodorising by the Romans, who both took
it internally and made garlands of it to ward off intoxication and
strong odours. The remedy has been known in this country at least
since the 16th century, and appears in John Gerard's herbal guide
of the 1590s.
Kate Vesey, Long Melford, Suffolk.

QUESTION: Who first 'carried the can'?

☐ THIS derives from the most responsible and critical job in Army
– emptying the latrines.
David Brinicombe, Ealing, London W5.

QUESTION: Was there ever a real ACME corporation (as endorsed by Wile E. Coyote), and if so, what did they make?

☐ THERE were thousands of ACME corporations, making just about everything you can think of. In the days before companies adopted the uninspired practice of naming themselves with initials – AA Sprockets, ABC Lard Importers, or whatever – there was far more imaginative competition to find appropriate names that would secure that all-important first entry in the telephone directory. The Greek word for highest point, or perfection, was the acme of solutions.
John Porter, Sutton, Surrey.

QUESTION: In July 1994 comet Shoemaker-Levy collided with Jupiter. What action could be taken if we had several months' warning that a comet was due to crash into the earth? Has any serious consideration been given to this, and are there appropriate bodies to plan for such an emergency?

☐ IN 1991, Nasa conducted a series of studies of the asteroid (or comet) impact threat to the earth, and ways in which to avoid it. These were followed up by a Near-Earth Object Detection Workshop which concluded that over 2,000 objects larger than one kilometre across lie in earth-crossing orbits. Luckily, the Nasa team also concluded that it was feasible to avert similar catastrophes by deflecting the path of the object. Deflection methods would either involve a 'kinetic-energy impact' – i.e. a series of non-nuclear missiles shot at the object – or, for larger objects, a huge nuclear explosion close-by. However, the team also decided not to proceed beyond the theoretical because of the high cost in the face of a low-risk factor.
Jeff Craig, Edinburgh.

☐ COMETS, asteroids and rogue satellites heading for England

and Wales are a responsibility of the Home Office, which funds emergency planners in metropolitan districts, fire and civil defence authorities, London boroughs and county councils. Our job is to get city, town and county halls in shape for the next disaster. We do what we can, but the obliteration of Mother Earth is not a priority right now. There are quite enough disasters around already before we ransack municipal basements to find the old civil defence plans for survival after World War Three.
Simon Turney, Emergency Planning Unit, South Yorkshire Fire and Civil Defence Authority.

QUESTION: Would the presence of a long 'lifeline' on the hand of just one young deceased person automatically make palmistry invalid?

☐ No. THE length of the lifeline does not in any way determine how long you will live. The line refers to the quality and the kind of life you will experience.
Annabel Ingram, Juniper Green, Edinburgh.

QUESTION: To the best of my knowledge, lions are not found in the Far East, yet the lion has been a favourite object for Chinese sculptors for thousands of years. How come?

☐ NEITHER are dragons.
Mark Crompton, London E13.

☐ LIONS are 99.9 per cent confined to Africa, but used to be more widespread. Human behaviour ensures their distribution is constantly shrinking. The last remaining lions in Asia inhabit a few square miles of the Gir forest on the western coast of India. Human encroachment is a serious problem there and it is doubtful whether the lion in Asia will be with us much longer.
Roger Panaman, International Carnivore Protection Society, Oxford.

QUESTION: How does an electrical testing screwdriver work?

☐ THE electrical testing screwdriver contains a neon bulb, which can glow with an extremely low current, and a very high value resistor to limit the current to a safe value below the level which can be felt as a shock. When the blade touches the live wire and the person touches the small metal stud on the end connected to the bulb, a current flows and the lamp lights. The puzzle for most people is that the person does not have to be earthed, or indeed connected to anything, for it to work, so how can any current flow? The answer is that household mains is alternating current, at 50 cycles per second. The electrician has a small capacitance to earth, through which the current can flow without any direct connection. As the voltage increases in each cycle he charges up, only to discharge and reverse as the voltage reverses. The lamp is lit by these tiny currents which flow to charge and discharge him. The device will not work on direct current or low voltage supplies such as batteries. Do not try the technique with any other type of lamp or without the high value resistor if you want to survive.
Professor Harvey Rutt, Department of Electronics and Computer Science, University of Southampton.

QUESTION: Who was Pete in 'for Pete's sake'?

☐ THIS mild profanity is a reference to St Peter.
G. A. Wilkinson, Waterlooville, Hants.

QUESTION: Since the nomenclature of both the Labour and Conservative parties gives a very poor indication of their true nature and purpose, what names would be more fitting?

☐ 'CONSERVATIVE' is very apt for the Tories. 'Con' stands for confidence trick; 'serve' indicates the self-service which is the essence

of Toryism; 'Vat' is the tax which they have more than doubled; and 'ive' is short for 'I have', the phrase greatly beloved of Tories. The Labour Party, on the other hand, badly needs a new name, since the Tories have made real work such a scarce commodity.
Brooke Harvey, North End, Essex.

☐ I WOULD disagree with the questioner that the Labour Party's name no longer reflects its purpose. The Labour Representation Committee was established in February 1900 with the aim, as the name suggests, of increasing the representation of the labouring classes who at that time had no voice in Parliament. It became the Labour Party in 1906. Although socialists were present at its birth, the vast majority of the early membership of the Labour Party – as today – were more interested in improving the conditions of ordinary people (often called by the Victorians 'the labouring classes') than of creating a socialist paradise. To call the Labour Party socialist – as its opponents have always done – is, at best, misleading. The aim of the party has not changed; nor should the name. It still represents the interests of the labouring classes, although of course recent history shows that the Labour Party does find it difficult to persuade people of this. Ironically the Conservative Party might perhaps be renamed the Radical Party. The term 'Radical' in recent years has shifted in meaning from somebody being on the left of politics, as the great Manchester radicals like Cobden and Bright were, to being on the right.
Simon Fowler, Secretary, Labour Heritage, Kew, Surrey.

☐ 'OPPOSITION' and 'Government'.
Andrew Ogden, The Park, Nottingham.

QUESTION: 'An event has happened, upon which it is difficult to speak, and impossible to keep silent.' What was Edmund Burke referring to?

☐ HE WAS referring to the case of Warren Hastings. This was a

great public scandal until its lengthy duration resulted in most people losing interest. Hastings was a British governor-general of India until he was impeached in 1786 and then tried before the House of Lords. Burke, who made the comment in 1789, was a prime mover in the case against him. The charges ranged from fighting unnecessary wars to maladministration and financial impropriety. The trial lasted seven years (1788–95), at the end of which Hastings was acquitted.
Mark Pack, York.

QUESTION: What is a 'Dutch Uncle' and why?

☐ ACCORDING to *Brewer's Dictionary of Phrase and Fable* (1990), the derogatory implication of a number of English phrases which include the word 'Dutch' (Dutch courage, Dutch comfort) derives from the Anglo-Dutch wars of the 17th century. To talk like a Dutch Uncle means to reprove firmly but kindly, as the Dutch were not noted for their discipline.
John Davies, History Department, Liverpool Institute of Higher Education.

QUESTION: Exactly when will the world's oil run out, and will there be any alternative convenient energy available at that time?

☐ THE rate of consumption of oil is not constant. Fuel efficiency measures may decrease the rate of consumption, or, more likely, increases in use in less-developed areas will increase the rate of consumption. Also, it is not known exactly how much oil exists. Geographers usually distinguish between a resource – that is, the total amount of oil on the planet – and a reserve, which is the total amount of oil we know about and can extract economically. Clearly, the reserves of oil are always changing with new finds, or improvements in technology, or changes in price. At best, all that

can be said is that current reserves at current rates of consumption should last until at least 2030. Undoubtedly, however, oil will run out some day if we continue to use it at anything approaching current rates. Whether we have an alternative depends on many factors. One thought is that as oil becomes more scarce the price will increase, which will force industry and governments to act to find alternatives. The sceptics argue that even if there is sufficient foresight for this to happen, the transition may well be difficult with increased potential for conflict as organisations fight (perhaps literally) for the remaining reserves.
Mark Payne, Montacute, Somerset.

□ REGARDING alternatives, the main uses for which oil is particularly convenient are transportation – uniquely so, in the case of aviation fuel, for which no real substitute has yet been found – and certain grades of lubricants, which as yet have not been re-created synthetically. However, for all other purposes, oil is going out of favour, primarily on environmental grounds. In almost all instances, including motor transport, the substitute fuels will be natural gas (methane), which is cheap, plentiful (it exists in greater quantities than oil), safe, and far cleaner than coal or oil.
Nicholas Perry, Croydon.

QUESTION: Has anyone called Bill Posters actually been prosecuted for his crime of the same name?

□ OF COURSE Bill Posters hasn't been prosecuted – everybody knows he's innocent.
Roger Darby, West Moors, Dorset.

QUESTION: White wine is bottled in clear glass. Why then does red wine come in green bottles, and beer in brown bottles?

□ MANY white wines are bottled in green glass. The first bottles (*c.* 1700) were made of coloured glass because clear glass was impossible with the technology of the day. In addition, coloured glass protects red wines and beers from direct sunlight, which can bleach out the anthocyanins which give the drink its colour. In the last century or so, some wines have gone into clear glass for various reasons: pink wines and sweet wines to show off their natural colour; Louis Roederer's 'Cristal' Champagne because the Tsar of Russia asked for it; and some Italian dry whites to emphasise their lightness and delicacy. Some German wine even comes in blue glass bottles.

John Radford, Ilkeston, Derbyshire.

QUESTION: How effective (or otherwise) were this country's anti-aircraft defences during the blitz of 1940–41?

☐ In 1940–41 our guns were not successful at shooting down many German aircraft by day or by night. In daylight, however, they did help to break up enemy formations, hampering attacks. This aimed fire was controlled by optical predictors and height finders which were used until radar took over. By night there was little better to do than barrage firing, which made a reassuring noise for the populace and also made it more difficult for the enemy to make an accurate attack. Improvements in radar, and the development of electronic predictors, finally brought accuracy around the clock. In the little-known guns-only defence of Antwerp against flying bombs in early 1945, the British and US heavy anti-aircraft guns started off with a kill rate of 65 per cent, and at the end were killing over 97 per cent.

D. C. Bennett, Earith, Cambs.

QUESTION: Apart from a means of identity, is there any other reason as to why we have fingerprints?

☐ God, in his infinite wisdom, knew that lager would need to be

served chilled. He thus created 'fingers with treads' to stop glasses with condensation on the outside from slipping.
Chris Rees, Cardiff.

QUESTION: A large proportion of the calories I consume as food will be used to keep my body warm. So can I lose weight by increasing the rate at which I lose heat, for example by wearing thinner clothes or turning down the heat in winter?

☐ THE human is a warm-blooded animal, which entails main-taining body temperature within a narrow range, outside which vital organs cease to function. Considerable effort is devoted to keeping the body core temperature steady in environments as diverse as the Saharan desert and Antarctica. The body has a variety of mechanisms for preserving heat, clothing being only one. The fat under the skin which troubles the questioner is one of these adaptations. In a cold environment the blood vessels in the skin would contract, diverting blood to the body core. Only when the body core temperature fell would a person begin to shiver in an effort to make more heat. The energy consumed would be very small, and use muscle sugars rather than fat. In the long term one's appetite would increase to lay down a better layer of fat under the skin. If anyone wishes to lose weight, then it is far better to increase the amount of exercise he or she takes.
Roger Hackney FRCS, British Association of Sport and Medicine, Nottingham.

QUESTION: Serial killers, rapists etc are often described in news reports as having 'piercing' or 'staring' eyes. Is there any physical/psychological reason for this? Should one, in general, be wary of men with piercing eyes?

☐ PROBABLY not, but watch out for the ones with beards.
Joseph Cowen, Vauxhall, London SE11.

☐ IT IS usually witnesses, who have seen rapists or killers shortly after they have committed a violent assault, who describe them as having 'piercing' or 'staring' eyes. The offender is probably scared witless that he has been noticed and is revealing wariness of anxiety, not intensity or prescience. Before he attacks, he is more likely to seem inoffensive, otherwise he would never get near his victims. So, men who have 'mellow' or 'blinking' eyes probably pose more of a risk.

David Canter, Department of Psychology, University of Surrey, Guildford.

QUESTION: Is anything unthinkable?

☐ NOT that I can think of.
Bob Livermore, London E3.

☐ THE dictionary definition of thinking is 'to use the power of reason' – we assume thinking has a purpose about it. In that sense, dreaming is unthinkable as we cannot 'think' dreams. It is the unstructured nature of dreams that makes them hard to recall or describe. Aspects of the future are unthinkable in the sense that Bach could easily have played jazz but was unable to think in those terms because he didn't have the relevant musical concepts to think with. The process of thinking entails an objective to reach and the appropriate mental images to attain that objective. If these are missing then the concept is unthinkable.
S. Hayward, London NW2.

QUESTION: Baby boys sometimes produce breast milk in the first few weeks after birth. Would it be possible for a man to breastfeed a baby?

☐ BABIES of both sexes often have pronounced breasts at birth and may produce breast milk due to high hormone levels in their mothers' blood. It is also not uncommon for adolescent boys to develop breasts at puberty – although it may be a surprise to them. A man's breasts can produce milk and men have been recorded as breastfeeding (albeit extremely rarely and possibly largely as a way of comforting the baby rather than providing any significant nutrition). In order to breastfeed well, however, a man would need to take an array of hormone tablets and injections. Initially he would need oestrogens and progesterones to develop the milk ducts and glands, which would also change the shape of the rest of his body. Prolactin and oxytocin would then need to be added to start the production and release of milk. At the same time, the man would need to start trying to express milk or have a baby willing to work for little reward. In fact there is a device which enables the baby to suckle, providing the stimulation necessary to maintain hormone levels, while taking formula milk from a tube in the corner of his mouth to provide nourishment at the same time. This is occasionally used by mothers who have adopted babies or otherwise need to increase their milk supply, while maintaining the baby's interest. It will be seen, then, that it is possible for a man to breastfeed, but if this man is also doing the shopping, cooking, washing and looking after the emotional needs of the baby, he may well take to the bottle.

Rosemary Dodds, Policy Research Officer, National Childbirth Trust, London W3.

☐ ACCORDING to Gould and Pyle's Anomalies and Curiosities of Medicine, published in 1896 and still the definitive volume on medical weirdness, it is indeed possible. They mention six cases, including a man of 55 who had suckled all his wife's children, and they also mention a report from 17th-century missionaries in Brazil describing a tribe whose women had shrivelled breasts and whose children suckled exclusively from the men.

Ian Simmons, Leicester.

QUESTION: What is the purpose of the white squares, perhaps one metre across, painted at intervals on the surfaces of motorways such as the M11 and M25?

☐ THE white squares on motorway surfaces are used by the police

to measure speed. A police car drives between the squares (which are in pairs, usually about 0.2 miles apart), measuring the time taken at a given speed. This is then used to judge the speed of other vehicles. Similarly, they provide a reference point for speed measurement when a vehicle is being followed by a patrol car.
Dr Jeremy Vanke, Public Policy Manager, RAC, London SW1.

QUESTION: The total money supply continues to grow even during a depressed economy. Since normal business transactions result in a straightforward transfer of money from one person or company to another, this means that somebody is creating money. Who is this, and is this a contributing factor in the problem of inflation?

☐ MOST definitions of the money supply comprise deposits held in banks and building societies, and these are dependent on saving/consumption ratios, interest rates and other allied factors. Banks and building societies are financial intermediaries between depositors and borrowers and cannot 'create' something out of nothing. They simply lend and borrow real wealth in its monetary form. The reason the money supply defined in these terms has grown over the last few decades has been largely as a result of price rises themselves, because the higher the price level, the higher the sums deposited will tend to be in absolute terms. The only institution which can really create money is the Bank of England, which can issue notes and coins – the value of which does not correspond to real wealth created in the economy, injecting a spurious excess monetary demand into the economy which causes prices to rise. The amount of notes and coins in circulation in the British economy since 1938 has risen from about £450 million to approximately £16,000 million, a rise far in excess of that required by increases in population, production and trade. In the same period the price level has risen 30-fold. The Bank of England claims it simply issues notes and coins to meet the demands of the banking system. However, this seems an inadequate explanation because,

as the questioner implies, both notes and coins in circulation and prices have continued to rise throughout the post-war period even when growth, industrial output and retail sales have all been falling. The real answer would appear to lie in the attitude of the monetary authorities who may well continue to believe that a stimulation of currency will help spur economic activity. As the economic history of Britain, America and other countries has demonstrated, there is no evidence to support this belief.
D. A. Perrin, Little Acton, Clwyd.

☐ D. A. PERRIN'S response is erroneous. The ability of the commercial banks to create credit is fundamental to economic activity. Based on the assumption the depositors will not simultaneously withdraw, the banks are able to lend a multiple of the sums deposited with them – currently about eight times. The allocation of these funds is crucial to economic management but is often misguided – twice in the last 20 years fuelling inflationary property booms. A further source of the recent growth in money supply is credit card lending. The abolition of credit controls over financial institutions in the 1980s unleashed massive increases in consumer spending leading to 'demand pull' inflation. The Bank of England's issue of notes and coins constitutes a tiny proportion of what is regarded as money.
Jane and Tony Abramson, Leeds.

QUESTION: Do fish sweat?

☐ OF COURSE. That's where all that salty water comes from.
Len Clarke, Uxbridge, Middx.

☐ FISH are poikilothermic – their body temperature follows that of their surroundings – so sweating as means of temperature control would be unnecessary. However, the tissues of marine fish have a lower concentration of dissolved salts than the sea, so they lose water by osmosis across their gills, where the blood is in

intimate contact with the surrounding water. This water is replaced by drinking sea water, and the excess sodium chloride absorbed as a result is excreted back across the gills. So although marine fish do lose both water and salt to their environment, the process is not 'sweating' as we normally understand the word.
Michael Hutton, Camberwell, London SE5.

QUESTION: Who invented car alarms, and where does he/she live?

☐ I HAVE an original scale-model of a car alarm patented by my father in the late 1920s, which I doubt even your irate questioner would have found environmentally offensive. Designed not to activate when sat on by a cat in the middle of the night, it's very simple. When the owner left the car, he or she turned a key which triggered a hinged plate in the exhaust system. This plate diverted the engine fumes into another pipe which was capped by a large brass whistle. Thus the vehicle would only make an intrusive noise when it had actually been stolen. Sadly, however, this invention would offer no protection to modern carphones and stereos.
Stuart Kerr, Chiswick, London W4.

QUESTION: WHY hasn't society evolved so that we take our eight hours' sleep between 8 p.m. and 4 a.m., thus optimising the hours of daylight all year round?

☐ BLAME the industrial revolution – we forgot how to coexist with nature. I think they call it progress.
Sally Keyworth, Fenstanton, Cambs.

☐ IN MANY farming communities in Britain, it is usual, when the season demands, to rise at daylight and work until nightfall. In many parts of Africa and the hotter countries surrounding the Mediterranean, the 'siesta' is used to break the working day which

starts earlier than Britain's and often ends later, thus avoiding the
hottest part of the day. In Norway, during the summer, it is not
unusual for people to start work around 6.30 a.m., and finish
before 4 p.m., thus maximising the daylight hours. In
Johannesburg, the business day usually starts before 8.30 a.m.,
and most people are up long before then.
Adam Henderson, Leeds.

□ BECAUSE the pubs don't shut until 11 p.m.
G. S. Jones, Farnham, Surrey.

**QUESTION: My father has maintained for years that Billy
the Kid was shot and killed, not by Pat Garrett, but by the
owner of the house in which he was staying. Is there any
evidence to support this theory?**

□ EVERYONE 'knows' that Pat Garrett killed Billy the Kid in Pete
Maxwell's house at old Fort Sumner around midnight on 14 July
1881 – but (to paraphrase John O'Hara on the death of George
Gershwin) you don't have to believe it if you don't want to. Con-
spiracy theory fans have been having fun with the proposition for
years. It is generally believed that Billy was staying with Celsa
Gutierres, a married woman who had been his mistress. Making
her carpenter husband Sabal the killer is a wonderful new twist to
the story. However, most researchers are fairly satisfied that at the
time Kid was killed it was not Celsa who was his sweetheart, but
Pablita, Pete Maxwell's teenage sister, who was pregnant with his
child and who was hastily married off to one Jose Jaramillo within
months of the Kid's death. So the owner of the house in which he
was killed, rather than staying, also had a good motive for wanting
the Kid out of the way. But whether those midnight doings at Fort
Sumner were indeed any darker than history records we shall
probably never learn, although it would be interesting to know
upon what information the questioner's father bases his theory.
Other stories abound: my favourite has the Kid discovered in bed

with Pablita and shot *in flagrante delicto*, an enviable way to
shuffle off this mortal coil.
Frederick Nolan, Chalfont St Giles, Bucks.

**QUESTION: Is it possible to carry out a genuine altruistic
act, bearing in mind that it ceases to be so at the slightest
feeling of pleasure or satisfaction?**

☐ SPONTANEOUSLY laying down one's life for another must surely
count as such.
Anthony F. Bennett, Chichester, West Sussex.

☐ I WOULD imagine that standing for the Tories in a 'safe' Conservative seat at a by-election is truly altruistic. There surely could
be no pleasure or satisfaction in either the campaign or the result.
Vincent Quirk, Skelmersdale, Lancs.

☐ ALTRUISM, as 'regard for others as a principle for action' (OED),
is in the act, not in the gratification or otherwise which one might
feel in doing the act. Regard for others, although maybe the
priority in altruistic acts, does not necessarily exclude regard for
yourself.
Adam Thompson, Brussels.

**QUESTION: Has any research ever been carried out to
prove, or disprove, the existence of 'a sense of direction'?**

☐ IN HIS delightful booklet, *The Compass in your Nose* (Kennedy,
1977), Lionel Kennedy describes his four-year research project to
test his hunch that a sense of direction is a real and measurable
human attribute. Starting with 1,400 volunteers ranging in age
from 10 to 72 (but mainly students), he began a series of elegant
experiments in which he and two assistants tested volunteers' responses to a strong electro-magnetic field which was switched on

and off in an isolated part of a university lab. Subjects appeared unable to detect the field. However, after open-air trials, mainly in Brighton and Oxford, Kennedy found a significant proportion of subjects displayed a 74 per cent success rate in 'returning to a start point'. Tests without audiovisual suppression produced a higher success rate, but he attributes this exclusively to 'ambient cues' – such things as one-way traffic systems, the sound of the ocean, and road signs! About two-thirds of his successful subjects were male.

Oscar Jedleigh, London SW1.

QUESTION: With so many phobias recognised and named today, is there a fear of phobias, or a fear of fear? Assuming it is something other than craven cowardice, what is it called and what are its symptoms?

☐ IT IS no longer the practice to name individual phobias, as this does not aid our understanding or treatment of them. Phobias are generally classified into agoraphobia, social phobia and simple phobias. The last two usually relate to a particular object or situation, hence it is unlikely, per se, that fear itself would feature in this context and I have never seen it. However, fear of going crazy or doing something uncontrolled is a recognised feature of panic disorder which is characterised by physical symptoms of anxiety such as hyperventilation, a feeling of 'butterflies' in the stomach, sweating and palpitations etc. Treatment is available for all the conditions mentioned.

Daniel S. Allen (Dr), Senior Registrar in Forensic Psychiatry, Fromeside Clinic, Bristol.

QUESTION: Is 'A question sender' the most appropriate anagram of Notes and Queries?

☐ DO INANE requests; send a risque note.
Steve Dungworth, Harrogate, N. Yorks.

☐ INSANE quest doer.
P. F. McGinley, Wakefield, West Yorks.

☐ O, SEND a request in.
Jack Griffiths, Ferring-by-Sea, West Sussex.

☐ SEND a note, Squire.
C. Campbell, Fleet, Hants.

☐ ENQUIRERS' sad note.
Andrew Peel, Canterbury, Kent.

☐ REQUEST non-ideas; sender so antique.
Gerry Abbott, Chorlton-cum-Hardy, Manchester.

☐ ENQUIRE, as stoned; I end reason quest.
Claire Whieldon, Keele, Staffordshire.

QUESTION: What differences would there be were the earth not to have a moon, and what would be their consequences?

☐ WEREWOLVES would wonder what was going on.
A. O'Reilly, Nottingham.

☐ THE earth's surface could never have been turned into a mixture of land and ocean without the moon's tidal drag working over billions of years, and advanced life could never have appeared if our world had been all land or all water. In 1988, Dr Jerome Pearson of the Flight Dynamics Laboratory in Dayton, Ohio, pointed out that the ocean tides, directly caused by the moon, and the emergence of tidewater zones which alternate between flooding and drying out, probably helped life to emerge on land. Also, the huge gravitational tide of the moon was responsible for the earth's molten core, which has opened and closed ocean basins and separated continents, isolating gene pools and speeding up evolution. Additionally, the moon has probably served as a partial

shield against meteoric bombardment from space, further enhancing the prospects for intelligent life.
Tony Martin, Nunhead, London SE15.

☐ TONY Martin is wrong on what causes the tides. If the moon did not exist, our tides would be almost unchanged because they are caused almost entirely by the sun. The gravitational force between two bodies is proportional to the product of their masses, divided by the square of their separation. The sun's mass is 27 million times greater than the moon's, giving a gravitational force 176 times greater. The effect of the moon is, therefore, negligible.
D. Fitzgerald, Ilkley, West Yorks.

☐ D. FITZGERALD correctly states that the sun produces tides on the Earth. These tides, however, have less than half the magnitude of the tides produced by the moon. It is not the strength of the gravitational pull of the moon that matters, but the difference in the strengths of the gravitational field due to the moon at the points on the earth nearest to, and farthest from, the moon. This depends on the mass of the moon, and on the ratio of the diameter of the earth (7,900 miles) to the distance from the earth to the moon (239,000 miles). The same is true in the case of the sun. Even at 93 million miles, the gravitational field due to the sun is much stronger than that due to the moon, but it is changing more slowly with distance. When the sun and moon are in line, their tides add up to give a large rise and fall (spring tides). When they are pulling at right-angles to one another, their tides tend to cancel out (neap tides).
Jim Stacey, Thornton, Liverpool.

QUESTION: On what basis do hospital out-patients' departments work out how many they can see in a given time? Do they ever get it right?

☐ THE consultant doctor decides how many patients he or she can see at a clinic, and the length of time the average patient will need.

Despite individual variations, by the end of a clinic the estimated time per patient will usually have proved pretty accurate. The system breaks down because many consultants start their clinics late and can never catch up. In 1967 I carried out a work study in the out-patient department of Essex County Hospital, Colchester. Of 102 clinics studied, only one started on time. Scheduling the starting times 15 minutes later had no effect; the doctors were still late starting. At Black Notley Hospital, all clinics started at the same time and all patients had the same appointment time: to coincide with the arrival of the only bus.
Don Gardiner, Widford, Ware.

□ THE number of patients seen is entirely dependent on the number of lines on the page in the diary for that day.
Ann Hazell, Stevenage, Herts.

QUESTION: Why did Hitler not invade Switzerland?

□ Because a stable, working Switzerland served him better, providing a base for business deals, an important railway link to Italy, a safe haven for spies and securing diplomatic contact with enemy forces. 'Six days a week Swiss work for Hitler, on the seventh they pray for victory of the Allied forces,' went a joke in those times. The German share of Swiss exports (mainly weapons, ammunition, high-tech machinery, food) increased from 15.5 to 42 per cent between 1937 and 1942. Not only civil goods made their way from or to Germany through Switzerland: weaponry was transported up to October 1941, and forced Italian labour as late as 1943. The allied forces even considered bombing the Gotthard line in 1944. Money robbed by the Nazis during the war was transferred into Swiss bank accounts. Although aware of the fate of those fleeing the death camps in Germany, the Swiss authorities refused to take in more people. Germany really had no reason for invading Switzerland, as this country worked so well for the Nazis. If there was a winner in the Second World War, it was the Swiss.
Thomas Schwager, St Gallen, Switzerland.

QUESTION: Next year I shall be attending an international school in Hong Kong. A part of this will require me to display English culture, including national costume, songs, dances and recipes. Any ideas?

☐ JOIN a Morris team. They may not be able to help with the recipes, but you'll certainly be able to learn some traditional English dancing, probably some English folk songs, and Morris kit is the closest you'll find to a national costume.
Sally Wearing, President, Morris Federation, Earlsdon, Coventry.

☐ THE questioner should contact: the Centre for English Cultural Tradition and Language, University of Sheffield; the English Folk Dance and Song Society, London; the Folklore Society, London; any museum with a good collection of costume and an interest in traditional gear. For recipes, any large library with a good topographical collection, but do not discount the Women's Institutes and Townswomen's Guilds. National costume really doesn't exist, but regional, trade and local costume does.
Derek Froome, The Folklore Society, Hale, Cheshire.

☐ 'ENGLISH' culture perhaps existed between the departure of the Romans from the British Isles and the arrival of the Danes. Since then, England – which can only have a geographical meaning – has been under permanent foreign (British) domination. Our most famous rulers, Knut (Danish), Richard Lionheart (French), Henry VIII (Welsh), George I (German), and now the Greeks, have left the area of land called England without any culture of its own. We have no costume, songs, dances and recipes that have amused our British rulers and therefore been allowed to survive. Our language is a 'mish-mash' of Danish and French with just about anything else we can take on. Our football yobs wave the British flag at 'English' matches. Our national drink is tea – brought back by the British. Our ancestors were press-ganged into the British navy, conscripted into the armies, and died in British pits and factories to make the British owners rich. The Irish, Welsh, and Scottish

were further away from London, more protected by their mountains and sea. They still have a culture.
Andrew Moss, Greiveldange, Luxembourg.

☐ SALLY Wearing may not be aware of the non-European origins of the Morris dance. J. A. Rogers, in his book *Nature Knows No Colour Lines* (1952) cites a number of authorities to show that the name 'Morris' is a corruption of 'Moorish', and hence that the dance has an African origin. Dr Johnson's dictionary (1755), for example, has 'Morris dance, that is Moorish or Morrice dance'. Shakespeare used the term 'Moor' to refer to all black Africans, as was the common usage since long before his time. The African origin of the Morris dance is further reinforced by the fact that, in times gone by, white dancers blackened their faces to dance it. The main argument of Rogers' book is that there has long been a black presence in England – and in much of Europe – which has left many marks on our culture, including this, the most English of dances.
Charlie Owen, London N4.

☐ ONE traditional English dance might be appropriate. It requires 12 Englishmen, 11 clad in white and the 12th in a white coat. The dance starts with one of the 11 screaming at the man in the white coat. The latter replies by solemnly raising the index finger of his right hand. The 11 in white then leap in turn into the air with the man who uttered the initial scream, slapping hands and displaying unreserved ecstasy. After one minute of this display, the 11 suddenly stop and begin to clap rhythmically, all the while staring into the mid-distance. They are joined in the applause by the audience for approximately one more minute. The dance then ends. This dance is called The Dismissal of the Australian Batsman (sometimes also called 'The Waugh Dance'). It is performed at most four times every five days during periods of the English summer.
Stuart Newstead, Oxford.

QUESTION: What would be the consequences were our monarch to develop a strong, public and inflexible moral aversion to some aspect of government policy, e.g. nuclear weapons?

☐ THE Queen could express her feelings by: (i) joining the Peace Tax Campaign to ensure that none of her taxes went on nuclear defence expenditure; (ii) breaking into the gardens of Buckingham Palace to protest at the desecration of Western Shoshone lands caused by nuclear testing; (iii) wearing a CND badge on all public appearances; (iv) as head of both the government and the armed services, cancelling the Trident contract forthwith.
Claire McMaster, Vice-chair, CND, London N7.

QUESTION: Is there anything wrong with being a Champagne socialist?

☐ NOTHING, if you can add some much-needed fizz and sparkle to the Labour Party.
Annette Maloney, St Leonards on Sea, East Sussex.

☐ NOT if we are all given an equal chance to get to the bottle.
Mary-Rose Benton, Stourport on Severn, Worcs.

QUESTION: Why did the First World War produce better poetry than any other war? Is it true only of Britain?

☐ THE British poetry of the First World War is uniquely powerful because the circumstances of the war contrasted with the imagery which contemporary writers and politicians had developed to describe an ideal England. The 'heart of England' was a network of rural pathways, ancient ruins and markers of buried pre-history. The trenches in France and Flanders were like a terrible inversion

of this ideal national landscape. British First World War poetry was the distillation of the best aspirations of Victorian culture meeting the worst consequences of the modernity which the culture had generated. The special resonance of that moment could never recur.
Dr Paul Barlow, University of Northumbria, Newcastle upon Tyne.

☐ THE best German war poetry never became as well-established because, when the anthology of First World War German poetry was due to be published as part of the national collection, the Nazis took over and the original editor was replaced by a party member more interested in the *Heldentod* (dying for the Fatherland) than any anti-war experience.
John Warren, Oxford Brookes University.

☐ HOW about the *Iliad*? Or numerous sagas and Border Ballads, and 'The Cattle Raid of Cooley'?
N. MacDonald, Lenzie, Glasgow.

QUESTION: Are there any organisations dedicated to the preservation of unpleasant creatures, rather than those which look good on T-shirts?

☐ YES – the Conservative Party, which is dedicated to the preservation of financial speculators, corporate asset-strippers, arms dealers and tobacco barons.
Nick Gotts, Leeds, West Yorks.

☐ THE Phasmid Study Group is dedicated to the breeding, conservation and study of stick insects, which suffer from an image problem. However, the PSG produce T-shirts, emblazoned with a larger-than-life picture of a female Jungle Nymph, and I think these look outstandingly good.
Joanna Clark, University of Glamorgan, Cardiff.

□ ANY organisation devoted to preserving creatures presumably does not regard them as unpleasant. Organisations specifically dedicated to less popular creatures include the Amateur Entomologists' Society and the Invertebrate Conservation Centre of London Zoo, whose projects have included breeding *Partula* snails. There are also many projects organised by the Biological Records Centre whereby amateur enthusiasts can contribute to surveys for scientific and conservation purposes, of groups as obscure as slime moulds, flatworms, fungus gnats, woodlice and fleas.

Martin Harvey, High Wycombe, Bucks.

QUESTION: Is a fourth – or higher – spatial dimension a reality that exists but eludes human senses and imagination, or is it an abstract concept for which there is no room in the real universe?

□ THE fact that we cannot comfortably fit our right-hand foot into our left-hand shoe is evidence that space has only three dimensions. Consider a two-dimensional experiment: two paper shapes are laid out on a table, one in the shape of an R, the other a mirror-reversed R. By simply moving the shapes around on the two-dimensional surface of the table, you cannot make them exactly coincide, the reason being that they have no axis of symmetry. In contrast, an E, which does have an axis of symmetry, can be made to coincide with its mirror-image. However, if you let one shape move in the third spatial dimension, by lifting it up and turning it over, you can make it coincide with its mirror-image counterpart. The apparent differences between these two-dimensional objects disappear once they are allowed to move in three spatial dimensions. The three-dimensional right foot and left foot are just like these shapes: they cannot be made to coincide as things are (having no plane of symmetry). But were they able to rotate in a fourth spatial dimension, their differences would disappear. Nature is full of objects which have no plane of symmetry. A molecule of adrenaline, for example, has no plane of symmetry, and can occur in either a 'right-handed' form or a 'left-handed' form. The fact that these different forms have different physiological properties should convince us that there is no fourth dimension of space.

Dr Robin Le Poidevin, Department of Philosophy, University of Leeds.

☐ THE fourth spatial dimension is simultaneously at right angles to any direction in which we care to point. However, being 'trapped' in the three dimensions we can't actually point in this direction. Also, even if we could detect the extra dimension, we would not be able to 'see' it because our retinas are two-dimensional surfaces and to see a four-dimensional object in its entirety, we would need three-dimensional retinas. The best we could hope for would be to see three-dimensional slices of the objects in series as we scanned it, just as hospital scanners are used to view slices of the human body. There exist some computer programs which show the projection of, say, a hypercube (the four-dimensional analogue of an ordinary cube) rotating. The images are perplexing and some people claim to be able to get an idea of the appearance of the actual hypercube through watching these real-time images. According to some of the latest theories in physics, space consists of many more dimensions than we can actually detect. The fourth and higher dimensions are postulated to be a physical reality.

Dr Khurram Wadee, Ealing, London W13.

☐ THE contradiction between the two respondents can be resolved by analysing what we mean by 'space'. Dr Le Poidevin's symmetry examples certainly show us there are only three dimensions to our everyday, common-sense kind of 'space', the 'space' we can perceive and move our feet in. Physicists dealing with superstring theory, however, have developed persuasive theories using an extra six spatial dimensions. These higher dimensions, however, are curled up into tiny circles, or similar closed surfaces, and are so small they are invisible on casual inspection (something in the range of $1/10^{33}$ across). This curling up of dimensions is

analogous to our observing, say, a piece of string from a distance and seeing it as a line, then moving closer and observing that it actually has an extra, circular dimension. If we could observe any point (say, a subatomic particle) at a large enough magnification, we would similarly see that it is not a point, but has further dimensions in unexplored directions.
Mark Howard, London NW6.

QUESTION: What *is* the difference between right and wrong?

☐ THE present government has demonstrated that the right can almost invariably be wrong.
Ted Tranter, Birchington, Kent.

☐ IN A logically sound language, there would be no such adjectives as 'right' and 'wrong': these words do not describe objective qualities but attitudes. Any meaningful statement about right and wrong implies someone's approval; either your own, or that of the circle in which you move, your religion, your god, a consensus of opinion via democratic process, etc. The use of such words as 'approved' and 'disapproved' has the advantage that it helps us clarify our minds on whose approval we are referring to.
Richard Benjamin, Ethical Society, London WC1.

☐ RICHARD Benjamin is wrong simply to assume that 'right' and 'wrong' do not refer to objective qualities – this is still a hotly contested issue in moral philosophy. If, as I expect, Mr Benjamin is working with a conception whereby the only objective properties are the ones turned up by physicists, then no doubt he is right. However, under this conception not only would the adjectives 'right' and 'wrong' have to disappear from Mr Benjamin's 'logically sound language', but so too virtually every other adjective we commonly use. This ought to make Mr Benjamin suspicious that maybe there are objective criteria relating to human conduct that

make certain adjectives, including right and wrong, objectively applicable. Biting someone's face off just does seem objectively wrong, given the sort of lives we might intelligibly be expected to want to lead as human beings. Secondly, he seems to be pedalling a long-since discredited 'emotivist' theory of moral discourse by identifying 'right' and 'wrong' with 'approval' and 'disapproval'. It is simply false to claim that a sentence such as 'I believe euthanasia is right' means the same as 'I approve of euthanasia'. I might well approve of euthanasia but the question whether euthanasia is right surely remains to be answered. Similarly, the fact that whole communities might approve of certain behaviour – for example, capital punishment, enslaving other cultures, etc – does not mean that such behaviour is right.
Robert Avon, School of Humanities and Social Sciences, University of Wolverhampton.

☐ ROBERT Avon fails to recognise that the right road for one traveller is the wrong road for another. It has nothing to do with the objective quality of the road. 'Right' and 'wrong' are used together to measure the quality of something, just as 'hot' and 'cold' are used to measure temperature, and 'north' and 'south' to measure directions. Used independently of each other, they are meaningless, the toys of philosophers.
Sam Micklem, Eldwick, West Yorks.

QUESTION: When did we start the absurd practice of ironing our clothes, and why do we persist with this futile activity?

☐ THE Chinese have used smoothing irons for two millennia, and in royal Korean tombs, *c.* AD 50, was found a box-iron – hot stones were its heat-source. In Europe, the pressing of wet linen had been done with a smooth surface, either weighted or screwed down on to the cold, and probably damp, cloth ('press' as in cider or cheese press). The cloth was folded: the resulting crisp creases can be seen

in many paintings. Heated metal irons were essential in tailoring and hat-making to shrink-shape wool cloth: in the 16th century they were used to give the perfect flat finish to the newest status garments, shirts and shifts of linen so fine-spun and woven that its costliness was shown off at neck and wrist. Since ironing is a time-consuming occupation, unwrinkled clothes became, and have remained, the ideal luxury – every time light linen, or later cotton, fabric is worn it should be washed, and patiently ironed, preferably by laundry-maids, with special instruments for the frills.
Ann MacDonald, London.

☐ IRONING was invented to occupy one's mind while watching television.
John Gray, Norwich.

QUESTION: Did Adam and Eve have navels?

☐ IN GENESIS 1:26, God (displaying his own disconcerting tendency to plurality) says: 'Let us make man in our own image, and let them have dominion over the fish of the sea.' So 'man' was a collective being from the beginning. As for Adam and Eve, the names occur much later on in the text, after the fall, and mean something like 'red' or 'earthy' and 'living' or 'lively'. So they're symbolic qualities, and were presumably consciously attached to symbolic persons. It took a later, less-aware culture to start treating these allusive stories as literal histories. So the first humanity wasn't very different from present-day humanity, belly-buttons and all, and the power of creation stories can still be recaptured by those who gaze beyond their own navels.
David Newton, Chelmondiston, Suffolk.

☐ 'YES' is the short answer. It could be argued that the Adam created in God's own image was navel-less: sexual reproduction came on to the scene only after the expulsion from Eden, and the navel is a mark of our fallen state. In the last century a creationist rearguard action against Darwinism centred on Adam's navel. Philip Gosse's book *Omphalos* (Greek: navel) argued that, although Adam was created, his body looked as if he had once been born; similarly, although the animals in the Garden of Eden were created as adults, they looked as if they had been born and grown in the normal way. Gosse's master-stroke was to extend the argument to the Earth itself, which 'appeared' as if it dated back millions of years. However, neither creationists nor evolutionists were impressed with this, and the case for a scientifically respectable creationism duly perished.

Phil Edwards, Manchester.

☐ MY THEORY is that when God had finished making man he realised that Adam just didn't look right with that expanse of smooth featureless abdomen, so he created the belly button. Later, when placentation became just the thing, it was the perfect place for the umbilical cord to attach to the foetus.

Dr Kitty Smith, London N8.

QUESTION: Why are those suffering from dyslexia able to form 'correct' drawn images but 'incorrect' written ones?

☐ IN DRAWING there is no requirement to use the phonological codes and sequences required for writing. This takes 'load' off the working memory and allows the spatial skills required in drawing to act without hindrance.

Liz Brooks, Executive Director, The Dyslexia Institute, Staines, Middx.

QUESTION: What is the logic behind the use of yellow headlights? If they have a proven safety advantage, why haven't we adopted them in Britain?

☐ YELLOW headlights do not have a proven safety advantage. Seeing distances in white and yellow light, under realistic conditions, with and without glare from opposing headlights, was

investigated by the Road Research Laboratory in the 1950s. It was found that: for equal wattage white light was better; if the wattage of yellow light was increased to overcome loss of intensity there was a very slight increase in seeing distance in yellow light, especially with glare; but drivers preferred white headlight beams.
Barbara Preston, Marple Bridge, Stockport.

☐ SINCE January, all new cars manufactured in France have white headlamps. Yellow headlamps are an anachronism dating from the Occupation and were intended to enable German soldiers immediately to identify French vehicles at night.
Richard Baker, Bingham, Notts.

QUESTION: Whatever happened to Fotheringhay Castle, the scene of the beheading of Mary Queen of Scots? There is certainly a large mound still in existence but no stones, walls or any surface signs.

☐ FOTHERINGHAY Castle has shared a fate similar to that of so many medieval buildings. The standing structure of the castle has been demolished, and only the defensive works – in the form of a substantial earthen mound and enclosing moats – are visible. This is the site of the original 'motte and bailey', and part of the moat of a subsequent larger bailey. The succession of stone and timber buildings, including a stone keep, chapels, a great hall and domestic buildings that once crowded these defences, were periodically demolished or altered before abandonment in the 17th century. Demolition followed and, according to the Royal Commission on Historical Monuments, by the 19th century the few remaining structures were pulled down by the owner, who used some of the salvaged materials in his own buildings. Traces of former walls, floors and yards are still preserved below the turf, but only one visible fragment of limestone masonry, reputedly from a tower on the motte, is today visible, having been placed by the river earlier this century. Like so many other deserted medieval castle, village

and manor-house sites across Northamptonshire, the medieval earthworks have proved far more durable than the buildings they were erected to protect.
Kim Lanning, Graham Cadman, Planning and Transportation Department, Northamptonshire County Council.

QUESTION: How can I cure myself of my childish and figure-fatal sweet tooth?

☐ A SWEET tooth is indicative of a lack of chromium in the diet. The craving for sweet things happens because the body knows that very low blood sugar is life-threatening. Eating something sweet causes the levels to soar, which is very useful for emergency treatment for serious hypoglycaemic attacks but not recommended as regular practice. Once the blood glucose level is high again, insulin is produced to bring the raised levels under control. The mechanism which balances insulin production cannot function without chromium, which is easily destroyed through modern farming methods (over production and crop-spraying). So it is lacking in the modern diet and is almost certainly responsible for the onset of diabetes in many people. Take a supplement of 100–150 mcg GTF Chromium daily with food and the sweet craving will disappear, as well as the likelihood of becoming diabetic. Eat a balanced diet to include wholegrains, fruit, vegetables and fatty fish, avoiding animal fats and cheese.
Rodney Quixley, Nutritional Consultant, Battersea, London SW11.

☐ I WAS a chronic addict, losing most of my teeth as a result. My remedy was to promise to pay £5 to my son every time I ate a sweet or chocolate. This was over 20 years ago and I've only had to part with one fiver since then. My daughter-in-law struggled for many years to give up smoking, finally consulting a hypnotist who charged her £32. This had no effect except that, having paid out so much, she decided she wouldn't smoke again, and hasn't.

I suggest the questioner promises to pay me the sum of £500 (say) every time a sweet or chocolate is consumed – £5 is all I'm asking for the treatment.

John Gibberd, West Wittering, West Sussex.

QUESTION: What are the 'Lyme' and 'Lyne' that Newcastle and Ashton are 'under'?

□ LYME was the ancient name of a large district on the uplands of the Pennine massif on the northern borders of Staffordshire, the south-eastern and eastern borders of Cheshire and the south-eastern borders of Lancashire. Not only does the name appear in Newcastle under Lyme and Ashton under Lyne (Asshton under Lyme, 1305), but also in a range of toponyms such as Lyme Park, Lyme Wood and Limehurst in Lancashire; Lyme Hall and Lyme Handley in Cheshire; Chesterton under Lyme in Staffordshire; and even in the final syllables of Audlem (Cheshire) and Burslem (Staffs). The distribution of placenames containing 'under Lyme' follows the 400-foot contour along the western edges of the Pennine massif, indicating that the Lyme was a region above this height. The name Lyme is pre-Anglo-Saxon but is of disputed etymology. It appears to be either a derivative of the British word *lemo*, 'an elm tree', perhaps a British *lemia*, 'the district where the elm trees grow', or of a British *lummio*, giving Primitive Welsh *lim*(m) in some such sense as 'the bare or exposed district'. The latter derivation would suit the appearance of the moors massif in modern times and probably its condition on the arrival of the Anglo-Saxons, who adopted the name from the Celtic inhabitants. However, a notable stand of elms in a region where any tree was rare could well have given rise to a district name based upon such a feature.

Professor Barrie Cox, Department of English Studies, University of Nottingham.

QUESTION: Is there a Letsby Avenue anywhere in England and if so, are there any police officers living there?

☐ I RETIRED from Flatfoot County Police Department in 1989.
Watt Sauliss, Sunshine, Arizona.

QUESTION: About 100 years ago the French launched a ship which ran on six large wheels supporting a hull carried clear of the water. It was said to be very fast, stable and efficient and there was no drag. What became of the ship and the principle?

☐ THE roller-ship *Ernest Bazin*, launched in 1899, is described by Lt-Cdr R. T. Gould in *The Star Gazer Talks* (1943, p.70). The claims that it was very fast and efficient must have been anticipatory. Gould explains: 'On trial the best she could do was about 8 knots. This was due to the wheels carrying with them, as they turned, a film of water which, slowly dripping off, caused the back half of each wheel to be heavier than the front half.' But he adds that she 'showed her sea-worthiness by crossing the Channel and touring the East Coast, where she aroused a good deal of interest. In the end, she was broken up at Hull.' Bazin's idea might be worth reconsidering in the light of modern materials technology. If the wheels could be coated with some unwettable plastic, perhaps his hopes would at last be realised.
George Toulmin, Cheltenham, Glos.

QUESTION: How often do people take the opportunity to declare that 'these persons may not be lawfully joined in holy matrimony'? What happens when they do?

☐ FIFTY or so years ago, as a small bridesmaid, I thought that a shout of 'I object' from the congregation was just a regular part of each and every wedding ceremony. When it happened there was at first some talk between the vicar and the man who had called out. The bridal party, myself included, then trooped into the vestry with the objector. The objection, as I learned some years later, was from the father of the bride. He and the bride's mother were separated and the bride, being under 21, needed parental consent. He had not been asked, had only just discovered the wedding was taking place and had gone along to uphold his paternal rights – perhaps taking the odd drink or so on the way to boost his resolve. The vestry deliberations ended with him giving his consent and we all went back for the marriage service to proceed without further hindrance.

Carol Hammerton, Mickleover, Derby.

☐ THE words quoted are laid down in the 1662 Book of Common Prayer for reading the banns – although a similar invitation is included in the Marriage Rite itself. Their primary purpose was to discover any clandestine or private 'spousal' of marriage, contracted by either party, which would invalidate the proposed public ceremony. In 1753 such pre-contracts were outlawed by statute – and at the same time parental consent was made essential for the marriage of persons under 21 (now 18). The banns changed function so that they have become the means whereby parental consent is established or denied. If a parent, legal guardian or their representative objects during a service to the reading of the banns for the marriage of a minor, then the marriage ceremony is cancelled. The couple's options are: to wait till they are both over 18, to move to Scotland or to apply through the courts for a licence to marry, overriding the parental objection. A parent who has not objected to the banns cannot stop the marriage by objecting at the ceremony. Anyone present, however, can declare that a general legal impediment exists. These are: that one of the parties is under 16; that they are not male and female; that they are related within the prohibited degrees; that one is already married; that the ceremony is defective (e.g. if the minister is not an ordained deacon of the Church of England). The Prayer Book states: 'The solemnisation must be deferred until such time as the

truth be tried.' False or frivolous allegations would result in heavy damages.
Tom Henne!l, Withington, Manchester.

QUESTION: What is the difference between bribes, paid to foreign politicians, and consultancy fees, paid to British politicians?

☐ THE difference is not unlike tax evasion and tax avoidance. In both cases, the objective and, hence, the end result is the same. The issue is not intention, but declaration. If it is not declared, then it is illegal. If it is, then it is merely unethical. In a 'fair' world, however, there is no difference and there can only be one interpretation: corruption.
Dr M. Russell, London W1.

☐ FOREIGN politicians generally still possess some notion of public responsibility. Therefore they need some extra incentive to be persuaded to support decisions and policies which are against the interests of those they supposedly represent and favour the rich, the powerful or the crooked. British politicians, however, are quite willing to do such things (cf the dismantling of British Rail, the coal industry and the Post Office) without apparently needing any outside inducement. So the answer is: the bribes are necessary, the consultancy fees are not.
Michael Hutton, London SE5.

QUESTION: Was Leslie Halliwell (*Filmgoer's Companion*) having us on, or was there really a 'dignified German character actor' in Hollywood called Gustav von Seyffertitz who sometimes went under the name of G. Butler Clonblough?

☐ GUSTAV von Seyffertitz was an Austrian. Born in Vienna in 1863, he became one of the most popular villains of silent and early sound films. A veteran of the stage, both in Europe and America, he made his first film appearance in 1917, adopting the name G. Butler Clonblough until the end of the First World War. He was a superb Moriarty opposite John Barrymore in *Sherlock Holmes* (1922) and his chilling portrayal of the villainous baby-farmer Grimes in *Sparrows* (1926) elevated this otherwise ordinary Mary Pickford drama into the realms of horror. His other movies included two directed by fellow Austrian Josef von Sternberg – *The Docks of New York* (1928) and *Shanghai Express* (1932). He also appeared with Greta Garbo in *The Mysterious Lady* (1928) and with Anna Neagle in *Nurse Edith Cavell* (1939). He died in 1943. *Trevor Smith, Copnor, Hants.*

QUESTION: Why are lesbians called 'dykes'?

☐ JANE Mills, in her book *Womanwords*, says that the word probably started out as 'dite' as in hermaphrodite – on the grounds that any woman who spurned a man's advances must be part male. *Ann Collins, Balsall Heath, Birmingham.*

QUESTION: Why was sailors' rum ration called 'grog'?

☐ IN 1742 Admiral Vernon was concerned about the drunkenness of the Fleet and ordered the rum ration to be diluted. In later years the regulation mixture was two parts of water to one of rum (a 'Nor-wester', for special occasions, was one part water to one of rum). The Admiral habitually wore a voluminous cloak made from grogram and was known as 'Old Grog', hence the name for the diluted rum. 'Grog-blossom' was the name given to a red nose, blotch or pimple caused by excessive drinking. Originally issued twice daily ($\frac{1}{4}$-pint of rum to a pint of water), it was cut to one issue in 1824 and reduced to a 'half-gill tot' in 1850. Issue to

officers ceased in 1881 and to warrant officers 1918. Grog ration to ratings ended on 1 July 1970, being replaced by beer.
Roger F. Squires, Hodge Bower, Shropshire.

QUESTION: Why do things *peter* out?

□ THERE must once have been a staff member at *Punch* magazine called Peter. Anyway, I once submitted a piece to that publication, only to have it returned. On the rejection slip was scribbled: 'Good scene, but peters out.' Just my luck.
Michael J. Smith, Swaffham, Norfolk.

□ BEFORE the invention of percussion caps, a cannon or musket was first primed with gunpowder, then fired by touching the priming pan with a slow-burning cord that had been soaked in a constituent of gunpowder, saltpetre (or potassium nitrate). Occasionally, it would stop burning or 'peter out'. To this day, certain regiments in the army in dress uniform carry the historical remnant of this device on the shoulder and through the epaulette. The original was also braided to keep it in compact form.
Reg Williamson, Whitehill, Staffs.

QUESTION: What is the origin of the phrase 'taking the mickey'?

□ MICHAEL Barrett was the last man to be publicly hanged in Britain – for an explosion at Clerkenwell Gaol in 1867, which was an attempt to free a leader of the Fenians, Richard O'Sullivan Burke. Irish settlers were to become known as 'Michael Barretts', a term of derision later shortened to 'Micks'. The stereotype of the Irish being stupid gave rise to the term 'taking the mickey'.
David Glinch, London SE6.

□ ACCORDING to both James Macdonald's *Dictionary of Obscenity,*

Taboo and Euphemism (Sphere, 1988) and R. W. Holder's *Dictionary of Euphemisms* (Faber, 1987), 'Mike Bliss' or 'Mickey Bliss' was Cockney rhyming slang, and 'taking the Mickey' was therefore 'taking the piss'. E. J. Burford, in *The Orrible Synne: A Look at London Lechery* (Calder and Boyars, 1973), also reports that 'micgan' was Old English for piss, from the old Norse 'migan', and that this was the root of the expression.
P. Cross, Highbury, London N5.

☐ P. CROSS is right to identify the origin of the phrase in Cockney rhyming slang. However, to suggest that it owes something to the Old English 'micgan' is to overlook the medical term for the same process, micturition.
Neil Grant, Kings Heath, Birmingham.

QUESTION: In 'Ode To Billy Joe' by Bobby Gentry, what is it that Billy Joe and his girlfriend throw off the Tallahatchee Bridge?

☐ BOXES full of that dreadful Bobby Gentry record.
James Canwin, Leicester.

☐ WHEN 'Ode To Billy Joe' was first released, the common belief was that Billy Joe McAllister and his girl threw their newborn baby off the Tallahatchee Bridge. However, according to the 1976 film inspired by the song, what Billy Joe and his girlfriend really threw into the river was a rag doll. (The doll, incidentally, had been the subject of another Bobbie Gentry song, 'Benjamin'. In the film, the action symbolises the passage of boy and girl into adulthood, discarding childish ways. The film, which was scripted with Gentry's blessing, also resolved the mystery of just why Billy Joe jumped off the bridge at all: he couldn't come to terms with a gay encounter he had had with the sawmill owner who employed him. In the final scene, the Bobbie Gentry character leaves town because her

family mistakenly assumes she is having Billy Joe's child: pretending to have it is her way of keeping his heroic image alive.
Stephen Barnard, Hatfield, Herts.

QUESTION: It is customary to take fresh fruit to people in hospital. Is this nutritionally sound, and are particular fruit to be preferred or avoided?

☐ THE custom of giving fresh fruit to sick people dates from the time when it was usual to fast when sick. A fasting patient breaks the fast with small, easily digestible meals. A meal of fresh, ripe, juicy raw fruit is ideal for this purpose.
Alan Ashley, Bramford, Ipswich.

QUESTION: What is the greatest coincidence ever?

☐ I WAS just about to ask that very question.
Martin Chinnery, Blackheath, London SE13.

☐ SURELY it is the meeting of a sewing machine with an umbrella on a dissecting table at precisely the moment when surrealism was looking for a definition of beauty.
Brian Birch, Cottingham, North Humberside.

☐ THAT Ernest Saunders developed acute Alzheimer's Disease when he was sent to gaol for his part in the Guinness fraud, was released as a result, and then became the only person ever to make a full recovery.
John Davies, Eston, Cleveland.

☐ THAT the relative sizes of sun and moon and their relative distances from the earth mean that we get the sort of eclipse effects we see. Unless, of course, it's not a coincidence but a matter of design.
(Rev) S. Parish, Warrington.

QUESTION: Why are Granny Smith apples so called? Who was she and where did she live?

☐ THE original Granny Smith tree grew from a pip thrown out by Mrs Thomas Smith of Ryde, New South Wales, Australia. Trees of the variety were fruiting by 1868, and were brought to the UK in 1935. (See John Bultitude, *Apples: A Guide to the Identification of International Varieties*; Rosanne Sanders, *The English Apple*.) Apples do not grow true from seed, so a tree grown from a pip will be unique, and you can name it after yourself. The odds are very much against you coming up with anything worthwhile, but both Cox's Orange Pippin and Bramley's Seedling were raised by amateurs.
R. G. Pratt, Hay-on-Wye, Hereford.

QUESTION: Of the various amphitheatres built in ancient Greece, that at Epidaurus is among the largest and is still used. It will accommodate 14,000 people, but where in ancient times did so many people come from? Epidaurus is in an empty part of Greece and is unlikely to have been the local theatre for more than a few small villages.

☐ THE magnificent theatre at Epidaurus was built in the 4th century BC as part of the sanctuary of Asclepios, the god of healing. Far from being in an 'empty part' of Greece, Epidaurus was then an important centre, a city-state of the Argolid peninsula, which at one time had controlled the island of Aegina. With the development of the cult of Asclepios, it became what we would now call a spa town, famous throughout Greece for the healing qualities of its water. As a place of pilgrimage as well as healing, Epidaurus would have had no difficulty in accommodating 14,000 visitors. The great drama festivals held at the site derived from the 5th-century Athenian festival of Dionysus which originally had a religious connotation as well as being an entertainment. Greek drama

was concerned, among other things, with the destiny of humans in relation to the fickle powers of the gods.
David Wilson, London W10.

☐ THERE are no amphitheatres in Greece, only theatres. An amphitheatre is a Roman construction, elliptical in shape, like two theatres put together, and was used for gladiatorial contests.
Mary Lambell, Reigate, Surrey.

QUESTION: Are there any logical reasons for cannabis to be illegal?

☐ ANY centralised and undemocratic State feels the need to be able to control societal elements who are inclined to deviate from standard modes of thinking and behaviour. Cannabis tends to produce these traits to some degree in those who use it. Therefore it is logical for the State to give itself the power to arrest such users.
Dr Richard Lawson, Green Party Health Speaker, Congresbury, Avon.

☐ IT IS likely that cannabis-smoking may cause lung damage, but it is often difficult to separate the effects of marijuana from tobacco, as both substances are smoked together in a joint. Other research has suggested a connection between marijuana use and depression but, as this link is only correlational, one cannot be sure that this demonstrates a causal connection. People may smoke it simply because they are prone to anxiety and depression. In the 19th century, cannabis was used as a treatment for depression, as well as other ailments. There seems to be no entirely logical reason why cannabis should be illegal, especially when we consider the fact that alcohol and tobacco are legal.
E. B. Thomas, South Ockenden, Essex.

☐ I'M THOROUGHLY in favour of making Ol' 'Mary Jane' legal but intellectual honesty compels me to put forward the fact that we do not have a means of detecting whether drivers are 'under the influence' of hash, as the breathalyser does for alcohol. If one of

your readers can assure me that such means do exist, then as far as I'm concerned the last logical reason is washed away. The next question is: what on earth has logic got to do with passing laws?
Michael Cule, Bourne End, Bucks.

QUESTION: When not in use, what is the correct position to leave the toilet seat, lowered or raised?

☐ IF THE loo in question is used by both sexes, lowered please. The unexpected contact of bare flesh and cold porcelain is traumatic.
Anne Bryson, West Kirby, Merseyside.

☐ SO NOW we know! Anne Bryson reveals the real reason women get mad when men leave the seat up – they don't bother to look before they plonk themselves down! Right, now let's settle this: we'll all leave both seat and cover down after use and then we'll all have to check before the action starts.
Christopher Turner, Sevenoaks, Kent.

☐ THERE need be no gender war – seat and lid should both be replaced! Every time the toilet is flushed, fine droplets of probably harmful bacteria explode upwards over an area of four cubic feet. Wise people limit infection.
Margaret Williams, Isleham, Cambs.

QUESTION: Would it be possible to make human mother's milk into cheese?

☐ THE effort would have little success because the amount of casein in human milk is too little and mostly of the wrong type for the usual cheese-making enzymes to yield a good curd.
Alan Long, Vega, London SE13.

☐ ROBERT Plot in his *Natural History of Staffordshire* (1686) records that at Cannock he met one Mary Eagle 'who could draw two quarts of milk from her breasts per diem . . . where of she

could make two pounds of butter per week . . . which she sold to some Apothecaries hereabout at a good rate, it being useful (as she said) in all sorts of swellings, Aches of the head, sore Eyes'. She gave Plot a sample but before he could test its efficacy he found it had grown rancid.
Michael Paffard, Keele, Staffs.

QUESTION: What is the origin of the word 'juggernaut'?

☐ JUGGERNAUT is derived from Sanskrit and modern North Indian languages such as Hindi. 'Naut' here is Lord (*nath*) of the universe (*jagat*). The compound, Jagannath, is a title for the Hindu god, Vishnu, especially in his eighth incarnation as Krishna. Huge lorries are called juggernauts because the epithet of the deity had come in English to be associated with the enormously heavy chariot (*rath*) which bears Jagannath in procession at the annual festival (Rathayatra) at the town of Puri ('Jagannath Puri') in Orissa in north-east India. This has been reported by European travellers since about 1321 and reports mentioned worshippers dying, crushed under the massive wheels. Western observers' usually disparaging accounts led to an intermediate usage of juggernaut for any 'institution to which persons are ruthlessly sacrificed' (OED, 1933) before it was applied to 'a very large lorry for transporting goods by road, especially one that travels throughout Europe' (*Collins Dictionary of the English Language*, 1979). During the past 150 years, juggernaut served in a derogatory sense as a verb and an adjective as well as a noun.
Eleanor Nesbitt, Senior Research Fellow Religious Education, University of Warwick.

QUESTION: Who invented the standard paper sizes (A3, A4, etc)? How did he or she persuade so many countries to adopt it, and why did the USA reject it?

☐ THE equivalent size to A4 letter paper in the USA is 216 mm ×

298 mm, almost the same as A4 which is 210 mm × 297 mm. As
we say, if something works, don't fix it!
David Griffiths, Seattle, Washington.

**QUESTION: Is it possible for the same electron (or any-
thing) to exist more than once?**

□ THE answer depends on whether there is any continuity between two existences. If there is, then there is only one continuous
existence. If there is no continuity, then the first existence has
ceased to be and any other subsequent existence is another entity
occupying another stretch of Space-Time.
Donald Maw, Mansfield.

**QUESTION: Can anyone confirm that somewhere in a field
in the North of England there used to be a sign saying
'Please do not throw stones at this notice'? Are there other
examples of this kind of helpful public information?**

□ THERE is a sign at the back entrance to the botanical gardens
in this town that says: 'Slow Down – You are entering a work
zone.'
Paul Mestitz, Greelong, Victoria, Australia.

□ IN A coffee-bar in Sincelejo, northern Colombia, the following is
displayed: 'Bread with butter: 100 pesos. Bread with margarine:
80 pesos. Bread without butter: 60 pesos. Bread without margarine: 40 pesos.'
Bernardo Recamán, Bogotá, Colombia.

□ THE strictures against 'throwing stones at this notice' seem
positively tame compared to the list of prohibitions posted at a
beach called Wilderness, Cape Province. They read: 'The following are prohibited. No: picnic between sunset and sunrise; bad

language; firearms; singing; playing of musical instruments; use of loudspeakers; dumping of rubbish; camping; animals; damage of vegitation (sic); washing of crockery or laundry; gatherings; alcohol. Thank you.'
Beverley Roos, Cape Town, South Africa.

☐ SEEN in a field in West Yorkshire: 'Beware of the Bull. Entry Free. Bull Will Charge Later.'
Mrs Ray Tantram, Great Bookham, Surrey.

☐ PRINTED on toilet paper tissues at the Harwell Laboratories in the 1970s: 'Not for resale.'
Dr J. G. Booth, Department of Physics, University of Salford.

☐ IN THE Raemoir House Hotel near Aberdeen there used to be a sign on a door which read: 'Room for shooting guests only.' The room is now the manager's office.
Colin Millar, Oyne, Aberdeenshire.

☐ THE NSW Public Works Department had a portable toilet with a sign: 'Please do not place your handbag in the urinal.'
B. Kesteven, Hurstville, New South Wales, Australia.

☐ SEEN at the tip of Great Camanoe Island in the British Virgin Islands (1962–64): 'No trespassing without permission.'
A. S. Batham, Taupo, New Zealand.

☐ I AM told that in Belize, in a place called 'The Dump', there was a football field with a sign saying: 'Anyone throwing stones will be persecuted.'
R. E. G. Smith, Maseru, Lesotho.

☐ OUT in the wilds of Connemara there is a gaunt granite mono-lithic monument, with a plaque reading: 'On this spot in 1897 nothing happened.'
Ruth Smith, Cambridge.

144 Notes & Queries

□ OUTSIDE Shap Abbey in Cumbria stands this notice: 'Admission Free. Special terms for parties.'
Marcus Cousterdine, Blackpool.

□ A NOTICE which reflected the spirit of the question was written in chalk on a wall in Cambridge not long ago. It read: 'This graffito is biodegradable.'
Bernard Cashman, Biddenham, Bedford.

□ IN RECENT years there was a blue heritage plaque on a house in Zinzan Street in Reading which stated: 'William Hogarth (1697–1764) never lived here.' It has since disappeared. Maybe they found out it wasn't true?
Maxine Wicks, Bishopston, Bristol.

□ MY FAVOURITE road sign is in Chesham, Bucks, where the highway authorities – having spent large sums of taxpayers' money to build a relief road with two lanes in each direction – now instruct motorists: 'Use Both Lanes.'
Geoffrey Allen, Pavia, Italy.

□ THERE is a sign at the edge of a pasture in Belgrade, Maine, which states: 'If you can't cross this field in 9.9 seconds or less, DON'T TRY IT. The bull can make it in 10.'
E. A. Mayer, Belgrade Lakes, Maine, USA.

□ WHEN we lived in Massachusetts in the 1960s, I distinctly remember a sign on a high-tension electricity pylon saying: 'To climb this structure means instant death. Anyone found doing so will be prosecuted.'
Nicholas O'Dell, Phoenixville, Pennsylvania, USA.

QUESTION: Is there such a thing as a positive stereotype? If so, examples, please.

□ STEREOTYPES (structured sets of beliefs about social groups)

have long been shown to have a pervasive and pernicious influence on judgments about individuals who are members of various ethnic, religious and other social groups. Some scholars argue that stereotypes are inherently 'bad' or 'wrong' because they are illogical in origin, resistant to contradiction, morally wrong and so on. However, they are not always negative. First, stereotypes may concern 'ingroups' (of which we are members) or 'outgroups' (of which we are not members). The former tend to be positive and the latter negative. Second, most stereotypes probably consist of a mix of positive and negative characteristics. Even virulently racist stereotypes often include positive traits (e.g. 'athletic', 'musical') as well as negative traits (e.g. 'aggressive', 'lazy'). The same is true for anti-semitic stereotypes (e.g. 'intelligent' vs 'mean'). Third, the questioner might consider nurses and find they have a predominantly positive stereotype ('kind', 'humane', 'sensitive', 'caring', etc). All this is not to deny the social significance of negative stereotyping. The problem is that often the 'positive' stereotypical characteristics ascribed to outgroups are patronising and/or concern relatively unimportant dimensions of comparison between groups.
Miles Hewstone, Professor of Social Psychology, University of Bristol.

☐ I TAKE it quite positively when I am occasionally called a 'typical bloody *Guardian* reader'.
Ian Casson, Preston, Lancs.

☐ TRULY positive stereotypes are produced entirely within one culture and are usually seen in a positive light only by a small section of the community. Guns N' Roses, whose tours are famed for reckless excess offstage, are one example. Their appeal to young rock fans is based on a shared view that their lifestyle is to be aspired to. The exploits of such heroes become, quite literally, legend. These legends could not exist without the creation of a stereotype that wilfully ignores the fact that rock stars are merely human, and instead credits them with superhuman sexual stamina, God-given talent and the kind of constitution that can withstand drink and drugs that would kill the rest of us. Anyone who has ever idolised another person in this way has done something to create a positive stereotype.

Neil Nixon-Bearsted, North West Kent College of Technology, Dartford.

QUESTION: Have there been any authenticated cases of psychic powers being used to solve a murder?

☐ THERE is not a single authenticated case of a 'psychic' doing anything for the police that they cannot do for themselves. Stories to the contrary are fun to read (and good for the psychic's reputation), but they all collapse under examination, as many diligently researched books have shown. Not surprising, since no one has so far been able to demonstrate any psychic ability, of any kind, under well-designed test conditions. The best source of information on this subject that I've found is Prometheus Books UK (081-508 2989), who stock many excellent books on psychic claims.

Ian Rowland, Streatham, London SW16.

QUESTION: I was putting some heavy books in a bookshelf on the second floor of my home and wondered how many I could put before there was a danger of the floor collapsing. Is there any way one can find out?

☐ ALL houses should be capable of carrying a uniformly distributed floor loading of 30lb per square foot of floor area or a concentrated load of 300lb over an area of one square foot. Thus for a room of 200 square feet in area the permissible total uniformly distributed load is 6,000lb. If the questioner does have anything approaching 6,000lb to support he should really consult a structural engineer like me.

R. E. Brand, C Eng, F I Struct E, Hastings, Sussex.

☐ WHENEVER a client raises the possibility of one of the bespoke bookcases made by our company cascading towards the cellar, I suggest we consider the humble piano of yore, which must have been heavier than a few Penguins. A structural survey I once witnessed involved the gentleman conducting the survey jumping in the middle of each floor without benefit of discernible instrument. I might recommend this to the questioner as an excellent cure for the possible confusion between a given volume's weight and its weightiness.

W. Milne, Calgari Cabinets, London N19.

QUESTION: Are there any valid arguments, other than religious ones, as to why it would be better for the planet for the human race to continue rather than to become extinct?

☐ THE questioner asks whether or not it would be better for 'the planet'. This is a problem of values. The planet, in so far as it is a material object, clearly has no values of its own, since values are a product of consciousness. The planet could no more experience pleasure in the continued existence of life than it would lament its passing. It therefore follows that any positive attributes the planet is thought to possess exist only because of their presence in the mind of a living being capable of experiencing them. So far as we know, humans are able to experience more complex and varied responses to the world than any other animal. This opinion may be no more than 'speciesist' vanity, but the existence of anything approaching human levels of creative thought in other animals is so far unproven. In any case, whatever other animals think, we can only answer this question from within our own value system. To this extent it answers itself. The beauties and pleasures of the natural world which we experience are only recognised as such because we are here to do the recognising. If we didn't exist, neither would these experiences. The planet is valuable only as long as someone is here to value it. Our existence is thus a

necessary condition for the continuation of the planet itself as something which is meaningful.
Dr. P. Barlow, Sunderland University, Tyne and Wear.

☐ DR BARLOW'S answer is based on the assumption that 'better' necessarily means *'morally superior'*: this makes nonsense in the context. In the English language it can also mean 'in a superior physical condition', as when we say that someone is better after an illness. In this sense the planet would obviously be better without the human race. In these days of efficient contraception and when there are few family businesses left to keep going, the main motives for perpetuating the human race must be to satisfy the parental instinct, to attempt to achieve some sort of immortality, or to keep Debrett's Peerage in business. However, it may surprise the questioner to know that two Christian sects, the Albigenses and Cathari in the 11th to 13th centuries in southern France and elsewhere, condemned procreation on the grounds that it increased the amount of evil in the world which they saw as a battleground between spiritual good and material evil. They were condemned as heretics and became the victims of a crusade led by our Simon de Montfort.
Robert Sephton, Oxford.

☐ IT WAS not *our* Simon de Montfort, Earl of Leicester, born in 1208, who led the merciless crusade against the Albigenses and Cathars in south-west France. It was Simon IV le Fort, Sire de Montfort, who was appointed to lead the crusade in 1209, following the assassination of the Papal Envoy, Pierre de Castelnau, near St Gilles. Meanwhile, *our* Simon de Montfort was a babe in arms.
F. Paul Taylor, Frodsham.

☐ I WONDER if Robert Sephton realises that by introducing the Albigenses and Cathars into the debate, he undermines his own argument. These sects, like other forms of Manicheism, believed that all matter was evil. For them, the world would be a better place if all biological life was extinguished. By this logic, a healthy

planet is a dead planet. So keep up the good work, all you polluters out there!
Flavia Dunford-Trodd, Liverpool.

☐ IF IT is acceptable and rational for a parent to step in front of a speeding bullet to save a child, which most people would agree on, then it is also acceptable and rational to wish for my/our extinction in order to save the planet. All one needs to do is give a plausible defence of what one is trying to save. If there are two alternatives – the complete extinction of all life on Earth or the extinction of all human life – which do we choose? According to Dr Barlow, who says that 'the planet is valuable only as long as someone is there to value it', one might as well make the decision with a pin. This I cannot accept. The second alternative leaves the planet intact and with a wealth of biological diversity, whereas the first leaves just another dead planet. There is a difference. The real question is, is this the alternative that faces us?
Giles Radford, Ashford, Kent.

QUESTION: Is it true that if you drink coffee soon after drinking orange juice, the coffee destroys the vitamin C in the orange juice?

☐ THE Coffee Science Information Centre (CoSIC), which reviews worldwide research on all aspects of coffee and health, can find no scientific evidence for this. Coffee actually contains trace amounts of some vitamins and minerals, especially the B vitamin (niacin), although the contribution from coffee to overall daily vitamin and mineral intake is generally very small. Professor Vincent Marks of the University of Surrey has confirmed that, as far as he is aware, the suggestion that coffee destroys vitamin C is 'simply one of those myths which can spread from no scientific grounding whatsoever'.
Sophia Papadopoulos, CoSIC, Oxford.

QUESTION: Why are women generally smaller than men?

☐ SINCE Neolithic times, men have generally been taller than women. However, the difference in height has been reducing over the years and, from research I carried out some years ago, it seems that the difference in height between the sexes is now less pronounced. Even so, it is not likely that women and men will eventually be the same average height. Much of the growth in our long bones occurs before puberty. Hormonal changes at puberty slow down the rate of growth, and because females reach puberty at an earlier age than males they have a shorter time in which their long bones can grow.
Graham Jones, Thatcham, Newbury, Berks.

☐ IT'S because God, like the Japanese, improved on his earlier model by making a more compact and sophisticated design.
Dinah Pollock, Huyton, Merseyside.

☐ DINAH Pollock is wrong about men being the earlier model. For a few million years, life was female, self-producing only. We only invented men because we were getting bored.
Mary-Rose Benton, Stourport on Severn, Worcs.

☐ WOMEN are smaller than men as a result of an evolutionary process known as sexual selection which may take one or both of two forms: intra- and inter-sexual selection. Intra-sexual selection, which normally consists of competition between males for females, leads to a larger body size and a lower threshold for aggression in male animals. Conversely, inter-sexual selection leads to 'sexy' traits in males (i.e. those characteristics which females find attractive). Current theory suggests that human males are larger as a result of inter-sexual selection, leading to the conclusion that in our evolutionary past females chose to breed with larger males (perhaps because larger males were perceived as superior hunters or were more successful in competition with other males). The question is very important since, if sexual selection is responsible for differences in characteristics between the sexes, then two interesting consequences may arise. First, since the vast majority of animal species where males are distinctly bigger than females are polygynous (one male to several females, with most males not breeding), it may be argued that we are also 'naturally' polygynous. Second, if the current behavioural differences between the sexes have a genetic component, then characteristics which feminists presently deplore in males (e.g. sexual jealousy and a lower threshold for physical aggression) may be a result of female choice in our evolutionary ancestry.

Dr Lance Workman, University of Glamorgan, Pontypridd.

QUESTION: Can the temperature of a vacuum be measured? If so, what is it the temperature of?

☐ YES, with a thermometer. Suspend it in a hollow sphere, pump out the air and heat the sphere until it is red hot. The thermometer soon approaches the temperature of the walls. Not in contact with any matter, it is measuring the temperature of radiation – mostly infra-red and some visible light. Alternatively, point your thermometer out into space, as has indeed been done. It reads −270°C, which is the temperature of the microwave background radiation from the glowing embers of the big bang.

Dr John Samson, Department of Physics, Loughborough University of Technology.

☐ WHAT Dr John Samson is measuring in his experiments is the temperature of the residual molecules, since an absolute vacuum is not achievable. Radiation has wavelength, frequency, intensity and direction but not temperature.

Edward Gulbenkian, Mitcham, Surrey.

☐ THE temperature of something is a measure of the average kinetic energy of its molecules. In the theoretical perfect vacuum,

there are no molecules and hence the idea of temperature is without meaning.
David Henderson, Nuthurst, West Sussex.

☐ RADIATION most certainly does have temperature because it has energy, measured by the vibrational frequency of its photons. Photons can be treated as particles in a manner akin to atoms and molecules. You measure the temperature of a vacuum cavity by taking the energy spectrum of the radiation flying about inside it. In fact, the temperature of outer space as measured by the 'background radiation' is taken as evidence for the Big Bang hypothesis of the origin of the universe. Since then the expansion of the universe has diluted the original high temperatures down to a background of about four degrees 'Absolute'.
Peter Rowland (MSc, PhD), Dulwich, London SE24.

QUESTION: Is counting sheep an effective cure for insomnia?

☐ NOT according to William Wordsworth. In his poem 'To Sleep', he states:

> A flock of sheep that leisurely pass by,
> One after one; . . .
> I have thought of them all by turns, and yet do lie
> Sleepless!

Mary Baldwin, Evington, Leicester.

QUESTION: What is the significance of the sign of the cross keys?

☐ THE cross keys, one of gold and one of silver, the insignia of the Papacy, symbolise the power of the keys conferred by Christ on the first Pope, St Peter. In Matthew (16:19) Christ says: 'And I will give unto you the keys of the kingdom of Heaven: and whatsoever thou shall bind upon Earth shall be bound in Heaven: and

whatsoever thou shall loose upon Earth shall be loosed in Heaven.'
In Britain the cross keys appear in various forms on the arms of
the Archbishop of York and of the bishops of Winchester, St Asaph,
Gloucester, Exeter and Peterborough. But most frequently they
are seen adorning public house signs.
*John Davies, Department of History, Liverpool Institute of Higher
Education.*

☐ I DISPUTE the suggestion that Cross Keys public houses are
named after the crossed keys of St Peter. Although never as common as on the Continent, in the middle ages crucifixes were
erected at crossroads in the UK. Where these were dedicated,
villages were sometimes named after them. Thus we have
Crosspatrick and Crossmichael in the Borders, Crossmaglen
(Magdalen) in Northern Ireland and several Cross Keys. I suspect
that these latter, and the pubs so called, derived from Cross Jesus,
or Cross Caius as it would have been written then (and pronounced as in Gonville and Caius College, Cambridge). Furthermore, all the Cross Keys pubs I recall are on crossroads.
David Beattie, Chester.

☐ THE cross keys are also found in a tarot card, the Hierophant.
They represent the keys to the conscious and unconscious minds:
the gold relating to the conscious and the sun, the silver to the
unconscious and the moon. The keys are seen to unlock the gates
of higher consciousness or knowledge, and the Hierophant himself
symbolises the gateway reached through ritual and tradition.
Madeline Lees, Diss, Norfolk.

QUESTION: Why an elephant symbol for US Republicans, and a donkey for the Democrats?

☐ THE elephant was used in 1874 by an American cartoonist,
Thomas Nast, to represent the ponderous weight of the Republi-
can vote. Nast continued to use this beast in relation to the Repub-
licans until it became indelibly identified with them. Nast also had
a hand in popularising the donkey as a symbol of the Democrats

in the 1880s but the first use of this animal dates back to the 1828 presidential campaign. Andrew Jackson's opponents had derided him as a jackass but it was an image Jackson used in his favour, as the 1828 election swept him to victory.
Derek Frankland, Lancaster.

QUESTION: Who awards the gold medals that appear on Continental beer bottles, and why do British breweries never appear to win any?

□ THE main Continental-based international award system for beers is the La Monde Selection, which is held every year. It is their medals which can often be seen on Continental beers. British brewers do win these awards – Charles Wells's Best Bitter, Bombardier, has won gold medals at La Monde for six years in succession, and these are featured on the latest countermounts, bottles and cans.
Tom Wells, Charles Wells Ltd, Bedford.

QUESTION: The *Collins English Dictionary* of 1979 features the word 'pornocracy', defined as a 'government or domination of government by whores'. What events, historical or otherwise, brought this word into being?

□ DURING the 9th and 10th centuries, with the break-up of the Carolingian empire and the resultant internecine wars, foreign invasion and the rise of local feudal lords, the Papacy became marginalised and lost its political authority and spiritual prestige. Between AD 914 and 963, the landed aristocracy under the leadership of a Roman senator Theophylact, his wife Theodora and their daughter Marozia came increasingly to dominate the Curia. Marozia, mistress of Pope Sergius III and mother of his son, the future Pope John XI, took control of Rome. In a move characteristic of her egregious family, the Crescentii who held power on

and off throughout the 10th century, she had her Pope son imprisoned until her other son, Alberic, took up the reins of power (AD 932). This period is known as the 'Pornocracy'. Whether Theodora and Marozia were whores in the true sense of the word is a moot point. One suspects, however, that to a male-dominated Church the very idea of women being in control of the Curia must be anathema and, by its very definition, an obscenity.
Colin Andrew, London NW1.

QUESTION: Why does Coventry have an elephant as part of its coat of arms?

☐ THE oldest Coventry seal dates back to the late 13th century when the crest had two sides: on one an elephant bearing a triple-towered castle standing before an oak tree; on the other, St Michael overcoming a dragon among oak trees. Although the elephant was not a familiar beast in medieval England, it was known by repute through the Bestiaries. These books of supposed natural history contained fanciful accounts of various beasts, birds and monsters, but their real object was to give religious and moral instruction. In these books, the elephant was depicted with a castle on its back and according to legend was unable to bend its knee and was thus considered a symbol of civic pride. It was also supposed that because of this disability the elephant slept leaning against a tree trunk. To capture an elephant, hunters would saw partly through a tree trunk so that the elephant fell to the ground. A legend of the elephant was thus connected with 'tree', which formed part of the name of Coventry i.e. Coffers Tree. The use of the elephant and castle on a shield as the coat of arms of Coventry is probably as old as the city's charter of incorporation (1345).
Sue Ling, Press and Publicity Officer, Coventry Council.

☐ ACCORDING to one medieval tradition, the elephant was regarded as the opponent of the dragon (who ate the young of the elephant). Coventry, in the Middle Ages, was regarded as the birthplace of St George and thus the saint and the elephant are associated by their battles against the scaly beast. A more plausible explanation is that, in the coat of arms, the elephant is seen carrying a castle which is a corrupted illustration of the Indian howdah, a symbol which has customarily been associated with the wool trade. As Coventry was a leading centre for the export of cloth and wool in the medieval period, the elephant and castle, representing security, strength and quality, was the ideal choice as a heraldic device for the city's armorial bearings.

Elaine M. Treharne, Publications Office, University of Warwick, Coventry.

☐ THE Coventry Morris Men who (with permission) wear the city coat of arms on their baldricks, are often asked this question when dancing in public. The answer we usually give, which has some plausibility, runs as follows: the Manor of Cheylesmore, which included most of what was then the city, was owned by the Black Prince, who married the daughter of the King of Spain (Castile). She became known as the 'Infanta de Castile' which, corrupted to 'Elephant and Castle', became the device on the coat of arms. Whether the young lady was overweight to earn this epithet, I don't know. We believe that the Elephant and Castle area in south central London was also owned by the Black Prince, which adds further weight to the theory. The city's current logo is of another famous medieval lady, Godiva, who rode naked through the town in defiance of her husband as a protest against his implementation of a hated poll tax.

Rev Dick Wolff, Earlsdon, Coventry.

QUESTION: What are the Incompleteness Theorems of Kurt Goedel? Is their relevance confined to mathematics?

☐ EARLIER this century, Kurt Goedel and other mathematicians proved various theorems which set limits on what can be calculated and what can be proved in mathematics. The first and best known of these was Goedel's Incompleteness Theorem, which states that any (sufficiently complicated) mathematical system contains statements which can neither be proved nor disproved. While the techniques used in proving the theorem have been of use in mathematical logic and computer science, the main impact of the theorem is philosophical. While the theorem sets important conceptual limits on what mathematicians can hope to do, it has remarkably little impact on what they actually do. Most of the results related to the incompleteness theorem show that there is no universal method for doing things such as showing that two mathematical objects are the same, or solving certain types of equation. However, no one would really expect the existence of any practical way of doing these things. The philosophical implications of the theorem are more interesting. By showing there is no set of basic assumptions from which all mathematical truth can be deduced, it seriously upset many philosophers. Like many scientific and mathematical discoveries, it attracted its fair share of strange interpretations. It has been claimed that the theorem demonstrates the impossibility (and the necessity) of God's existence. More recently, the limits it sets on mechanical reasoning have been used to claim that computers could never achieve our level of intelligence. As there is every reason to believe that we are also subject to these limits, the argument leaves a lot to be desired. The classic book *Goedel, Escher, Bach* by Douglas Hofstadter gives a sound and remarkably comprehensive account of why the theorem is true and what it implies.

Thomas Lumley, Exeter College, Oxford.

QUESTION: In Chapter 9 of *Three Men in a Boat* there is a reference to what was presumably a popular song of the time: 'He's got 'em on'. Is anything still known of this masterpiece?

☐ IT IS most likely the song also known as 'Arry' by E. V. Page (c. 1880). Like others of its kind it satirises the custom among young 'swells', as they were called, of assuming the manners and dress of their social and financial superiors doing the 'la-di-da'. In

Jerome's book, in the context in which the song is mentioned, the narrator describes the presence of 'provincial 'Arries and 'Arriets'. The implication is obvious if the words of the song are known. One verse and the chorus (note the last line) go:

> 'Arry's fond of two guinea suits,
> Just suits 'Arry.
> Curly hats and polishy boots;
> Crackpot, 'Arry.
> 'Arry's bags are loud and light,
> And thirteen bob they are,
> And 'Arry's ring looks well (at night)
> While doing the la-di-da.
> There you are then, 'Arry! I say 'Arry!
> By jove you are a don,
> Oh 'Arry! 'Arry!
> There you are then, 'Arry!
> Where are you going on Sunday 'Arry?
> Now you've got 'em on.

Ron Williams, Salisbury, Wilts.

QUESTION: A recent article on climate and weather in the Fortean Times mentions that Eskimos visited Scotland during the 'little ice age' of the mid-18th century. Is this true?

☐ IN ABERDEEN there are two kayaks in the Anthropological Museum of Marischal College. In an exhibition there a few years ago several accounts of Eskimo visits to Scotland were recounted. During the late 17th and early 18th century there were several records of strange men in canoes seen fishing off the Scottish coast. They were called 'Finmen' in the belief that they came from Finland. Around 1730 an Eskimo kayaker came ashore near Aberdeen but died soon after, and his is one of the canoes now in the museum. A century later an Eskimo named Enoolooapik was brought from Labrador to Aberdeen aboard the ship *Neptune*. He

stayed for about a year, becoming a popular figure around town and occasionally giving kayaking demonstrations on the River Dee.
Dr Warren L. Kovach, Pentraeth, Anglesey.

QUESTION: What are the economic reasons (in layman's terms) for not sending butter mountains, etc, to feed starving Somalians?

☐ IT IS vital to draw a clear distinction between food given for emergency relief and the greater part of food aid, perhaps three-quarters of the global total, which is not granted in response to a particular emergency. In the face of an emergency, there are no economic arguments, at least none I find convincing, against shipping EC surpluses to feed those who are starving (provided the surpluses are the appropriate type of food – powdered milk, beef and butter are of little use). The failures observed in practice are due to political and bureaucratic factors, not economics. Most food aid is given to governments who then sell the food; it is the economic criticisms of this practice that the questioner may be thinking of. While food aid can be deployed effectively, so that it benefits the poor and malnourished, the dumping (selling at below local market price) of EC surpluses does little if anything to help the recipients. African farmers, broadly speaking, are efficient. Given the appropriate incentives and opportunities, most African countries could be self-sufficient in food. But because of massive subsidies from the Common Agricultural Policy, EC surpluses can be sold on African markets at prices below the production costs of local farmers, thus driving down the local price and eroding incomes. This is one of many factors discouraging African farmers from growing food crops. There is no economic argument against food aid to the starving, but there are strong arguments against dumping subsidised EC food on local markets.
Dr Oliver Morrissey, Department of Economics, University of Nottingham.

QUESTION: I remember an occasion during the Lord
Mayor's Show in London when some animals got out of
control and a lion was gored to death by elephants on the
Embankment. At the time, around the late 1920s, I was a
young boy and I remember reading about it afterwards. I
have found no reference to the event since. Can readers
shed any light?

☐ I WAS a student at King's College, London, from 1927 to 1931
and the incident took place in either 1928 or 1929. As customary,
students gathered on the Embankment close to the rear entrance
of the college, with a life-sized model of a roaring lion, called
Reggie, painted red and mounted on a wooden platform. As each
part of the Lord Mayor's show passed they raised Reggie aloft and
cheered. When the elephants passed, they turned on the students.
Mounted police scattered and the students, with Reggie, dodged
across to the river side of the Embankment and hid from view.
After a while the elephant keepers got their animals under control
again and the procession resumed. I was one of the students already on the river side of the Embankment and saw it all. The
evening's London press made much of the affair. No one was hurt
to my knowledge, Reggie survived and the press suggestions that
the students were irresponsibly provocative were strongly denied
by the president of the students' union. I tell my own grandchildren of the affair and the questioner can safely tell the story to his.
N. E. Blake, Faversham, Kent.

QUESTION: What, according to orthodox Christian teaching, happens to the souls of the dead? There seem to be two
opposing views. One has it that the souls (after a possible
spell in Purgatory, some say) go pretty directly to Heaven,
the other that they remain with their bodies until the last
day, when Christ will come in judgment.

☐ ORTHODOX Christian teaching certainly seems to hold two ir-
reconcilable views. The Scriptures, however, are clear that man,

far from possessing an immortal soul, has 'no pre-eminence above
a beast ... all go unto one place; all are of the dust and all turn to
dust again' (Ecclesiastes 3:19). In truth, the whole notion of the
soul is generally misunderstood as being a sort of disembodied
spirit. As the earliest use of a word in the Hebrew Bible can often
throw light on its later use, it is instructive to look up the first
reference to a '*nefesh*', the Hebrew word that is frequently trans-
lated as 'soul'. 'And God said: "Let the waters bring forth abun-
dantly the moving creature that hath life [*nefesh*] and fowl that fly
above the earth in the open firmament of heaven".' (Genesis 1:
20). There is no ambiguity here; if the creature were to die, it
would no longer have 'life' or a 'soul'. The claim, therefore, that
the soul goes to Heaven (or Purgatory – a placename unknown in
Scripture) has no foundation in the Bible. God has, however,
promised that those who have heard the message of the Gospel
and understood the promises made to Eve, Abraham, Isaac, Jacob
and David (see Galatians 3:8) and thus are responsible, shall be
raised for judgment at the coming of Jesus, the Messiah: 'And at
that time shall Michael [Hebrew: 'Who is like God'] stand up, the
great prince which standeth for the children of thy people ... And
many of them that sleep in the dust of the earth shall awake, some
to everlasting life and some to shame and everlasting contempt'
(Daniel 12:1,2). The 'everlasting life' promised to those who are
counted worthy is described in the Book of Revelation: 'They shall
be priests of God and of Christ and shall reign with him a thousand
years' (20:6). This millennium will culminate in all things being
subdued unto God and 'then shall the Son also himself be subject
unto him that put all things under him, that God may be all in all'
(1 Corinthians 15:28).
K. Ritmeyer, Skelton, York.

☐ MR RITMEYER'S Biblical quotations are misleading, in that they
are used to support a very human argument, and ignore the spiritual. In Acts 7, the martyr Stephen, a man 'full of the holy spirit
and wisdom' says in his dying moment: 'Lord Jesus, receive my
spirit.' In his parable of the rich man and Lazarus, the Lord

Himself speaks of afterlife (Luke 16). My advice to the questioner is to accept the definition that 'soul' is the amalgam of a physical body and an intelligent life-force ('spirit'). The Bible makes it absolutely clear that when the physical frame expires, the 'spirit' goes into the custody of the Lord of Creation, Jesus Christ.
James Fasey, Toton, Nottingham.

QUESTION: Can anyone provide information about the fire at Alexandria in Egypt which destroyed the great library there among other things? When was it, do we know what was lost, and what were the consequences?

☐ THE library was the first research institute in world history. Alexander the Great's successors as rulers of Egypt, the Ptolemy I and II, developed it in the 3rd century BC. It contained the greatest collection of handwritten papyrus scrolls in the ancient world, perhaps numbering over 700,000 and a foundation for the systematic study of the arts and sciences was established. Even the Old Testament came down to us from mainly Greek translations made in the library. The library was deliberately burnt down by a mob *c.* AD 420 as classical civilisation disintegrated and the Dark Ages closed in. All that survived was a tiny fraction of its work and a cellar of the Serapaeum, the library annexe. The loss was incalculable but we do know, for example, that the work of Eratosthenes, a library director who had accurately calculated the size of the earth, and Aristarchus of Samos, who had postulated a heliocentric universe, the axis-rotation of the earth and its revolution around the sun, had to be rediscovered by Columbus and Copernicus 1,000 years later. Of the 123 plays of Sophocles only seven survived (one of which was *Oedipus Rex*). Much the same happened to the work of Aeschylus and Euripides.
Tony Martin, London SE15.

QUESTION: How do they decide who deserves to be

included in the credit titles shown at the end of a film or televison play?

☐ CREDIT where it's due.
Answer by Graham Guest, writer's refreshments by Brygida Guest, letter posted by Jane Guest, London SE19.

QUESTION: Can anyone name the piece of music used in the Scottish Widows advertisement in which a young woman, dressed in black, walks out of the building towards the rain?

☐ IT WAS specially composed for the commercial by Tony and Gaynor Sadler of Logorhythms.
Sarah E. Wilson, Scottish Widows, Edinburgh.

QUESTION: At what point in the last 1,000 years was our economy at its strongest?

☐ IN TERMS of Britain's share of world manufacturing output and exports, a strong currency and relative price stability: the 19th century. In terms of rapid growth of total output sustained over several decades, combined with reasonably full utilisation of labour and capital, and some movement towards a fairer redistribution of income and wealth: the post-war golden age of 1945–73. In terms of overall productive potential, in spite of the last 13 wasted years: today. Unfortunately, having a large productive potential is no guarantee that the potential will be used wisely or fairly, or even used at all, as three million unemployed workers and bankrupt entrepreneurs will testify.
Mark Harrison, Department of Economics, University of Warwick.

☐ THE economy in 1124 was facing a crisis similar to that of today, with high inflation and low confidence caused by 12th-century currency speculators. Henry I found a solution which was

both fast-acting and permanent. The Anglo-Saxon Chronicle of 1124 explains: 'When they came thither they were taken one by one and each deprived of the right hand and testicles below. All this was done in the 12 days between Christmas and Epiphany and was entirely justified because they had ruined the whole country by the magnitude of their fraud which they paid for to the full.' Similar sanctions applied to those responsible for economic policy today would no doubt produce a similar economic miracle.
Sean Kelly, Owen McLaughlin, Cambridge.

QUESTION: Is it better to give than to receive?

☐ YES. This morning I *received* a poll tax demand, a caustic letter from my bank, the local rag and a leaflet telling me of the joys of 'window replacement'. I *gave* all these to the dustman and felt absolutely wonderful.
Julian Smith, Kingston-upon-Thames, Surrey.

☐ THIS was discussed by E. M. Forster in *A Passage to India*, where he wrote (on page 154 of the Penguin edition): 'Like most Orientals, Aziz overrated hospitality, mistaking it for intimacy, and not seeing that it is tainted with the sense of possession. It was only when Mrs Moore or Fielding was near to him that he saw further, and knew that it is more blessed to receive than to give.'
Richard Lewis, Arlington, E Sussex.

☐ I REFER to Michel Eyquem de Montaigne in *Essays*, Book 2, Ch. 8: 'He who confers a benefit performs a fine and honourable action, but the act of receiving one is merely useful. Now the useful is much less lovable than the beautiful. A beautiful action is stable and permanent; it furnishes a permanent gratification to its performer. A useful action, on the other hand, easily disappears and is lost; and the memory of it is neither so fresh nor so pleasing. These things are dearest to us that have cost us most; and it is harder to give than to receive.'
Brian Taylor, Bonsall, Derbyshire.

☐ IN ALL the many answers given so far, nobody seems to have tracked down who first said it, in order to give the saying some context. It is, in fact, probably the best-attested saying of Jesus of Nazareth, though it occurs in none of the four Gospels. It does, however, appear in Luke's second volume, the Acts of the Apostles (20:35) where Paul, a contemporary of Jesus, makes the saying his final word at his last meeting with the Ephesian elders. Luke was there to jot it down. In the familiar translation, the passage runs: 'Remember the words of the Lord Jesus, how he said "It is more blessed to give than to receive".' Jesus himself undoubtedly practised what he preached – even to the extent of giving his life into the hands of his enemies and thereby making his death his supreme appeal to them and all humans to become their true, giving selves. As to the question: 'Is it better to give than to receive?' – the answer is, 'Try it!' It is the only way to find out.
Rev. Walter Gill, Hartlepool, Cleveland.

QUESTION: On the tramline north of Manchester is a station named Besses o' th' Barn. Who were the Besses?

☐ THOMAS Holt's *Pilkington Park* suggests two possible origins. The first is that Dick Turpin stabled his horse, Bess, at a barn in the locality. The other, which he favours, is that the name derives from an inn owned by a woman called Bess, which was next to a barn (Bess's at the barn). He notes that the name is not old, and the inn name can only be traced back to 1715, unlike most place-names in the area.
Paul Hindle, Department of Geography, University of Salford.

☐ IN 1859, Bessie Gagg lived with her husband John on a canal boat plying the Manchester, Bolton & Bury Canal. While moored at Bury they had a violent argument one Christmas – he assaulted her and she fell into the freezing water. She made off for Manchester on foot and took overnight refuge in a barn. Because of the freezing temperature she died there from hypothermia. The

barn was near to where the station is today, and it became known as Besse's Barn. The above facts are from newspaper reports of the inquest. How Besse's Barn became Besses o' th' Barn I do not know.
Kenneth Goodwin, Ramsbottom, Bury.

☐ EXTRACTS from the weekly newspaper *Manchester Magazine* in 1748 and 1749 make reference to Besses o' th' Barn, invalidating Kenneth Goodwin's theory. And the name was established well before Dick Turpin's Black Bess had learned to walk. There was, in fact, an old inn known as 'Besses o' th' Barn Inn' which stood on land now occupied by the Whitefield ambulance station. Close to the inn was a barn which was later replaced with stables. The 17th-century licensing records are incomplete but they do show that, for most of that period, there were between two and six ale-house keepers in the area. Only two of those listed were named Elizabeth (shortened to 'Bess' in those days). And of the two, Elizabeth Bamford is registered as keeping an inn or ale-house between 1674 and 1699, which is also about the time the name Besses o' th' Barn started to appear. Both the inn and the barn were famous landmarks.
Glenn Worth, Whitefield, Manchester.

QUESTION: A few years ago several articles appeared in the press relating to the alleged invention of a machine which could negate the force of gravity without any external fuel source. The inventor, Dr Sandy Kidd, claimed that his machine was operated by a complex configuration of gyroscopes which would revolutionise travel and make all present forms of transport redundant. However, Dr Kidd was refused development funding and emigrated to the United States to continue his work. Does anyone have further information about this device?

☐ DURING the past six months I have carried out my own research into this and similar devices and have obtained a copy of Mr Kidd's international patent application (in fact, there are two) and a copy of his book about his recent experiences with the commercial and academic worlds. The title of the book is *Beyond 2000: The Laws of Physics Revolutionised* and, while I no longer have a copy, I remember that Mr Kidd spent a somewhat unfruitful time at Dundee University researching his ideas before receiving interest from an Australian company, BNW. As far as I know, BNW's tests on Mr Kidd's machine proved inconclusive, and he is now back in Scotland continuing his research. It should be stressed that an external source of energy *is* required in order to set such a machine in motion. Conservation of energy, which must be regarded as *the* fundamental law of physics, really cannot be broken. The motive force claimed to be produced by a device such as Mr Kidd's is via the angular momentum to linear momentum conversion. As far as the scientific establishment is concerned, the main sticking point with such a device is the violation of Newton's Third Law, which states that for every force acting on a body there has to be an equal and opposite force acting on another body. This latter point has made it difficult, if not impossible, for patent applications to achieve granted status, giving rights of exploitation, as opposed to published status, which merely puts the invention into the public domain for scrutiny.

Ray Simpkin, Luton, Beds.

☐ AS PRINTED, the query contained four errors. Sandy Kidd is not a 'Dr'. Funding was generous, considering the nature of the project. Mr Kidd did not emigrate: he spent some time in Australia, not the United States. Thus the query demonstrates the reshaping of information in people's memories with lapse of time. With no news of the progress of the promising idea, the questioner eventually may have made an erroneous recall of hearsay items, which may already have been distorted. The interesting aspect is that the errors twisted the facts in the direction of accepted ideas: it was assumed that, as usual, support was not forthcoming in this country. Recalling that he had gone abroad, it was natural to assume that he had emigrated. The usual goal of emigrés of this

class is the US. The grant of a patent does not imply that the device will fulfil the stated aims. In the US and elsewhere some anti-gravity mechanisms have been granted patents – presumably the mechanisms were novel and could be constructed as described. One such is USA No. 2,886,976 (1959). The US is the place for curious inventions, for instance No. 1,087,186 (1914). This device consists of two interwound helical springs. Its stated purpose is to 'illustrate evidences of the Supreme Being'.
Mr R. A. Wiersma, Woking, Surrey.

QUESTION: Why is the Blackwall Tunnel under the Thames bent?

☐ THE first Blackwall Tunnel was built in the 1890s. It was constructed by driving from portals at the north and south ends, and also from two shafts close to the river. These four points are not in a straight line, so as the builders drove each section straight, there are sharp bends at the bottom of the shafts. This did not matter at the time, as only horse-drawn traffic and the occasional steam traction engines were on the roads; thus tight corners were not a constraint on traffic speeds. The second, east, tunnel was built in the late 1950s with curves to suit modern traffic conditions.
P. L. Sulley, C Eng, Yalding, Kent.

☐ A SURVEYOR once told me that bends were built into the Rotherhithe tunnel to prevent horses from bolting towards the light at the end of the tunnel.
Peter Lowthian, Marlow, Bucks.

QUESTION: How do creatures in the soil (rabbits, moles, worms, ants, etc) survive widespread flooding?

☐ THE mole's flexible nose allows it to sip the air trapped in the roof of its tunnel. When the flooding is widespread the mole's strong swimming powers come into play – for a creature which can 'swim' through peaty or sandy soil, swimming in water has no problems. Among the detritus at the limits of a flood you will see the new molehills where the animals have once more gone underground.

Roger Dobson, Ivegill, Carlisle.

QUESTION: Do we export Cheddar cheese to France? I prefer English Cheddar to any French cheese I have tasted, and I've never seen it on sale there. If not, do the French know what they are missing?

☐ I HAVE never seen Cheddar in the supermarkets or markets but it is on sale in the Paris branch of Marks & Spencer, albeit at an extortionate price. The French produce several cheeses similar in taste and texture to Cheddar, notably Raclette, Cantal and Conté, which melt quite nicely for cheese on toast. But the French usually cook with a rubbery French version of Gruyère, which is definitely not as nice as Cheddar. As to whether they know what they are missing, those French friends of mine who have eaten Cheddar at my house thought it rather nice. However, the French are very nationalistic about cheese and I doubt if any of them would admit that Cheddar is as good as anything they produce.

Louise Bolotin, St-Denis, France.

☐ MAGNIFICENT whole farmhouse Cheddars, cheesecloth-wrapped and weighing 1.75 kilos (4lb) can be found seasonally at the admirable Carmès cheese shop in rue de Levis, Paris 17. The price is 108 francs a kilo. Carmès also sells Stilton, Cheddar wrapped in red plastic (75f a kilo) and an orange confection called Chester (70f). I seem to be the chief and perhaps sole client for the farmhouse Cheddar, which is fine as there isn't enough for everyone.

Stephen Jessel, Paris.

QUESTION: In attempting to buy sou'westers for my two young children, I have been told repeatedly that such headwear is no longer available. Can this be true?

☐ THEY are on sale at Fleetwood Trawlers Supply Co., 240 Dock Street, Fleetwood, Lancs FY7 6NX (tel: 0253 873476).
Peter Woodworth, Poulton-le-Fylde, Lancs..

☐ I BOUGHT one yesterday from J. Barbour & Sons, Simonside, South Shields, Tyne & Wear NE34 9PD (tel: 091 455 4444).
Vincent Mulligan, Todmorden, West Yorks.

☐ I HAVE two – yellow for every day and black for formal occasions. This excellent and most useful item of headgear can be obtained from Greenbergs of Park Lane, Liverpool, in all sizes (tel: 051-709 7197).
Professor Robert Moore, Holywell, Clwyd.

QUESTION: Where can I buy rennet in tablet form? Shop assistants haven't even heard of junket (made with rennet and milk)! Help, please.

☐ WHY tablets? The liquid form works better. My bottle is labelled 'Essence of Rennet, manufactured by Ernest Jackson, Est 1817'. The Customer Services Department at Ernest Jackson and Co. Ltd, Crediton, Devon EX17 3AP, will provide 'a free junket recipe book containing 12 delicious junket dishes by Geraldine Holt'. Fifty years ago I had an equally delicious children's book called *Junket is Nice*, which featured a little girl sitting eating junket while a stream of passing characters speculated on what she might be thinking about. Eventually someone thought to ask her, to which she replied: 'Junket is nice!' If anyone knows where I can get a copy of the book, my grandchildren would appreciate it.
Elizabeth Newson, Nottingham.

☐ YOU don't need rennet to make junket. Epsom salts – medicinal, not garden salts – will do the job for you. To one quart of fresh milk, heated to blood temperature, add one small teaspoon of Epsom salts. This recipe was given to me by an old lady some years ago. I have never had occasion to try it but she always used it.
Mrs R. O. Uden, Shotley Gate, Ipswich.

QUESTION: What is sociology?

☐ OUR lecturer has offered us the following definitions: (i) The science of society, i.e. a discipline which tries systematically and objectively to examine and explain social behaviour within and between groups – for example, within a family or between the institution of the family and the political system; (ii) history with brains. Interestingly, our history lecturer has also offered us a definition of sociology as 'history with the facts taken out'.
Paul Turner, Wyke, West Yorks.

☐ SOME years ago I came across this definition of social work, which was coined by a working party of the British Association of Social Workers: 'Social work is the purposeful and ethical application of personal skills in interpersonal relationships directed towards enhancing the personal and social functioning of an individual, family, group or neighbourhood, which necessarily involves using evidence obtained from practice to help create a social environment conducive to the well-being of all.' I decided to study art instead.
Deborah Walsh, Stonyford, Stockport.

☐ ALTHOUGH social thought is as old as civilisation, as a specialised subject sociology is fairly recent in origin. It remained a vague current within philosophy until the turn of the century, when Emile Durkheim succeeded in having the first university chair created specifically in sociology; the study of sociological fact.

Without doubt, early sociologists saw themselves as having an active role in the pursuit of societal health, echoing Marx's view: 'The philosophers have only interpreted the world; the point is to change it.'
Rita Roberts, Sutton, Merseyside.

QUESTION: Hasn't this question about déjà vu been in Notes & Queries before?

☐ PLEASE refer to my previous answer.
Stephan Harrison, Tottenham, London N17.

QUESTION: What happened to Moral Rearmament?

☐ MORAL Rearmament, born in 1938 out of the Oxford Group, stresses the links between personal choices, faith and social and political conditions. It specialises in bringing people together across ethnic, political, class and religious divides. Some commentators have credited MRA with a role in the reconciliation between France and Germany after the Second World War and in the peaceful transition to independence of several countries. MRA faded from the headlines in the mid-1960s after the deaths of its two charismatic leaders, Frank Buchman and Peter Howard, and a split with its American wing, which became known as Up With People. Today, MRA works more quietly and is more decentralised. It is re-established in the United States and active in at least 48 countries. Major recent events included a seminar in Cambodia on reconciliation, and a conference on race in the United States. In Britain, MRA has focused on industrial and community relations, is based at 12 Palace Street, London SW1, and publishes an international magazine, *For a Change*.
Mary Lean, Moral Rearmament.

QUESTION: I have just been told that the people of Iceland enjoy the highest standard of living in the world. Can anyone confirm this?

☐ IN ICELAND they have a truly classless society where people build their dream homes on their own land. Reykjavik is a completely smokeless city where homes are heated by water from natural hot springs and electricity is produced by vast hydro-electric schemes – one of the cheapest ways of utilising natural resources to create power. I understand that unemployment is virtually unknown, the economy is dependent on the fishing industry, and all education is free. Iceland is also one of the most literate countries in the world – Reykjavik boasts more bookshops per head of population than any other city.
Ruth Booth, London SE4.

QUESTION: What are the destinations in the song 'Route 66' by Them, and what exactly does Van Morrison sing after 'Flagstaff, Arizona, don't forget Winona'.

☐ THE words of the song, written by Bob Troup and published in 1946, tell it all:
>   It winds from Chicago to LA,
>   More than two thousand miles all the way.
>   Get your kicks on Route 66!
>   Now you go thro' Saint Looey (sic) and Joplin, Missouri
>   And Oklahoma City is mighty pretty
>   You'll see Amarillo; Gallup, New Mexico; Flagstaff,
>   Arizona;
>   Don't forget Winona, Kingman, Barstow, San
>   Bernardino ...

'Have your fun on the A41' somehow does not have the same ring to it:
>   It winds from London to Birkenhead,
>   Just over two hundred miles like I said.

    Have some fun on the A41
    Now you bypass Chester, Warwick and Bicester,
    Birmingham City is jolly pretty
    You'll see Hemel Hempstead, Waddesdon, Berkhamsted
       too.
    Tring, Banbury, don't forget Aylesbury,
    Bicester, Watford and Wolverhampton . . .
Ah well, back to the day job.
Clive Ablett, Berkhamsted, Herts.

QUESTION: Why is there a United States naval base at Guantanamo Bay in Cuba?

☐ IN 1898, while Cuba was still a Spanish colony, the United States defeated Spain in a war that happened in the midst of a revolutionary struggle for Cuban independence. After the war, a convention was set up to frame a constitution for Cuba. The US attached a proviso to the constitution that deprived Cuba of real independence: this became known as the Platt Amendment (reproduced in full in the book *From Columbus to Castro – History of the Caribbean 1492–1969* by Dr Eric Williams, former Prime Minister of Trinidad). This clause basically made Cuba a colony of the United States and required that country to maintain a military presence on the island. The convention initially refused to accept the Platt Amendment but the United States made it clear that they would not withdraw from Cuba until the Platt Amendment was accepted, and so the convention backed down. In 1903 the United States 'leased' bases at Guantanamo Bay and Bahia Honda, agreeing to pay an annual lease of $2,000 which was to run for 99 years; in 1912 they surrendered Bahia Honda in return for a larger base at Guantanamo Bay for a rate of $5,000 annually. Incidentally, the Platt Amendment governed American relations with Cuba until the advent of Fidel Castro.
Mrs V. P. Connell-Hall, Peckham, London SE15.

☐ MRS Connell-Hall is correct to say that the US base at Guantanamo in Cuba traces its origins to the Spanish American War of 1898. This occurred when the US – for reasons which are hotly debated – chose to intervene in the Cuban war of national liberation against Spain. As a condition for subsequent withdrawal, it required 'independent' Cuba to accept the Platt Amendment, which justified subsequent US interventions in order to protect 'life, property and individual liberty' (sic). However, she is wrong to say that the Amendment remained in force until the revolution of 1959, for it was abrogated in 1934 by F. D. Roosevelt, whose 'Good Neighbor Policy' involved a renunciation of direct intervention in Latin American countries – not least because, in Cuba and elsewhere, such interventions had proved costly and counter-productive (see Bryce Wood, *The Making of the Good Neighbor Policy*). Conversely, the post-1934 Cuban regime was generally congenial to US strategic and economic interests. Castro's revolution changed all that, and his regime has had to suffer some less-than-good neighbourly policies. However, it did not have to abrogate the Platt Amendment, which was long dead, nor did it challenge the US presence at Guantanamo.
Alan Knight, Professor of Latin American History, Oxford University.

QUESTION: Does anyone use any of the hereditary titles created by Oliver Cromwell?

☐ YES. Look up Carbery, Baron 1715 in Debrett's *Peerage and Baronetage* in your local library and, if you read long enough, you will find my family and myself.
John E. D'Arcy-Evans, Staines, Middx.

QUESTION: I am off to the pub. It starts to rain. Will I be less wet when I arrive if I run there?

☐ IT DEPENDS. A professor from Harvard University, writing

in the *Mathematical Gazette* (October 1976) concluded that, to minimise the rain falling on the person over a set distance, the solution is 'to keep pace with the wind if it is from behind; otherwise run for it!' Or, on a damp journey to the pub, the questioner might like to remember: When caught in the rain without mac, Move as fast as the wind at your back. But if the wind's in your face The optimal pace Is as fast as your legs can make track.
D. R. Brown, Grantham, Lincs.

QUESTION: Can anyone suggest a use for a plastic squashed tomato?

☐ Place on the verge of a country lane as a warning to foolhardy hedgehogs.
David Jepson, Manchester.

☐ GIVE it tennis lessons then enter it for Wimbledon as the latest British hopeful: unseeded and out of shape.
Florence Huntley, Barnet, Herts.

☐ AT THE Hendon Music Centre Concert, Band 1 trumpets were asked to bring the squashed tomatoes for use as mutes, which they did. They were a very quiet success.
Norman Bar, Finchley, London N12.

QUESTION: Could anyone supply me with a job description for the Warden of the Cinque Ports in case the post becomes available?

☐ NO ONE can really give a job description of the post of Lord Warden of the Cinque Ports (the proper title) for it has long been a purely honorary one. Originally the Cinque Ports were responsible for the herring industry and for local naval defence, in return enjoying financial and other privileges. Today the Lord Warden's

only perquisite is the right of residence at Walmer Castle. The present Lord Warden is the Queen Mother, so the questioner might do better to look elsewhere for a rewarding post.
O. Killick, Dover.

QUESTION: Are there, or have there ever been, any famous Belgians?

☐ BELGIUM, a country not much bigger than East Anglia, has existed for about a century and a half. In this time it has produced the likes of: René Magritte (you just may have caught him on telly of late); Georges Simenon (wrote thrillers); Paul Delvaux (art again); Toots Thielemans (some jazzman, I think); Jacques Brel (sang songs); Adolphe Sax (inventor of the saxophone); Hergé (creator of an obscure comic hero called Tintin); César Franck; and of course Zénobe Gramme (without whom we could never weigh things in zenobes). Perhaps the questioner would care to name 10 world-famous post-1830 East Anglians.
Harry Campbell, Edinburgh.

☐ MY two favourite Belgians are Django Reinhardt, the superb and nimble-fingered gypsy guitarist, and Gerhardus Mercator who, at a time when everyone had finally settled on the idea that the world was round, made it flat again with his projection in map form.
Steve Becker, Leeds.

☐ CARAUSIUS, Emperor of Britain, AD 287–293.
Edwin Chapman, Reading, Berks.

☐ SO FAR no one has mentioned the greatest Belgian punk singer to have a UK Top 20 hit: Plastic Bertrand.
Dominic Rice, Sheffield.

☐ NO SELF-respecting train-spotter of 30–40 years ago would

want to leave out Walschearts (of steam valve gear fame) and who in the same group would forget the Belpaire boiler?
Robert Bracegirdle, Leicester.

QUESTION: Jean-Luc Godard dedicated his film, *Toutes les Histoires*, to Mary Meerson. Who is or was she?

☐ SHE was the partner of the irascible Henri Langois, founder of the Cinémathèque Française. An ample lady of unperturbable benevolence, she was the mother hen to the young roosters (among them Godard, Truffaut and Chabrol) who sat with her night after night in the front row absorbing American film culture. Since she could not see a foot beyond her nose, and the boys could not understand English, this gave rise to a fruitful tolerance for any shadows or garbled messages which passed across the screen and in turn made possible one of the most influential individualistic movements in film history (the nouvelle vague).
Peadar O'Leannain, London N19.

QUESTION: Why is a mirror image not upside down as well as being the wrong way round?

☐ THE short answer is that a mirror image is not the wrong way round (in the sense of a left/right reversal). Try this experiment: instead of designating your hands 'left' and 'right', place a glove on (say) the right hand and call them 'gloved' and 'ungloved'. Now stand in front of a mirror so that you are facing north. Your (right) gloved hand points east. So does the mirror image's gloved hand. Your (left) ungloved hand points west. So does that in the mirror. Your feet point down and your head up – so do those in your reflection. What has changed? You face north – your mirror image faces south. This is the only reversal.
R. Thomson, Brighton.

☐ CONSIDER looking at a book in a mirror. The key is that one has

to turn it round to face the mirror. If you turn it around its vertical axis, right and left are reversed, so you get 'mirror' writing. If you turn it around its horizontal axis you do not get mirror writing: it is upside down, and not right–left reversed in the mirror. In every case, you see what you have done to make the book face the mirror. The same holds for yourself. Usually you turn around vertically to face a mirror – but you can stand on your head, then you are upside down and not right-left reversed. The history of this ancient puzzle dating back to Plato, and its solution, are discussed in *Odd Perceptions* by R. L. Gregory (Routledge, 1986) and in the *Oxford Companion to the Mind* (OUP).
Professor Richard Gregory, CBE, FRS, Department of Psychology, University of Bristol.

☐ I TRIED various contortions with books in front of mirrors trying to fathom Professor Gregory's reply. All I got when I turned the book on its horizontal axis was mirror writing which was also upside down. Maybe I don't know my Plato from my Aristotle but I think the Prof is pulling our legs. It all depends on how you define 'wrong way round'. A mirror simply reflects every point straight back. There is no left–right inversion and also quite consistently no top–bottom inversion either. Our feet remain on the floor, our heads remain in the clouds, our left hands remain on the left and our right hands remain on the right. Inversion only occurs if we imagine ourselves to be our mirror images ... maybe that's where Prof Gregory's speciality – psychology – comes in.
Brian Homer, Gwynedd.

☐ PROFESSOR Gregory is certainly not 'pulling our legs', as Mr Homer suggests. Quite the reverse(!). Mr Homer claims that he saw mirror writing which was also upside down, which would be a refutation of the original question. Writing seen in a single mirror can be either upside down or the wrong way round but it cannot be both. Write the word 'bow' on a piece of paper. Turn it around a vertical axis to face a mirror. In the mirror it looks like 'wod', which is rightleft reversed. If the paper is instead turned around a

horizontal axis to face the mirror, the word looks like 'pom', which is upside down but not right–left reversed. The word Mr Homer would claim to see is 'moq'. It would not be possible to observe this with only one mirror. The rest of Mr Homer's answer is sensible and is not inconsistent with Prof Gregory's perfectly reasonable answer. This question is a speciality of the professor's, as can be judged from his contributions to *New Scientist* a few years ago. Nevertheless, the really intriguing question is psychological: why do we think of people or objects seen in mirrors as being the 'wrong way round' and why do we find it disturbing to see them? It is contrary to our perception of the 'real' world, where people greet each other by shaking their right hands, and the hands of a clock go round in a clockwise direction. It is as disturbing as the recent clever TV ads for Tennents Pilsner, where the tape is run backwards but still almost makes sense in 'real' time.
Dr Roger Owens, Wedmore, Somerset.

QUESTION: Is there an easy way to make money?

☐ YES! For further details send £1,000 to Peter Andrews, Finance Department, Vencourt House, London W6.
P. Andrews, London W6.

☐ WHILE I would not endorse such activity, my own antics as a child come to mind. I would sometimes accompany my father to the supermarket, wearing a big coat. While his gaze and that of anybody else was elsewhere I would slip a block of pre-packed cheese into my pocket. The following day I would return it, saying it was mouldy, and gain a refund. When I was a little older, I got a paper round. The man who ran the shop would go into the back to fetch the newspapers. During this time I would slip a few packets of cigarettes and some men's magazines into my holdall, which I later sold at school to the joy and titillation of the fifth formers.
O. Hemingway, Prestwich, Manchester.

☐ THE questioner should try getting others to do work in a project for which he gets the payment. One option would be to start a newspaper column which involved some readers sending in questions that other readers then answered.
Neil Nixon, Maidstone, Kent.

☐ A CHARACTER in *Good as Gold*, Joseph Heller's satire on Washington politics, came to own a string of supermarkets. When asked his secret for the Midas touch, he maintained that it was very simple: find a loophole in the law.
Paul Becke, Edinburgh.

QUESTION: What is the safest action for a driver to take when the car or lorry behind you is totally filling your rear-view and side-view mirrors and you are driving as fast as the road conditions permit?

☐ TURN your headlights on and off a couple of times. The person behind will see the rear lights come on, assume that they are the brake lights and immediately ease off the accelerator. You can then drive on without losing speed, opening up the gap you need to give you use of your mirrors again.
Clare Tickell, London W12.

☐ UNTIL recently I would have said to pull into a lay-by and let him go past, but this does not always have the desired effect, as I found out. I had already tried all the usual things – accelerating away from him, slowing down in the hope that he would overtake, waving my hands about and flashing my fog lights on and off. The only effect that any of these seemed to have was to get him irritated: he came so close that I thought he was going to ram me, and started shaking his fist, flashing his lights and blowing his horn. I eventually pulled into a lay-by, but he pulled in behind me, jumped out of his cab and started hurling abuse at me through the window of my car. I reported him to the police and phoned his employer. The employer rang back leaving an apologetic message

on my answering machine, but the police said that there was nothing that they could do as I had not had an accident nor been physically attacked. The only solution I could offer is to move to Germany – I gather 'harassing people by driving too close' has recently been made a specific offence under German motoring law. Perhaps we should start a campaign to persuade the British government to follow suit.
Angelika Voss, Manningtree, Essex.

QUESTION: So what?

☐ JUST so.
Tony Stevens, Telford, Shropshire.

☐ SO THERE.
Graeme S. Smith, Maidenhead, Berks and Julie Farrington, Bedford.

☐ SO LUTION.
Andrew J. Penman, London NW1.

☐ SO IN love ...
'Cole Porter', London.

☐ BE IT; far so good; forth; to speak; so much for a silly question.
Michael J. Smith, Swaffham, Norfolk.

☐ THE question is a logical contradiction: 'So what?' challenges the question-and-answer format as being relevant to discussion while, being in the form of a question, explicitly accepting it. The questioner has a point, though. If we are seeking the truth then everything in thought is a mere approximation, and not the real thing by definition.
Rick Carless, Nottingham.

☐ 'So WHAT' is the title of one of Miles Davis's finest compositions, an anodyne version of which recently became the first jazz record to reach the charts in the UK for about 30 years when recorded by Ronny Jordan.
Keith Leedham, Harrow on the Hill, Middx.

☐ IF NOTHING really mattered, the questioner would not have asked; the question negates itself. Pseudo-sceptics should consider the unconscious dialectic of Jean de la Fontaine's dictum: 'Nothing is useless to the man of sense.'
Peter Mahoney, London SE22.

☐ IN HIS wonderful unfinished autobiography, *The Strings are False* (Faber), Louis MacNeice's opening sentence is made up of this question. He goes on to reply: 'This modern equivalent of Pilate's "What is truth?" comes often now to our lips and only too patly, we too being much of the time cynical and with as good reason as any old procurator, tired, bored with the details of Roman bureaucracy, and the graft of Greek officials, a vista of desert studded to the horizon with pyramids of privilege apart from which there are only nomads who have little in their packs, next to nothing in their eyes.'
F. R. Powell, London EC1.

QUESTION: In Shakespeare's sonnet no. 57, line 6 states: 'Whilst I, my sovereign, watch the clock for you.' What did an Elizabethan clock look like?

☐ MANY 16th-century clocks retained the medieval weight-driven wheel mechanism. This was suspended on a stout 'post-frame', and could be made large for church and palace, or small for domestic use. It was produced as little as six inches high, though with several feet of weighted rope/chain dangling beneath. The windable coil of tensile steel we call a spring was invented *c.* 1500: clock-works powered this newer way could be fixed between front and back plates of metal (the 'plate-frame' clock), and were portable. Most clocks were rectangular boxes of engraved brass or other, decorated, metals; they had a dial-face with one pointer, indicating only the hour: rarely, there were separate dials with a pointer for minutes. No glass. A half-dome-shaped metal bell struck at the hour (and sometimes halves and quarters) surmounts many models. Optional extras include dials for position of the moon and other astral bodies, chimes, processions of figures circulating at hours etc, and an alarm (very common). Plate-frames with springs allowed fantastic inventions – e.g. a blackamoor pointing with sword-tip at the time marked on the Equator of a globe. The same mechanism, compressed, became a 'watch' – around three inches in diameter, two deep, owned by the rich and often carried around for them by a servant or favourite. Shakespeare was familiar with such luxury toys, and the sonnet seems to be making a joke about them.

Ann MacDonald, Plymouth.

QUESTION: Do the pictures on which Mussorgsky's 'Pictures at an Exhibition' was based still exist and would they be strong enough physically (and intellectually?) to travel to the UK?

☐ IT WAS thought for many years that all the pictures had been lost, but this is not quite true. A 1939 issue of *The Musical Quarterly* contained an article by Alfred Frankenstein which located a number of them, and from which this information is drawn: The painter, Victor Hartmann (1834–1873), was a friend of Mussorgsky and the other composers of 'The Five' in St Petersburg. Like them he was trying to develop a truly nationalistic style – in his profession of architect and designer. In his case this largely consisted of adorning his buildings with coloured tiles, carvings and other examples of Russian peasant handicrafts. Probably for this reason, most of his commissions were for temporary buildings (fairs, exhibitions, etc) or fashionable household objects (lamps, clocks, etc). He also travelled widely in Europe, where he painted many watercolours of places he visited. After his

sudden death, a memorial exhibition of his work was arranged by a mutual friend, Vladimir Stassov, who also suggested that Mussorgsky commemorate the event in music. Copies of the exhibition catalogue are now extremely rare, but show that over 400 pictures were displayed. At the end of the exhibition, the paintings were dispersed: many back to the private collections. By 1939, only 65 could be traced. Strangely, three of the pictures immortalised by Mussorgsky do not appear in the catalogue at all (The Old Castle, The Market at Limoges and Bydlo). Stassov said later that many works were added to the show after it opened but it was he who supplied the titles for the first edition of the music, when it was finally published five years after Mussorgsky's death. These titles have been printed, unquestioningly, ever since. It is certainly interesting to see the reproductions printed in *The Musical Quarterly*: Baba-Yaga's Hut turns out to be an ornate design for a clock – but as the author of the article admits, they can be a disappointment: Mussorgsky's music leads to expectations of something grander and stronger.
Terry Jenkins, Pinner, Middx.

QUESTION: What is happiness?

☐ IT IS the name of the hit single by Ken Dodd in 1964. The refrain line, 'I thank the Lord that I've been blessed with more than my share of happiness', confirms that happiness refers to the state of enjoying unusually low tax payments. A chilling warning that such a state is inevitably transient was provided by his hit single the following year: Tears.
David Wirth, Twickenham, Middx.

☐ HAPPINESS is wanting to be where you are, when you are.
A. J. Evens, Southsea, Hants.

☐ HAPPINESS is 'a warm puppy' (Charles M. Schulz: *Peanuts*); 'a warm gun' (Lennon and McCartney, 1968); 'being single' (car

bumper sticker); 'good health and a bad memory' (Ingrid Bergman); 'seeing Lubbock, Texas, in the rear-view mirror' (anon); 'a warm earpiece' (British Telecom ad); 'yes, but ecstasy is a warm codpiece' (graffito); 'a cigar called Hamlet' (cigar ad); 'egg-shaped' (egg ad).
Colin M. Jarman, London N22.

☐ HAPPINESS is having your complete answer published in Notes & Queries.
David Farrell, Cardiff.

☐ HAPPINESS is recognising the utter futility of responding to Notes & Queries.
David Hunter, Sheffield.

☐ THE brief responses you have so far printed do not answer the question. It is easy to see what happiness is not. Happiness is not being wealthy, for even those in possession of wealth may be vulnerable; it is not having good health, for even those sound of body may be disconsolate; it is not being loved, for even those in receipt of love may desire more; it is not in pleasure, for pleasures are transitory and unlikely to be appreciated by those lacking happiness. Obviously these things can be conducive to happiness, yet plainly are not sufficient for it. Happiness is a way of being. One is happy when one is able to flourish. One flourishes by developing and expressing one's abilities in activities and causes which one finds meaningful or just worthwhile, though one may in fact not know that one is flourishing and thereby happy.
Dr Keith Seddon, Director of Studies, The Philosophical Society of England, London SW19.

QUESTION: Who were the Peculiar People? Have they ceased to exist, and what were their peculiarities?

☐ ACCORDING to *Nelson's Encyclopaedia* (1911) they were 'a sect

of faith-healers founded in 1838 by John Banyard who reject medical advice except in surgical cases, relying on prayer and anointing with oils. Members have been frequently tried for manslaughter.' The title was also assumed by a London sect, the 'Plumstead Peculiars'.
Jim Miller, Redhill, Surrey.

☐ MY WIFE and her mother were members in the late 1940s and '50s. The 'Peculiars' had a great community spirit. My wife's parents had moved from Manchester to Grays, Essex, in the 1930s and many of the chapel members there became their closest friends. As a young girl, my wife enjoyed the Sunday services in our local chapel, despite their uncertain length – the Spirit might move anyone to give testimony. Often, the congregation would be chatting on the pavement outside the chapel after service, and the Spirit would move someone to sing – so they would all go back in and carry on, unaccompanied, and with great gusto. As they were not supposed to do any work on a Sunday, many members would cook the Sunday meals on Saturday. The Sunday School was great fun, and often visited other Peculiar chapels by coach and train to share their Sunday worship and to go on picnics. The Peculiar People took their name from Titus 2:13-14: 'Looking for that blessed hope, and the glorious appearing of the great God and our Saviour Jesus Christ; who gave himself for us, that He might redeem us from all iniquity, and purify unto himself a peculiar people, zealous of good works.'
David Collins, Harpenden, Herts.

☐ THE title also comes from the first book of Peter 2:9 which reads: 'But you are a chosen generation, a royal priesthood, a holy nation, a peculiar people, that ye should show forth the praises of Him who hath called you out of darkness into His marvellous light.' Other more modern translations have 'a purchased people', a 'special people', a 'people belonging to God'. The Peculiar People still exist but are now known as the Union of Evangelical

Churches. They are orthodox evangelical churches and in the mainstream of evangelical Christian beliefs.
L. B. Gunn, Claygate, Surrey.

QUESTION: Is it true that John Major had a walk-on part in the cult series, *The Prisoner*? A friend who worked in television in the 1960s reckons he appeared in the episode entitled 'The Girl Who Was Death'.

☐ THE character bearing an uncanny resemblance to John Major in *The Prisoner* episode was the mechanical sailor in the fairground booth: it had the same fixed grin and unnatural hand movements. Even in those days, John was not Number One.
Donald Warden, Headington, Oxford.

QUESTION: What are the 10 longest novels ever published?

☐ THE novel is generally defined as a piece of fiction, usually in prose form, of about 50,000 words or more. However, we can include works originally published in periodicals – authors such as Dickens and Joyce wrote some novels through them – as well as bound trilogies where the work has a continual singular narrative focus. In the light of this, here are 10 well-known works that may answer the question, though not in any accurate order of size. The first two were found listed in the *Guinness Book of Records*:

1. *Les Hommes de Bonne Volante* – Louis Frigoule (4,959 pages).
2. *Tokuga-Wa Ieyasu* – Sohach Yomacka (40 volumes).
3. *The Man Without Qualities* – Robert Musil.
4. *A Dance to the Music of Time* – Anthony Powell.
5. *Remembrance of Things Past* – Marcel Proust.
6. *Clarissa* – Samuel Richardson.
7. *The Wanderer* – Fanny Burney.

   8. *War and Peace* – Leo Tolstoy.
   9. *Camilla* – Fanny Burney.
   10. *The Lord of the Rings* – J. R. R. Tolkien.
C. Norton, The Sheffield/Hallam University Literary Society.

☐ IF C. Norton is right to include trilogies and novel sequences, then surely such works as Lawrence Durrell's *Avignon Quartet* (1,367 pages) and Henry Williamson's *Chronicle of Ancient Sunlight* (which he certainly regarded as a single work of fiction) should be allowed. Incidentally, Hugo's *Les Miserables* (1,232 pages) is certainly longer than *The Lord of the Rings* (1,172 pages including appendices).
Nicky Smith, Streatham, London SW2.

☐ LET'S not forget the extraordinary 18th-century Chinese novel *The Story of the Stone* (also known as *The Dream of the Red Chamber*) by Cao Xueqin. This moving, charming novel runs to 2,354 pages in the five-volume Penguin edition – about half as long again as *War and Peace.*
Glenn Oldham, South Ealing, London W5.

QUESTION: A Cambridge graduate recently claimed: 'Six of the 12 most important discoveries since the birth of Christ were made within half a mile of my rooms.' Assuming the claim is valid, what were the 12, and which were the six?

☐ IF THE 'importance' of a discovery is measured by the extent to which it altered the world, here is my list of 12, none of which has very much to do with Cambridge. Movable type; heliocentric solar system; human blood circulation; electromagnetic induction and radiation; explosives; antibiotics; mechanical clockwork; telephony; vaccination; mercantile capitalism; digital computing; genetic inheritance and plant and animal breeding. You will

notice, of course, that at least four of these were 'discovered' by people with close Scottish connections.
Dr Iain Stevenson, London WC2.

☐ DR IAIN Stevenson notes that 'none' of his list has very much to do with Cambridge. I disagree, as discoveries at Cambridge include: theory of gravity; DNA; atomic theory; Darwin's theory of evolution; digital computing; electricity and electromagnetic induction. The other six discoveries were: heliocentric solar system; internal combustion engine; printing; mechanical clockwork; explosives; antibiotics.
Douglas Ellison, London SE16.

☐ DOUGLAS Ellison's list of six 'discoveries at Cambridge' is wide of the mark. Electricity: Galvani, Volta, Ampere, Ohm, Oersted and Franklin, had no connection with Cambridge, or even England. Electromagnetic induction: the discoverer, Faraday, worked at the Royal Institution in London. Digital computing: Babbage was at Cambridge but produced no functioning computer, so could he really be the discoverer of digital computing? The credit seems really to belong to IBM at Harvard and Ferranti at Manchester. Theory of evolution: after three undistinguished and rather wasted years at Cambridge Darwin had a five-year voyage in HMS *Beagle*. On his return he married and settled in Kent where between 1837 and 1844 he formulated his theory of evolution. Atomic theory: the scientific atomic theory (as opposed to speculation) is due to John Dalton, Manchester in 1803. DNA: the discovery was shared between Cambridge and King's College, London. Theory of gravity: the famous apple tree was in the garden of Woolsthorpe Manor, near Grantham, where Newton spent the plague years 1665–7.
Norman Thorpe, Whalley, Lancs.

QUESTION: **Which law governs the use of amber flashing**

roof-lights on a pick-up truck or similar? Am I allowed to use them on my car?

□ A FLASHING or rotating beam of light which operates through 360 degrees is defined as a warning beacon and is covered by Road Vehicles Lighting Regulations No. 1796/89/3(2). Blue warning beacons are restricted to emergency vehicles and a green beacon may be used by a medical practitioner. Amber warning beacons can be used on a number of municipal, emergency or recovery vehicles, although none of these would normally be a private car. However, a four-wheel vehicle incapable of exceeding 25mph must not be used on an unrestricted dual carriageway without at least one amber warning beacon. This does not apply to cars used before 1947.
Christopher Sawyer, Stevenage, Herts.

QUESTION: Which of the following paints should an ecologically-sound artist use: acrylics, gouache, oils, watercolours, ink, ceramic?

□ THE question can be approached in two ways: (i) the responsibility of the artist; and (ii) the responsibility of the manufacturer. Vegetable colours such as Indigo, Madder Lake, and Quercitron Yellow Lake are still available but are of little interest to painters who want their work to last, as they fade. Casein, derived from dried curd cheese is (if you are prepared to consume dairy produce) about the most eco-friendly binder for artists' paint. It can be bought as a powder (lactic casein *not* hydrochloric casein), which is mixed with water into a paste. An emulsifying agent such as ammonium carbonate can be added. This solution is then ground with pigment to make a water-soluble paint. Casein can also be made into an oil-emulsion (meaning that it thins with water but has an oil content), by adding, drop by drop, cold-pressed linseed oil. Such a paint is available ready-made from Sax Oil Colours. This oil-casein emulsion avoids the use of turpentine or white spirit as thinners (although these two mild solvents evaporate completely and are much less harmful than cellulose-based paints, which are applied heavily in industry). Artists' ranges of paints tend to include pigments such as cadmiums and cobalts, which if used incorrectly could be toxic. Their toxicity with regard to use by artists is negligible when compared with the amounts used by industry. If you are worried about toxic pigments, then choose earths and synthetic organic pigments (Kremer Pigment). It would also be wise to consider paints which are manufactured with health and safety in mind. Lascaux is a Swiss-based firm which produces acrylics. During manufacture, all waste is packed and removed by the government; all water used during manufacture, even the water with which workers clean their hands, is filtered before release. Its 'Studio' range of acrylic colours is used in around 50 art colleges in the UK, combined with its 'Screenpaste' medium, to provide a 100 per cent water-based screen printing programme, complying with new COSHH regulations. The only cleaning agents used are water-based, enabling colleges to save money on rag bills, solvents and the costly installation of extractor fans. The 'Studio' range of colours avoids use of the cobalt or cadmium pigments, replacing them with synthetic organic pigments such as azos and quinacridones, which are safer and in fact more reliably lightfast.

Pip Seymour, A. P. Fitzpatrick Art Materials Service (UK agents for Kramer Pigment/Lascaux/Sax Oil Colours), London E9.

□ THE questioner has left out arguably the most ecologically-sound paint, egg tempera. This is of very ancient origin (9th century at least) and needs only a free-range egg yolk (a natural emulsion), water and the pigments of the artist's choice. That it has to be mixed up as one goes along means that it has not been subjected to the manufacturers' need for shelf consistency (egg tempera sold in tubes is a mixture containing oil and preservatives). Water colour comes a close second – made with plant medium gum arabic. One can even make up oil paints just using linseed oil and pure turpentine for thinning – avoiding added

stabilisers and extenders. I would avoid acrylic as it has a hi-tech recipe. It has been correctly stated that the earth pigments are the most benign but I also use, with care, poisonous cadmiums and cobalt in preference to the modern synthetic organics whose long-term effects are unknown.
Kay Wedgbury, Nailsworth, Gloucestershire.

QUESTION: Does anyone know if electronic mole repellers actually work, or is there a good alternative?

☐ NO. THIS expensive electronic gadget will shift one mole but you will need dozens of them to clear a small garden. And the moles will return so long as the land is damp and there are worms. On a Norfolk acre for 18 years my neighbours tried traps, cods' heads, smoke bombs, wine bottles, spurge plants, mothballs and twigs with rose thorns. The moles are still there. The Universities Federation for Animal Welfare carried out prolonged tests with non-poisonous chemicals and the Agriculture Ministry tried gum acacia, but the moles learned to scrape it off worms or pass them by. Strychnine will kill and give an agonising death (watch the household pets!). But the moles will always come back.
Mr Leslie Jerman, Richbrooke, Epping, Essex.

☐ I KNOW nothing about electronic mole repellers, but Jeyes Fluid works wonders.
Sheila Clegg, Aberdeen.

QUESTION: As sexual indiscretions are no longer an essential ingredient in a political scandal, what indiscretions – individual or collective – are necessary to bring down a British government?

☐ FOR the present government to admit to involvement in the: bombing of Pearl Harbor; Cuban missile crisis; assassination of John F. Kennedy and Robert Kennedy; break-up of the Beatles;

demise of English tennis and football; Watergate; great train robbery; Irangate; erosion of the ozone layer; Black Monday; Black
Wednesday; Brinks Mat robbery; creation of the poll tax; Mirror
Group pension fraud; Dianagate, et al. In fact, short of taking of
responsibility for the mess that this country is in and resigning
office out of decency, I see nothing bringing down a British
government, particularly the present incumbents, short of
Armageddon.
P. Sterling, London E5.

☐ IN THE case of the current government, the only indiscretion
necessary would be to tell the truth.
A. Bridson, Didsbury, Manchester.

QUESTION: Are there any professional bodybuilders who are vegetarians or even vegans?

☐ THE professional bodybuilders Steve Brisbois of Canada and
Andreas Cahling of Sweden claim to be vegans, although both
were meat-eaters earlier in their careers. Most modern bodybuilders follow a diet that is high in carbohydrate, moderate in
protein and extremely low in fat. The assumption that bodybuilders consume large quantities of meat is false, as both eggs and
milk are more easily assimilated forms of protein. A vegan diet
presents the difficulty of relying on vegetable and cereal proteins
to meet nutritional needs. However, this can be circumvented by
various food combinations, e.g. pulses and grains which, when
eaten together, provide the full range of amino acids and therefore
complete proteins.
Steve Large, Calne, Wilts.

☐ HORSES, elephants and bulls spring to mind as archetypal vegetarian and vegan bodybuilders. As for humans, body-building
drugs stimulate aggression, which is a condition alien to the spirit
of many vegetarians.
Alan Long, VEGA, Greenford, Middx.

☐ ALAN Long contends that aggression is 'a condition alien to the spirit of many vegetarians'. What a shame this has appeared in print too late to be read by that most famous vegetarian, Adolf Hitler.
John Moore, Norwich.

QUESTION: How did fishwives get such a bad press?

☐ BEFORE the invention of condoms, the Pill, and education for women, the avenues for women to support themselves other than by marriage were extremely meagre. Marriage was the be-all and end-all of existence, and an early grave from constant childbearing was the outcome. Women were connected with the sale of fish in London from medieval times – it was one way they could avoid marriage and earn money to live. They were permitted to buy fish from fishmongers but not to keep a stall and had to walk the streets carrying their wares. Billingsgate market was their headquarters and fishwives' 'scolding' (or language) became notorious. 'Billingsgate' was synonymous with foul language, and by the time of the Restoration the term 'fishwife' meant anyone who swore.
Olive Marshall, Market Harborough, Leicestershire.

QUESTION: It is often said that 10 per cent of the population is gay. Where does this figure come from and what is the evidence?

☐ THE generalisation comes from the Kinsey Report. But it is impossible to be precise about the real figure; recent American surveys give results between 4 and 17 per cent. Kinsey found that 37 per cent of his subjects had had homosexual experiences to orgasm. There are many problems in trying to get at the real figure. First, you need to define homosexuality: do you include all those who are homosexually orientated, or just those who practise?

Many homosexuals are unwilling to acknowledge their sexuality to themselves, let alone to anyone else (including researchers) – society hardly encourages gays to come out of the closet. Secondly, many gays are only 'out' in certain situations (for example, when in a gay bar), and act 'straight' for most of their lives. Thirdly, how do you deal with the undoubtedly large number of people who are bisexual? The 4 per cent figure probably represents those who are 'Out' in most situations in life (i.e. to parents and friends, or at work). Overall, 10 per cent is probably a good rule of thumb. That means that there are close to 4 million gays (over the age of 20) in this country, making this one of the largest minority groups.
Paul Hindle, Salford.

☐ PAUL Hindle is right in attributing the 10 per cent figure to the first Kinsey Report, but vague about the figure's true significance, and the evidence for and against it. Kinsey actually wrote that, among his sample of white Americans, '10 per cent of the males are more or less exclusively homosexual for at least three years between the ages of 16 and 55.' In the sensational press coverage that followed publication in 1948, this figure drew particular attention (the 4 per cent of men who were exclusively homosexual throughout their lives, and the lower corresponding figures for women, presumably had less shock value), and was taken up by the homosexual lobby, and later by the gay liberation movement. But as an index of the proportion of lesbian and gay people in the population, it plainly will not do, and Kinsey made no such claim for it – not least because he studied sexual behaviour, rather than sexual feelings. The incidence of gay desires – let alone potential gay desires – is largely beyond the scope of his work. For this, evidence from a range of disciplines can be taken into account. History, anthropology and sociology suggest that homosexuality may potentially be a natural aspect of almost anyone's sexuality. In pre-Roman Europe, male homosexuality was an essential part of the social fabric, and most males enjoyed both gay and straight relationships during a lifetime. In western society, women seem more open to development of sexuality in new directions (many

lesbians have left an exclusively straight lifestyle behind), while many subsequently heterosexual boys engage in 'homosexual play' during childhood and adolescence. All this suggests that sexuality is more mutable than many people believe, while the question 'what proportion of the population is gay?' has no meaningful answer – even the proportion who have gay sex can fluctuate wildly and for all sorts of reasons.
Leo Adamson, London SE14.

☐ LEO Adamson's observations, suffer from the problem of definition: who is a homosexual? Apart from a person who has gay relationships throughout his life, does it cover any or all of the following: (i) a person who earlier was heterosexual but now has gay relationships; (ii) a person who had gay relationships before but now has only heterosexual relationships; (iii) a person who has bisexual relationships? Is a person who had just one brief homosexual relationship in his life a homosexual? The problem was highlighted after the recent report from America that homosexuals' brains differ from those of heterosexuals; a letter to a newspaper asked whether, if a homosexual had heterosexual relationships, his brain would then alter! The confusion arises from Kinsey's view of homosexuality as a psychological state. The American discovery, however, confirms the thesis in my book *The Third Sex* (1990, Taprobane) that homosexuality is, in fact, a biological phenomenon. Homosexuality, the practice, then becomes distinct from homosexuality, the biological condition. It is seen, then, that every person who engages in homosexual acts is not necessarily homosexual: single-sex situations such as boarding school, the navy and the like are famous for such acts, and it is the Kinseyan classification of all those so involved as homosexuals that led to false conclusions and wild goose chases in psychological theories. Homosexual relationships, it is now seen, can take place between two biological homosexuals or between a biological homosexual and a biological heterosexual or even between two biological heterosexuals.
Gordon Wilson, London W5.

QUESTION: Is there any truth in the virility test for Eskimo priests who, standing naked on the ice, had to dry 14 damp towels with the heat of their body?

☐ I DON'T know about Eskimos, but Alexandra David-Neel, in her book *With Mystics and Magicians in Tibet* (Penguin, 1936) describes the practice of 'tumo' or 'gtumo' among Tibetan monks, which allows them to survive the winters in the hills above the snowline. This tumo is heat produced by the individual in a state of trance. After training, tumo students sit cross-legged by a frozen lake, and sheets are dipped in water and wrapped around the body. As soon as a sheet is dry it is re-dipped and placed back to be dried once more. At least three sheets have to be dried, and stories of 40 sheets in a night have been heard. Those who pass the test are called 'respas' and from then on go naked or wear a single cotton garment all year round.
A. C. M. Russell, Tweedmouth, Berwick-upon-Tweed.

QUESTION: If a murderer has killed his/her victim in order to inherit money (as often happens in 'whodunnit' stories), what then happens to the deceased's fortune?

☐ THE deceased's fortune would be shared among his/her next of kin – excluding the murderer. If the deceased has no close relatives, then any other family member has a right to claim the fortune.
Rachel Hutton, Hitchin, Herts.

☐ RACHEL Hutton has succinctly summed up the intestacy rules but, in addition, if there is a valid will, the murderer is struck off the list – the only instance when a person 'cut off without a penny' has no legal redress.
Cathy Baker, Twickenham, Middlesex.

QUESTION: Have there been any scientific investigations into the wearing of copper bracelets to relieve rheumatism and arthritis?

☐ AN ABSTRACT of a study in Australia by Walker and Keats was published in 1976. It reads: 'From over 300 arthritis sufferers, half of whom previously wore copper bracelets, three treatment-group-subjects were randomly allocated for a psychological study. This involved wearing copper bracelets and placebo bracelets alternately ... Preliminary results show that, to a significant number of subjects, the wearing of the copper bracelet appeared to have some therapeutic value.'
Robert Greenwood, Chatham, Kent.

QUESTION: What is the difference between a rechargeable battery and an ordinary one? What happens if I recharge a conventional battery?

☐ THE main difference is in the chemicals they are made from: rechargeable batteries have a nickel hydroxide positive electrode, and a cadmium negative – hence the name ni-cad. They normally have a much lower power rating than ordinary (or dry) batteries, and are not suitable for all uses. Dry batteries are made from a variety of metals, and are known as zinc carbon, zinc chloride, and alkaline. They can be recharged, but not in an ordinary recharger. If this happens, they will not be fully recharged and may leak (although not explode, as the battery-makers will have us believe). When a battery is being used, the zinc electrode oxidises and stops the battery from working. To recharge the battery, the zinc oxide has to be turned back to zinc (a bit like electro-plating). To do this, a special form of AC has to be used called Periodic Current Reversal. The circuit to create this is quite simple and a charger will cost less than £10. As it can recharge batteries up to 20 times, it soon pays for itself.
Chris Heathcote, Bicknacre, Essex.

☐ CHRIS Heathcote stated that rechargeable batteries have 'a lower power rating' than dry batteries. In fact they have a much higher power rating – you can jump-start a car with 10 small ni-cads. They do have a lower *energy capacity*, which means they have to be replaced more often to recharge. Even if dry batteries can be recharged up to 20 times, it still makes the more expensive ni-cads (rechargeable hundreds of times) a lot cheaper in the long run.

Ian Leslie, London SE24.

☐ A COMPANY here in Bury St Edmunds makes a device which can recharge conventional batteries several times. The company is Coltronics Systems Ltd (0284 755600) and the charger costs £39.95. I am not an employee, just a very satisfied customer.

Antony Hurden, Bury St Edmunds, Suffolk.

QUESTION: In 1940, motorists were required to immobilise their vehicles, when unattended, by removing the rotor arm – thus preventing theft by German invaders. Is this the solution to the problem of car theft and joyriders in the 1990s?

☐ THE removal of the rotor arm in a car does indeed disable it but modern distributors (in which the rotor arm is situated) often have the top cap screwed down rather then held on by quick-release clips. They are also less accessible than in older engines and are often near dirty engine parts, leading to a spoiling of clothes when you try to reach them. There is also the possibility that, as cars become more reliable, people no longer need to know what is under the bonnet and so have no idea where the rotor arm is or what it would look like.

Gordon Jackson, Manchester.

QUESTION: Why do humans have hair only on certain parts of their body and why those parts?

☐ WE ARE naked apes because, at a crucial stage in our evolution,

to protect ourselves from faster and stronger predators, we chose to live near lakes and rivers and became good swimmers. Since hair increases water drag, it was selected against a part from where it provided heat protection for the one part of the body to remain above the surface of the water – the head. Once bipedalism became established, initially because it enables a water-located primate to scan its environment, head hair continued in its heat-protecting function. In the aquatic stage of evolution, we developed our uniquely human system of temperature control in the form of millions of eccrine sweat glands. These largely displaced the scent-emitting apocrine glands of our non-aquatic primate ancestors. However, we retain a residual quantity of apocrine glands, concentrated under the arms and in the pubic area where the vestigial patches of hair serve to conserve and concentrate the glands' secretions.
Christopher Hill, Highbury, London N5.

☐ FURTHER to Christopher Hill's note, the millions of eccrine sweat glands also exude salt, as do our tears. We know how salty they taste. This suggests the crucial stage in our development was near the sea and our diet excessively salty. Perhaps our species was isolated by the sea for a long period leading to memories of seas engulfing the world (Noah), an isolated paradise with the growth of self-awareness and the recognition of nakedness (Adam and Eve) and a sea being divided to lead the tribe back to the promised land (Moses). Elaine Morgan's book *The Scars of Evolution* sheds much light on the possibilities.
B. W. Campbell, Bainton, Lincs.

QUESTION: How careful do you have to be in hitting an intruder over the head if you want to cause unconsciousness without killing him/her?

☐ AS SOMEONE who has practised various martial arts for over 10 years, and now teaches both self-defence and jujitsu, I can testify that there is no easy answer to this question. Practically, the answer depends on four factors. (i) The variation in the strength of the target skull. Some people have very thick skulls, some paper-thin. (ii) Assuming an averagely strong skull, one must then consider exactly where on the head you hit. Any strike on or around the base of the skull or upper neck is more effective, and thus potentially more fatal, than a simple 'klonk' on the top. The safest (but therefore least effective in KO-ing terms) place to hit the head would be downwards on to the front 'corners' of the skull. (iii) The next factor is what you hit them with. Unless specifically trained, or unusually strong, a blow, punch or chop with an empty hand is unlikely to render someone immediately unconscious, although it may stun them for long enough for other action to be taken. Using a weapon of any sort greatly increases the effectiveness of the technique and therefore the danger of killing someone. As a rule of thumb, though, the harder and sharper the weapon, the more dangerous it would be. Remember also that victims could equally damage themselves as they fall on the floor: contact with the edge of a table can be enough to kill. (iv) Finally, consideration of the legality of your actions is important. The law preaches a doctrine of reasonable use of minimum force. I would advise anyone confronted with an intruder to use force as an absolute last resort. Quite apart from the fact that the intruder will probably be better prepared for, and more inclined to use, extreme violence, avoiding the encounter and calling the police are far more sensible courses of action. If cornered, however, and with no other choice, by all means grab the poker or a golf club, but consider striking for less potentially fatal though equally debilitating areas of the body – the groin, elbows and kneecaps, for example.

Robert C. Avery, Maidenhead, Berks.

☐ HAVING spoken to a policeman over a theft, I mentioned that I kept a Number 2 wood handy in case of finding an intruder at a sufficient disadvantage. He then warned me of the problem of using too much force. I suppose the answer must be to use a 9 iron.
A. C. Cook, Middlesbrough, Cleveland.

QUESTION: Why are passenger ships, including ferries, usually steered from near the front or bow and freight ships, including tankers, from the rear or stern?

☐ MERCHANT ships used to fall broadly into three classes: tankers, dry cargo and passenger vessels. Even the first channel ferries were ordinary ships. These ships would be able to lift all sorts of cargo worldwide. Since then designs have multiplied and ships may now be designed to carry specific cargoes (e.g. gas carriers, container ships, offshore supply vessels) sometimes on specific routes. The traditional 'three island' ship – consisting of fo'c'sle, centrecastle and poop – was still being built in the late 1960s. Their design was aesthetically pleasing but they used up too much cargo-carrying space by having the engine room and accommodation midships. The ends of a ship can't generally be used for cargo, so tankers overcame this lost cargo space by moving the engine room and accommodation aft and simply stuck the bridge on top. This may give problems in seeing ahead under the bow, particularly when supertankers are in ballast and trimmed by the stern. Regulations govern the extent of this blind sector under the bow. Not all cargo ships have the bridge aft. Some container ships, log carriers, heavy lift ships and others have departed from this all-aft design and put the accommodation and bridge on the fo'c'sle. But this can be most uncomfortable for the crew in heavy weather. And there have also been instances of the (strengthened) bridge windows being smashed by heavy seas, leading to the prospect of the ship's nerve centre being washed out. Passenger ships and ferries do not have the same cargo-carrying constraints. The ship is one big accommodation block and it really doesn't matter where the bridge goes, except for the problems of seeing ahead. Passenger ship design is one area where naval architects still produce something graceful, looking like a ship. (Compare the floating shoe-box design of a car-carrier with the latest Scandinavian passenger ships.) Most passenger ship designs since the war have tended to put the bridge forward and the ferries merely continue this trend. There are other considerations which involve stability, construction techniques and materials, the intended work of the vessel and its ease of handling. For instance, the masters of ships being manoeuvred with precision (such as rig support vessels or tugs) will need good, all-round vision; in this case the bridge may be forward but will also give a good view aft.

Chris Haughton, Master Mariner, Fleetwood Nautical Campus, Blackpool, and the Fylde College.

☐ I AM sure Chris Haughton, in his reply, rightly assumed the questioner meant navigated or commanded rather than steered. However, as someone who often spent up to half his working day actually at the wheel, I feel the questioner may wish to be answered literally. Since it is the ship's master and his mates (not necessarily his friends) who navigate the ship, and the sailors who actually steer to the former's commands (a particularly mind-numbing job most of the time), then the man at the wheel does not technically need to see where the ship is going, although in pilotage waters, etc, it helps to be able to see the actual ship's heading and how she is responding. It therefore does not matter where the helmsman is situated as long as he is in contact with the bridge, has a wheel or tiller, a compass and a rudder indicator. The most obvious and practical place is on the bridge, although not necessarily there. I believe the helmsman on Grey Funnel Line ships can be located well away from the bridge deep inside the vessel.

Pete Mungall, Education Officer, RRS Discovery, Dundee.

QUESTION: Why do dolphins leap?

☐ IT'S usually done for a porpoise.
Peter Barnes, Milton Keynes.

QUESTION: In Dickens's story, A Christmas Carol, are Ebenezer Scrooge and Jacob Marley supposed to be Jewish?

☐ No, DICKENS did not intend Scrooge and Marley to be Jewish. If he had, he would have said so, both on their first appearance and in the list of characters it was his custom to place at the beginning of each book, as he did in the case of 'Fagin, a crafty old Jew, a receiver of stolen goods' in *Oliver Twist*, and in that of 'Mr Riah, a venerable Jew, of noble and generous nature' in *Our Mutual Friend*. The question was probably suggested by the forenames Ebenezer and Jacob, both indeed of Old Testament origin. Such names, however, were much used by 19th-century Nonconformists: Strict Ebenezer is actually the name of a particular Baptist sect. Surely Scrooge and Marley are intended to represent some of the less admirable and more puritanical and perverse aspects of the Protestant work ethic?

Michael Grosvenor-Myer, Haddenham, Cambridge.

QUESTION: **The following notice, carefully painted on wood and framed, was found in an antique warehouse and was believed to have come out of a pub: 'Do not spit on the floor, remember the Jamestown flood.' What was this flood?**

☐ THE questioner is almost certainly thinking of the Johnstown flood which occurred on 31 May 1889. According to the *Oxford Companion to American Literature*, some 2,200 lives were lost in the city of Johnstown, Pennsylvania, after a dam on the Conemaugh River was destroyed by heavy rains. The fact that such an event merits its own entry in a literary reference work is an indication of its significance to Americans and its impact on their collective folk memory. It is not particularly well known on this side of the Atlantic, however, and the following lines from John Stewart's song, 'Mother Country', were a mystery to me for many years: 'Boys? Hell, they were men; stood knee-deep in the Johnstown mud. It was during the time of that terrible flood.' According to Eric Partridge's *A Dictionary of Catch Phrases*, the saloons which abounded in the US before Prohibition all had 'No Spitting' signs, and comical variants such as 'Don't spit;

remember the Johnstown flood' were available in stores specialising in novelty items. Johnstown seems to be a particularly hazardous place to live, since there were further floods in 1936 and 1977, killing 25 and 85 citizens respectively.
Stephen Willis, Stalybridge, Cheshire.

QUESTION: If Henry VIII founded the Church of England to legitimise his divorce, why is it now against the canon law of the Church? Can the present head of the Church reverse this?

☐ THE question contains three fallacies: (i) Henry VIII did *not* found the Church of England. It was in existence centuries before the Normam Conquest brought it under the political control of the Bishop of Rome. The Church was reformed, not founded, in the 16th century in response to growing pressure from within the Church itself for greater freedom from Roman interference. The king gave his support to this movement because he, too, had his own problems with the Roman authorities. (ii) Henry VIII neither sought nor obtained a divorce. He sought to have his 'marriage' to Catherine of Aragon annulled on the grounds that the then rules of kindred and affinity had been broken. There is no doubt that the Pope would have granted such an annulment had he not been a prisoner of Catherine's nephew. After all, he had previously granted annulments to European monarchs on far flimsier grounds. But the annulment was refused, so Henry obtained one from Canterbury. His later 'marriage' to Anne of Cleves was annulled on the grounds of non-consummation, as some marriages are today. The bride and groom couldn't stand the sight of each other and spent their wedding night playing cards. An annulment means that a marriage never existed in the first place, as opposed to a divorce which recognises that a marriage did exist but does so no longer. The Church's canon law, based on the teaching of Christ Himself, forbids remarriage of divorced persons. (iii) The monarch is not the head of the Church. That position belongs to

Christ alone. The reigning monarch is 'supreme governor' of the Church of England and, as such, cannot constitutionally impose her (or his) will on the Church.
A. Tomlinson, Congleton, Cheshire.

☐ IT IS a general principle that canon law is subordinate to theology, and therefore cannot be changed in a way that implies an alteration in the fundamental doctrines of the Church, which ultimately derive from the word of God as witnessed in scripture. In the western Church, this has been taken to allow annulment and forbid divorce – although divorce is allowed in canon law in the eastern (Orthodox) tradition. Annulment is not a way out of the monarchy's current difficulties; first because the children of the annulled marriage would be debarred from succession to the throne, and second because there are no grounds for questioning the original validity of any of the current marriages. Catherine of Aragon, by contrast, had previously been betrothed and then married to Henry's deceased elder brother Arthur – both bars to a subsequent valid marriage with Henry. The marriage had only been able to proceed because the Pope had 'dispensed with' the application of canon law for this union. The issue under contention in the 1530s was whether the Pope had authority to make such a dispensation – which led in time to a denial of papal authority altogether.
Tom Hennell, Withington, Manchester.

☐ I REALLY must protest at the outrageous statement: 'Henry VIII did not found the Church of England. It was in existence centuries before the Norman Conquest brought it under the political control of the Bishop of Rome.' Wasn't it the Bishop of Rome (Pope Gregory) who sent Augustine to preach to the English? Was Bede an Anglican? Was it Anglicanism that Boniface took to Germany? The notion of an autocephalous Saxon Church is on a par with the belief that the Holocaust never happened. Henry VIII usurped the Pope's authority in England and appointed Cranmer as Archbishop of Canterbury to give him a divorce from his wife. He plundered the Church mercilessly. A movement for reform did not come from within the Church. Subsequently both Lutheran and Calvinist doctrines entered the new 'Church of England'. Then, under Elizabeth I, the 39 articles finally established the protestant nature of the Church of England ... and we blame the Communists for rewriting history.

Adrian Jarvis, Bickington, Devon.

QUESTION: Why does Bill Clinton wear white gloves when jogging?

☐ HE IS following standard medical advice to wear gloves for winter jogging. What he does not appear to realise is that the white gloves (for White House?) make him look less like the president than the butler.

Andrew Hoellering, Thorverton, Exeter.

☐ A PROBLEM for the serious long-distance runner is that at the beginning of a race one's hands are cold, but after a mile or so they will become quite warm. Bill Rogers, who 10 or 12 years ago was the leading marathon runner in the United States, solved this problem by using cheap white gardeners' gloves which he could later discard. The sports-clothing industry soon saw the potential of this and began to market such gloves, endorsed by Rogers, at high prices. I have not scrutinised my TV set closely to decide whether or not these are the gloves which Bill Clinton uses, but I suspect they are.

H. B. de Groot, Edinburgh.

QUESTION: At what stage does a foetus's heart begin to beat independently, and could this have implications for the debate on abortion?

☐ THE heart is beating by 18 to 25 days after fertilisation. At 21 days, the heart has been found pumping, through a closed circulatory system, blood whose type is different from that of the mother (*Growth*, New York: Life Science Library, p. 64). As for implications for the abortion debate, abortions are typically done at 9–12 weeks of pregnancy, i.e. 7–10 weeks after fertilisation (pregnancy is measured from the first day of the last menstrual period, so the baby's actual age is two weeks less). Even if there were any doubt about the fact that the life of each individual begins at fertilisation, abortion clearly destroys a living human being with a beating heart and (except in cases of anencephaly) a functioning brain. If the first right of a human being is his or her life, the direct killing of an unborn child is a manifest violation of that right.

Brendan Gerard, Hull branch chairman, the Society for the Protection of Unborn Children.

☐ THE foetal heart relies entirely on the umbilical cord for all of its supply of nutrients and oxygen from the placenta. Only after birth, when the umbilical cord is cut and the lungs inflate, will a small 'hole-in-the-heart', the foramen ovale, then close. This allows post-natal circulation of blood to begin independently.

Mrs A. Higgins (cardiographer), Battersea, London SW11.

☐ A FOETAL heartbeat can have no bearing on the morality of abortion, as human (and animal) rights depend on consciousness, whereas a heartbeat is merely mechanical. (A mature person in a persistent vegetative state is one whose damaged brain is capable of keeping the heart and lungs working, but not of any cerebral activity – no thought, no dreams, no sensation.) It is only when the foetus develops a functional central nervous system with the ability to feel pain that it acquires incipient human rights, and from that stage on it is reasonable to refuse abortion except on serious grounds (such as severe foetal defects).

Barbara Smoker, President, National Secular Society, London N19.

QUESTION: Is it now accepted that dowsing, or 'water divining', really works? If so, has it been explained scientifically?

☐ IN THE late 1960s, I joined Lancashire County Council's School Playing Fields Service as a technical officer, building and maintaining a vast acreage of school grounds. I noticed that all their area supervisors carried two copper welding rods in their cars. The last seven inches of the rods were bent at a right-angle to form a handle. They were used to detect old land drains which, if left uncoupled to the new sports field drainage, would cause trouble, as even land bulldozed to form a flat surface for the games pitches can continue to 'bleed' to these earlier agricultural drains. The technique is to walk arms forward with the welding rods held loosely, in line with the outstretched arms. When passing over a drain, the copper rods swing inwards and cross. It seemed to work for about half the people willing to try it and was highly regarded for its accuracy and for saving time in not having to search through old plans, or dig long trenches across soggy sports fields. On one occasion, I learned that the borough engineer of Middleton, near Manchester, was unable to locate a buried manhole on one of their playing fields. I walked the field with the two copper welding rods and, by planting garden canes wherever they crossed, I was able to plot the line of two old sewers. The missing manhole was found at the point of intersection. We never knew why it worked but most agreed that the rods were locating cavities rather than running water. We called it 'dowsing' and never used the technique for 'divining' water.
Alan Barber, parks management consultant, Nailsea, Bristol.

☐ ACCORDING to Terence Hines, a New York psychologist and critic of parapsychology, there has never been any evidence to show that dowsing really works, despite extensive controlled studies. He puts the movements of the dowsing rod down to small unconscious muscle twitches in the diviner's body. Most evidence for dowsing consists of anecdotal eyewitness reports, which are notoriously unreliable and are further complicated by the fact that witnesses tend to recall selectively only those dowsing attempts which are successful. Furthermore, dowsers frequently predict that water will be found at several locations. As well-drilling usually stops after the first success, other predictions which may have turned out to be wrong won't be tested. Also, vague predictions about depth may at first appear successful on the basis that digging deep enough will usually produce results. Add to all this the geological clues in the land which a dowser may pick up, albeit unconsciously, and you have a case for dowsing which appears not to hold water.

Jacqui Farrants, Romford, Essex.

☐ BIOMAGNETISM – the interaction of living matter (e.g. bees, carrier pigeons, whales) with the ambient magnetic field – has developed as a recognised science over the past quarter-century. At first, independently of that, Yves Rocard, professor of physics at Paris and a wartime resistance hero, used a dowser's services when needing water for a seismic laboratory in Normandy 35 years ago, and then sought an explanation of his success. In his four books (1962 to 1991) he attributed the effect to small differences between the earth's field at the right and left sides of the dowser's body. The hazel-twig or pendulum is not the detector but amplifies and indicates a muscular reaction. Although water is not magnetic, groundwater may correlate with magnetic anomalies – e.g. a ferruginous component of soil may be gradually deposited and concentrated. Despite the many difficulties in getting reproducible demonstrations, dowsing has achieved some respectability in garden and church archaeology (e.g. *Dowsing and Church Archaeology* by Professor R. N. Bailey et al, 1988).

Dr J. C. E. Jennings, London N6.

☐ WHILE with the Ministry of Defence, R. A. Foulkes conducted experiments to see if buried metal or plastic objects could be located by diviners (see *Nature* vol. 229, 15 January 1971, p. 163). On a 400-square grid, each square measuring 20 feet by 20 feet, he buried metal (dummy) mines, plastic mines, wooden blocks, concrete blocks and blanks. Twenty-two experienced dowsers were convinced they could sort them out but none did better than chance. Other experiments on water dowsing at Chatham were a little less rigorous but with the same negative result. Their last test included a search for a 42-inch water main eight feet down carrying a flow of 80,000 gallons an hour.

Dr A. Selwood, Harrogate, North Yorks.

☐ UNTIL I saw the letter from Dr Selwood, I had always assumed that diviners were able to detect metal under the ground. But I have never heard of a diviner who has come through a test to detect water. A prize of $10,000 was once offered by an American water association for detecting water flowing from a central tank through pipes buried beneath the ground. There were several pipes of different materials and water could be directed along any, or all of them, via a series of valves. The task of the diviner was to detect which pipes carried water. I never heard that anyone ever won the prize. This begs the question as to how diviners survive. Water diviners do not have much of a challenge in this moist country of ours. A borehole drilled virtually anywhere in Britain will encounter water eventually and in most cases it will be within a few tens of metres from the surface. It is upon this that the diviner relies, unconsciously or otherwise. I would not wish to give the impression that all water diviners are charlatans, because I expect that most who work at it for long enough build up useful experience. However, I am convinced that the performance with the 'rods' is nothing more than mumbo-jumbo. The difference between a diviner and a professional hydrogeologist is this: put a diviner in an area outside his/her experience and the diviner is lost; in contrast any half-competent hydrogeologist will be able to provide reliable advice virtually anywhere in the world. The catch is that the professional advice is usually expensive. Many diviners work in conjunction with a small drilling company and it is astonishing how frequently water is 'found' just by the track, and convenient for the rig. I used to work for one of the water

authorities, and it was not uncommon to receive requests for advice about water from hill farms and other households remote from the nearest water main. One day a farmer in the Lake District asked for information. It was clear from the address of the farm that it was situated on a rock formation known as the Bannisdale Slates which have no useful water-bearing capacity (they would not, after all, be much use for roofing otherwise). The farmer explained that a diviner had told him there was water below ground and a driller was standing by to construct a borehole to reach it. The advice sent to him was against drilling but the farmer ignored it, the borehole was drilled and found to be completely dry. The farmer was about £3,000 out of pocket.
Dr K. J. Vines, Plymouth.

QUESTION: A box of matches usually contains an average of 43. Why or how was this figure chosen?

☐ BEFORE decimalisation, boxes of matches cost 2d each (Swan Vestas 4d) and this price had been charged for many years. Fifty years ago the average content was 50 matches but after the Second World War inflation took hold. Since, with the contemporary coinage, any increase in price would have had to be at least 25 per cent, the average content was reduced to 49. Subsequently, the pace of inflation meant further reductions were in steps of two matches. Presumably, at current price levels it is now possible actually to change the price of a box.
D. J. Reade, Hanham Abbots, Bristol.

☐ MOST imported matches vary in contents from 30 to 35 to a maximum of 40 because they come in a smaller box. Bryant & May match boxes are larger and therefore contain an average of 43 per box.
Sharon Nibbs, Bryant & May, London W1.

QUESTION: Gutzon Borglum, the American sculptor, was

famous for his monumental busts of US presidents on Mount Rushmore. How did he carry out this work and when?

☐ BORGLUM, who had studied at the Beaux-Arts in Paris, began by sculpting the four torsos in miniature. He and his assistants then mapped the models by suspending a weighted string from a horizontal rod, which they rotated above the miniatures. By measuring the distance between the string and numerous key points on the heads, they produced a precise (notionally) three-dimensional grid, showing exactly where everything should be. These measurements, of which there were thousands, were then multiplied to produce a version of the grid gigantic enough to fit the mountain. To locate the key points on the granite rockface, Borglum's team measured the distance back from ropes suspended from a series of protruding poles fixed above. Despite its crudeness, this method proved very successful. Using a system of drilling and blasting, the heads were hewn from the rock. At one point the head of Jefferson had to be rotated slightly to his left when a vertical fault was discovered in the granite. This fault now runs visibly down the right side of the nose, the nostril of which is, incidentally, big enough to sleep in. Work on the 60-foot-high structure was stopped in 1941, the year Borglum died. By that time many people were sick of the delays, accidents and in-fighting. The monument was never finished, and if you visit Mount Rushmore today you can just see Lincoln's fingers starting to emerge from the granite, at the point where the work was abruptly halted.
Charles Mutto, London SW1.

☐ HE STARTED to deface Mount Rushmore on 4 October 1927. By 31 October 1941, the defacement was complete. The site for this sculpture is in the centre of Sioux Indian sacred land, the Paha Sapa (the Black Hills), ceded to the Sioux nation in perpetuity in 1868. It is said that Borglum wanted to carve full-length figures of the presidents but died before their completion. Perhaps if he

had started at the presidents' feet, instead of their heads, Americans would have a more appropriate 'shrine' to their democracy.
Ms Kim Hopkins (Cherokee Indian), London W5.

QUESTION: Is it true that the original saxophone solo on Gerry Rafferty's 'Baker Street' was performed by Bob Holness of Blockbusters fame?

☐ THE solo was played by Raphael Ravenscroft. The story that it was by Blockbusters' Bob Holness originates from the 'Believe It Or Not' column of the New Musical Express, which prints a weekly collection of blatant lies in an attempt to trap the gullible. It was, however, Holness who contributed the blistering lead guitar to Derek and the Dominoes' 'Layla'.
Paul Soper, Beaconsfield, Bucks.

☐ AS PAUL Soper rightly says, Bob Holness did play lead guitar on 'Layla' but, unfortunately, nobody outside the studio has ever heard his version. The original master tape of this memorable tune, with Bob playing, disappeared with the enigmatic Phil Spector and has never been seen since. Luckily for the record-buying public, Eric Clapton was in the studio when the original recording was made and managed to re-record it almost note for note, though never quite capturing the magic of Bob's original version.
Richard Ellis, Bottesford, Nottingham.

☐ SO. MY cover's been blown. The truth about Phil Spector and my involvement with the 'Layla' tapes is out at last. How in heaven's name am I going to face my fellow-members of my local Cavan O'Connor Supporters Club? Is there no privacy left? It's good to know, though, that some things are still sacrosanct. Have you ever considered just who was causing Elvis to giggle hysterically during that recording of 'Are You Lonesome Tonight?'... ?
Bob Holness, London NW.

QUESTION: I heard recently that from the Red Sea port of Eilat one can see four different countries: Israel, Jordan, Egypt and Saudi Arabia. Is a similar feat possible elsewhere?

☐ IF ONE stands at the summit of Snaefell mountain, Isle of Man, on a clear day one can see seven 'kingdoms': England, Wales, Scotland, Eire, Northern Ireland, Mann and the 'kingdom' of Heaven.
Pauline McCrorie, Lonan, Isle of Man.

☐ IT DEPENDS on what counts as a country. If one stands at the South Pole, one can see territory administered and claimed by New Zealand, Chile, the United Kingdom, Argentina, Australia, Norway and France. All these 'territories' consist of segments radiating outwards from the South Pole. Also, the base at the South Pole is American, so that makes eight nationalities converging on one place.
Peter Stockill, Middlesbrough, Cleveland.

☐ ON THE Zambezi, a few miles above the Victoria Falls, there is a point at which four national boundaries converge. This was brought about by South Africa's extension of South-West Africa into the 'Caprivi Strip'. The borders coincide at the river so presumably a swimmer could tread water in Botswana, Namibia, Zambia and Zimbabwe simultaneously.
Patrick O'Neill, Eastleigh, Hants.

QUESTION: What is a tune?

☐ THE orchestral player immediately recognises a tune and concocts a ribald lyric to fit it. Tchaikovsky wrote many tunes, Beethoven relatively few. Perhaps the classic symphonic tune is the occurrence of the Heinz beans advertisement, 'A million housewives every day ...', in Mendelssohn's Hebrides Overture.
Laurence Payne, Seven Kings, Essex.

☐ A TUNE is a series of sounds whose frequencies bear specific ratios to one another and whose durations bear specific ratios to one another. It must be so defined because its identity does not depend, within reason, on the actual frequency, called pitch, or on the actual rate of sound production. The durations usually relate to a repeated time unit called rhythm. In most western music, the available frequency ratios are set by reference to a scale found, for example, in the ratios of the sounds from a keyboard instrument and the commonest ratios are those provided by the 'white' keys. However, more readily recognisable and memorable tunes usually contain sequences in which the ratios of the successive notes approximate to simple fractions such as 2/3 or 5/4, or suggest that they may be related to sounds which contain a set of such simple ratios heard simultaneously. These multiple frequency units are called 'chords', a succession of which is often called harmony. A tune need not suggest a harmonic basis, and more than one such basis is acceptable within a given tune, but many of the sound sequences which are rememberable as tunes do have their harmonic basis. A common feature of many tunes is that the pattern established by the initial set of sounds is imitated in the continuation of the tune. But for those apparent requirements, one could devise more than 16 million tunes of eight successive sounds, using eight adjacent 'white' notes of a keyboard, each of which could also have various duration patterns. Use 12 notes and the number is astronomic. Yet a thematic index of every reasonably well-known tune contains about 16,000. An alternative definition of a tune is 'that which an arbitrary group of old grey men can whistle after they have heard it once'. A title derived from that idea was given to a long-running television programme containing remarkably little which would have satisfied this test.

Professor Sir James Beament, Queens' College, Cambridge.

QUESTION: There are many public houses called the Lamb and Flag. What is the origin of the name?

☐ THE earliest hostelry names were drawn for the most part from

chivalric and ecclesiastical heraldry and originally reflected
patronage and/or property of knightly families or of the Church.
The Lamb of inn names is the Agnus Dei, the Paschal lamb, which
was the emblem of St John the Baptist. It was also a blazon of the
Knights Templars, a military order founded *c.* 1118 to protect
pilgrims to the Holy Land. In both chivalric and ecclesiastical
heraldry, the lamb was often represented bearing the staff of the
Cross upon which flew a banner, itself decorated with a cross
motif, hence the hostelry name the Lamb and Flag. The earliest
example of the sign of the Lamb of which I am aware is a Norwich
instance recorded in 1504, but the elaborated sign of The Lamb
and Flag seems to have been current only from the 19th century.
*Professor Barrie Cox, Department of English Studies, University
of Nottingham.*

**QUESTION: In films about the Second World War, if a
submarine suffers a near miss from a depth charge the
crew get thrown about (understandable) and the lights
flicker (understandable) and water or steam escapes from
pipes which usually run along the walls of the control
room. All it seems to take to fix these is to turn a conveni-
ently placed stop-cock, whereupon everything is all right
again. Is this really what happened?**

☐ DURING a depth-charge attack the explosive pressure is distributed evenly around the hull of the submarine and the crew do
not get thrown around. The exploding charge produces a noise
which can be described as the loudest crack ever made and the
only movement of each crew member is involuntary muscle ten-
sioning and a momentarily slight sign of a protective crouch. This
reality cannot be reproduced on film and therefore the dramatic
presentation is to have the crew being thrown around. Yes, the
filaments of light do break, and dust and larger pieces of debris
are dislodged. I have no experience of pipes fracturing and allowing water or oil to escape, but isolation of any section could be

achieved by shutting valves, although a fractured pressure hull
valve would probably result in the loss of the boat.
H. J. Baker, Willesborough, Kent.

☐ THE effects of depth charging vary widely, depending on factors
such as water depth, the structure of the submarine and the position of each explosion relative to the submarine. In shallow water
the destructive range of a depth charge increases. I have experienced about 40 feet of a boat's hull being crushed in on one side.
All internal fittings, including hydraulic lines, in that area were
distorted or split, with consequent leakage of oil and water. With
riveted construction, hull distortion resulted in leaks which, when
spraying over electrical equipment, caused fires, fouling the air
and depleting its oxygen content. Compass readings, while these
were available, suggested that the boat was being swung bodily
by as much as 5 degrees by some explosions. This phenomenon,
together with the local crushing, indicated that the water-hammer
effect of a depth charge was by no means applied evenly over the
entire hull. It was certainly considered prudent to hold on tight,
and several crew members suffered severe bruising and lacera-
tions as a result of failure to observe that precaution.
G. D. Cuddon, Coventry.

**QUESTION: I heard recently that in the 1930s there was a
property in Bolton called Sod Hall, which my grandfather
wanted to buy. Did it, or does it, exist?**

☐ SOD HALL was a property off Clegg's Lane, Little Hulton, an
old district still referred to as 'near Bolton, Lancs'. It is shown on
the Ordnance Survey map, published 1 November 1950. The hall
is not mentioned in local guidebooks published by the Old Little
Hulton UDC, though many local people recall that a Victorian or
earlier building was there until a few years after the Second World
War. This was called Sod Hall Farm and was occupied by several
generations of the Shaw family. The farm was bulldozed in about

1960 to make way for new housing. The old name was revived by a tradesman who opened the Sod Hall Mini-Market and General Store almost opposite the original site, but the store closed a few years ago.
B. Rogerson, Swinton, Manchester.

☐ I CAN'T help the questioner, but on the Kent approaches to the Dartford Tunnel there is a house proudly called 'Llamedos'. I conclude that the owner is not Welsh but merely has an inverted sense of humour.
Peter Bourne, Ketton, Lincs.

☐ ON THE same lines, there is an ex-police house, now in private ownership, in the village of Hollesley, near the Suffolk coast. Its name these days is Evening Hall.
David Mackness, Ipswich.

☐ IN THE village Wisbech St Marys, in Cambridgeshire, there is a fancy house built a few years ago by a local entrepreneur with a reputation for doing regular battle with the authorities (particularly the planning department). The house is called Fockham Hall.
John Webb, New Romney, Kent.

QUESTION: Would the USA be radically different today if Kennedy had not been assassinated?

☐ WOULD Kennedy have avoided the urban rioting and the unwinnable land war in Vietnam that defeated the Johnson administration? Probably not – America would be no different today. In the domestic sphere, Kennedy was guilty of arousing too many expectations – particularly among ethnic minorities – that could not easily be fulfilled because of systemic constraints and, not least, his own political shortcomings. Arrogant in temperament, he was largely incapable of working with Congress. The legislative achievements of the Democrats in the late 1960s were implemented under President Johnson for the most part, and he was helped by the sympathetic consensus throughout America following the assassination. Even so, the pressure in favour of the Civil Rights Bill would eventually have led to its adoption whether Kennedy had lived or died. With regard to international affairs, it has to be said that Vietnam was Kennedy's war. He believed the superpower rivalry was entering a new phase, one of insurgency and counter-insurgency and, naturally, he wanted America to win it. (To this end, Kennedy created the Green Berets.) Unfortunately, the war in Indochina also diverted funds away from US domestic priorities. It seems probable that if Kennedy had lived for a second term, he would have faced the same problems which later tormented Johnson. The 'Camelot' legend would have been shattered for ever by 1968, and ironically, it would have been JFK's arch-enemy Richard Nixon – whom he defeated in 1960 – who would have dealt it the coup de grace by coming into office on a law-and-order platform as he actually did.

Tony Martin, London SE15.

☐ TONY Martin ignores clear evidence of Kennedy's intention to withdraw US forces from Vietnam. The Pentagon Papers (Senator Gravel edition, Vol. II, pp. 175–81) show that in July 1962 Kennedy directed McNamara to start planning the phased withdrawal of US personnel from Vietnam by the end of 1965. By May 1963 the plan was deemed in satisfactory shape. On 2 October 1963 Kennedy had McNamara announce from the White House steps the immediate withdrawal of 1,000 of the 15,500 Americans then in Vietnam (see, for example, O'Donnell and Powers, *Johnny We Hardly Knew Ye*, Ch. 1). There is no reason to suppose that, had he lived, JFK would have made a U-turn.

B. J. Burden, Bocking, Essex.

☐ B. J. BURDEN believes I ignored clear evidence of Kennedy's intention to pull US forces out of Vietnam quoting the Pentagon Papers (Vol. II). Yet the President had no discernible plans for a

complete withdrawal. Dean Rusk, JFK's secretary of state, stated unequivocally that he never heard the President even discuss total withdrawal. In a retrospective interview taped by John B. Martin in the spring of 1964, Robert Kennedy was asked directly: 'There was never any consideration given to pulling out?' Bobby replied: 'No.' Admittedly, President Kennedy signed a withdrawal memo on 11 October 1963 calling for the return of 1,000 'advisers', but this was as far as he was prepared to go. The memo was part of a White House ploy to scare President Diem of South Vietnam into making political reforms (as the State department informed the US embassy in Saigon). At an early stage of his administration's venture in South-East Asia, Kennedy told journalist James Reston: 'We have a problem in trying to make our power look credible and Vietnam looks like the place.' On 2 September 1963 he told Walter Cronkite: 'I don't agree with those who say we should withdraw. That would be a great mistake.' Instead, escalation would have been more tempting for Kennedy, especially given his enthusiasm for those counter-insurgency techniques that McNamara's enormous increase in military spending had secured.
Tony Martin, Nunhead, London SE15.

QUESTION: A fully-wound eight-day clock spring is dissolved in acid. What happens to its energy?

□ THE energy in a clock spring is known as 'strain energy' – energy caused by the distortion of a solid. The distortion affects the distance and forces between every atom in the clock spring. It is as though each atom were tied to its neighbours by pieces of stretched elastic. Winding up the spring stretches the 'elastic' more than usual. Dissolving the clock spring by acid appears to be a continuous process. However, it occurs atom by atom, which means breaking each bond one at a time. As each bond breaks, individual atoms fly off at high speed. They collide with the molecules in the acid, thereby increasing their own average speed. We sense this increase in speed as an increase in temperature.

Hence, when you dissolve a metal in acid it gets hot. The strain energy in a clock spring causes the atoms to fly off slightly faster than normal. You would find that the acid would be a fraction of a degree warmer when a wound-up clock spring was used compared to an unwound one.

Fred Starr, (BSc, CEng), London SW16.

QUESTION: I am at a loss as to the origin – etymologically and socio-linguistically speaking – of the word 'spiv'. I wonder if your readers can go beyond 'palindrome of VIPs'.

☐ THE suggested palindrome seems wide of the mark, particularly as its early usage appears to have been exclusively cockney working-class, usually with criminal connotations. My father, Bill Naughton, besides giving 'spiv' the currency which it enjoyed in the 1940s (thanks mainly to an article of his which appeared in the first issue of Charles Madge's sociological quarterly *Pilot Papers*, and later in the *News Chronicle*), suggested it was an acronym. In a volume of his autobiography, published in 1987 – five years before he died – he wrote: 'it was customary for the police from a certain West End police station to keep that area of London free of tramps and beggars. A man of disreputable appearance daring to walk around Belgravia would be taken into custody, and described on the charge sheet as "Suspected Person: Itinerant Vagabond" with the capital letters prominent.'

L. M. Naughton, Southgate, West Sussex.

☐ BREWER'S *Dictionary of Phrase and Fable* says that it is probably an abbreviation of 'spiffing', an old slang word meaning 'fine', 'excellent', an allusion to flash, dandified appearance.

H. G. Hereward, Toller Porcorum, Dorset.

☐ BILL Naughton may have given the word 'spiv' national currency, as L. M. Naughton says, but he was wide of the mark in

suggesting it had anything to do with people of disreputable appearance. Brewer's guess that it abbreviates 'spiffing' is also unlikely, as that was a public school word never used by cockneys. My recollection is that it came into being among South Londoners during the war and originally meant someone who dressed in a certain flash style in suits tailor-made by a Mr Spivack. Spivacks, or spivs, came to mean civilians who dressed in that style (at the time of the zoot suit in America) and could afford to throw their money around. Bearing in mind wartime conditions, most were petty black-market operators, some small-time criminals, sometimes itinerant, but not vagrants. Some spivs carried shivs (knives) so there was also an element of rhyming slang.
A. E. Meltzer, London SE13.

☐ WHEN I was an infant in wartime London, the cavity of my bassinette pram was often used to transport black-market goods around Bermondsey (with me gurgling disarmingly on top). I can therefore state with some authority that SPIVs originated during the Second World War as the characters who dealt in illicit Supplementary Petrol Issue Vouchers, which were even more precious than nylons.
Ron Birch, Stroud, Glos.

QUESTION: How can I become a ventriloquist?

☐ STUDY Hillary Clinton.
David Tebb, Guiseley, Leeds.

☐ GRACTICE.
Paul Tickle, Leicester.

☐ OBTAIN a copy of *Adventures of a Ventriloquist: Many Hints for Beginners* from my second-hand bookshop, for £6.50 including p&p.
Steve King, Boutle & King, 23 Arlington Way, London EC1R 1UY (071-278 4497).

**QUESTION: Postmodernists say there is no objective truth.
Why should anyone believe them?**

☐ AS THE question suggests, postmodernism is self-sabotaging,
like all sufficiently radical forms of scepticism and reductionism.
Unlike some earlier forms, however, it is based on an elementary
confusion between truth and certainty: although no person or
group can justifiably claim complete objectivity, it does not follow
that there is no truth, just that we should not place anything
beyond the possibility of revision. Since postmodernism is a
fashion statement rather than a philosophical position (I think
many postmodernists would accept this), it need not be taken
seriously intellectually. It is, however, morally pernicious: if there
is no objective truth, then it is not objectively true that *The
Protocols of the Learned Elders of Zion* is a forgery, or that the Gulf
war took place – Baudrillard has in fact denied that it did. Postmodernism also demonstrates, under the guise of opposing all-encompassing views of the world, the most extreme self-importance
and intellectual imperialism: claiming as it does that the world
consists only of texts, it implies that literary criticism encompasses
all other disciplines.
Nick Gotts, Leeds.

☐ IN RESPONSE to Nick Gott, what possibly needs clarifying is the
belief that postmodernism denies truth. Certainly there is within
the field of postmodernism a rejection of any single objective
'Truth' leading to ultimate enlightenment and so on, but there is
still an acceptance, indeed the promotion, of many subjective
'truths' rather than none at all. Truth thus becomes contextually
reliant rather than all-encompassing. Reality is another matter
entirely: I think that what Baudrillard was probably saying was
that the Gulf war wasn't a war as such, more a kind of movie war,
choreographed for the cameras. As to postmodernism being a
fashion: well possibly, but only insomuch as the dominant theories
of any epoch are fashionable. Finally, I believe that it confuses
matters to think of postmodernism as an 'it', as there are many

conflicting theories employing the term trying to get a hold of a
complex theoretical spatial temporality: the here and now.
Andrew F. Wilson, London E7.

**QUESTION: The phrase 'We'll head 'em off at the pass' is
one of the best-known Western film clichés. But in which
films does it actually occur – other than *Blazing Saddles*,
where Mel Brooks is well aware of its clichéd status?**

☐ IT IS older than the cinema, by a long way. In Sophocles'
Oedipus at Colonus, Theseus speaks roughly about catching a
hostage party 'where the hill road forks'.
Oonagh Lahr, Muswell Hill, London N10.

QUESTION: Are 'iron lungs' still in use in the NHS today?

☐ THE iron lung or tank ventilator was in widespread use in the
1940s and 1950s, particularly for people with breathing muscle
weakness due to poliomyelitis. The patient is enclosed in the iron
lung chamber from the neck down and ventilation is aided by
applying negative pressure to the chest wall. Although a cumbersome beast, the iron lung came back into vogue a decade ago and
was then used to treat a wider range of breathing problems including respiratory failure due to curvature of the spine and chronic
bronchitis, and breathing difficulties during sleep. Newer, more
sophisticated, models have been developed, but over the last five
years the technique of nasal positive pressure ventilation has
begun to overtake negative pressure ventilation as the treatment
of choice in these conditions. Probably around 100 individuals
continue to use the iron lung in hospital or at home in the UK.
*A. K. Simonds, Consultant in Respiratory Medicine, Royal
Brompton Hospital, London SW3.*

QUESTION: What is the origin of the classification of wood screws (e.g. 8 × 1)?

☐ THIS perverse and sentimental usage by the largest English screw-maker is a persuasive reason for preferring the imported competition. The '8' is the screw shank diameter in an obscure 'screw gauge' related neither to the wire gauge anciently used for (some) nails, nor to any other known number series. The second figure is the length in the obsolete inch measure. Under the 1963 productivity and efficiency initiative of the Confederation of British Industry and the British Standards Institute, this should have been dropped from carpentry (and all other building work) as far back as 1971. The metric equivalent of $8 \times 1 - 4.2 \times 25$ mm – can be grasped instantly by anybody without having served an apprenticeship, and readily and directly related to the job in hand. With the metric figures anybody can instantly and confidently pick up the correct drill bits for both pilot and clearance holes.
Vivian Levett, London SE21.

QUESTION: What was the good news that they brought from Ghent to Aix?

☐ AIX is besieged and about to surrender; the good news is that help is on the way. This is the implied meaning of line 46 of Robert Browning's poem, 'the news which alone could save Aix from her fate'. The explanation is Browning's, but he gave it with reluctance; he always insisted that the ride itself was what mattered. He said that he wrote the poem 'on board ship off Tangiers', when he 'had been at sea long enough to appreciate even the fancy of a gallop'. There is no historical foundation for the episode: according to Browning it reflects a 'general impression of the characteristic warfare and besieging that abounds in the annals of Flanders'.
D. Karlin (co-editor, The Poems of Browning, *Longman Annotated English Poets, 1991).*

QUESTION: I have heard that the Treasury uses a computer program to model the economy, and that it is in the public domain. How can I get hold of a copy to run on my PC?

☐ THE public version of the Treasury model is available on a subscription basis through the ITEM (Independent Treasury Economic Modelling) Club. There are three components: the model itself (a collection of mathematical equations); a database of historical and projected variables, and an operating system. The database consists of historical quarterly data from 1971 to present. Variables are projected for 10 years by ITEM for forecasting purposes. ITEM updates the database quarterly to include new data releases, while the model itself is updated annually (with the revised version as released by the Treasury). In order to solve the model, a user needs a PC with 1.5 Mbytes of memory, a maths co-processor and approximately 4 Mbytes of hard disk storage. It is also advisable to have VGA graphics capability. Naturally, the model comes with full documentation, as well as support from the ITEM Club. The annual subscription rate is £2,600 plus VAT.
Paul Droop, ITEM Club, London SE1.

QUESTION: Would it be possible to construct an airship which was propelled and steered by sails?

☐ A SAILING boat works because it uses the opposing forces imposed on it by the air and the water. Because the hull (usually with a deep keel) is largely in the water, it resists the thrust of the sails. The rudder, too, is in the water. Thus, when a wind comes from the side, sideways movement is prevented by the water, and the boat goes forward like a dried bean squeezed from between the fingers. An airship is not dipped in a more resistant medium. It is entirely immersed in air. Thus, there are no opposing forces involved. A sailing airship would simply be blown along, twisting

and turning in an uncontrolled way – which is exactly what happens to an airship now if it loses its power.
Gerald Haigh, project editor, Association for Science Education, University of Warwick.

☐ IT COULD be done. Gerald Haigh is right when he says that a sailing boat works because it uses the opposing forces imposed upon it by the wind and water. The problem is to generate these opposing forces in mid-air. There are two intriguing possibilities. The first is to adapt the principle by which unpowered, sail-less barges were once navigated on the river Hull in East Yorkshire. By dragging an anchor from the bow to reduce their speed to less than that of the tidal flow, such barges were able to steer effectively while travelling astern in the general direction of the current, the speed difference causing a steady flow of water over their rudders. An airship dragging an anchor over land, or a sea-anchor over water, could be steered in a similar fashion. An even better possibility might be to exploit the fact that wind speeds and directions are far from constant at different altitudes above a given point on the earth's surface. Thus, an airship flying at, say, 10,000 feet might be driven by a 15-knot wind, while at 15,000 feet the wind might be 30 knots. Obviously a 'mast' long enough to exploit this difference would be impractical, but 'sails' resembling a large kite or a modern steerable parachute could be launched up into the zone of faster winds, and the tension between airship and kite used to navigate in the same manner as a sailing boat. There are obviously many technical difficulties with this approach but, theoretically, 'tacking', i.e. zigzagging into the wind, should be possible. If Richard Branson is reading this and would like to contact me, I could develop for him the means of crossing the Atlantic by balloon from East to West. Cash up front, of course.
John Ramsey, London E3.

QUESTION: Makers of mains radio and television sets recommend unplugging if the house is to be left unattended

during a holiday. A fireman has recommended that they be
left plugged in but switched off at the mains socket to provide a route to earth should a condenser discharge. Which
is correct?

☐ THE fireman is wrong. Condensers, correctly known as capa-
citors, store electrical charge. In a TV or radio they would only ever
discharge through their associated circuitry within the television,
and not to earth. In any event most televisions nowadays are not
earthed – note the two-core (live and neutral) mains cable.
Charles Turner, Stockport, Cheshire.

☐ MOST mains sockets only have the live terminal wired up to the
switch, so if the socket has been wired incorrectly (i.e. live wire to
neutral terminal), when the plug is left inserted and the socket
switched off the appliance remains live even though it won't operate. Even with the socket wired correctly, the condition of the
switch could make the appliance unsafe if left. The safest way
would be to turn the plug upside down and insert only the earth
pin into the socket (this is possible because of its longer length).
Even though the pin cannot be inserted fully, there will still be a
connection because the earth terminal in the socket is close to the
surface. Also remove connection leads to outdoor aerials in case of
lightning.
Peer Czerwinka, Eccles, Manchester.

QUESTION: What happened to the only British serviceman to refuse repatriation at the end of the Korean war?

☐ THE marine, Andrew Condron, was indoctrinated in a Chinese
prisoner-of-war camp in Korea. The Chinese initially convinced
him that the Americans had used germ warfare, and this seems to
have influenced his decision to live on in China. As a result of this
Chinese propaganda coup, the British Foreign Office was concerned to know 'the state of Condron's mind' with a view to

persuading him to return to the West. However, this plan was foiled when Lt-Col J. L. Lindop of the Intelligence Division of the Admiralty confirmed to A. L. Mayall of the Foreign Office that the Navy 'regard Condron as a deserter and . . . he is liable to be arrested and charged with desertion . . .' Unsurprisingly Condron stayed on in China. By 1959, however, the Foreign Office considered Condron to be an embarrassment to the Chinese and monitored his conduct – and the Chinese reaction – with the greatest glee. The British Embassy in Peking reported that Condron was becoming disillusioned with the Chinese regime and uncontrollable. The embassy official spoke of 'song and drink on a fairly hearty scale' and concluded that 'while he is here, particularly if he is indeed becoming disgruntled, there is a chance of his becoming quite an embarrassment to them'. Drinking was not the only activity that the Foreign Office considered a potential embarrassment to the Chinese: Condron had 'involved two Chinese girls in serious political difficulties when he became too friendly' to them. The obvious relish of the Foreign Office at this was soon to turn to their own embarrassment when Condron began a relationship with a Jaqueline Hsiung Baudet, the illegitimate daughter of Philippe Baudet, a leading French diplomat. I am not sure what happened to Condron after 1959. I believe he married Jaqueline but I cannot confirm this. He faced arrest from the Admiralty if he returned to the West. He was disillusioned with the Chinese regime, unable to keep down a steady job and had vague plans to move to Czechoslovakia 'because it has the highest standard of living in the socialist bloc'. His girlfriend was being questioned for 'consorting with an Imperialist'. Indeed, the only positive thing to come out of Condron's experience, according to the Foreign Office, was that 'his Glasgow accent seems to have vanished'. This information was compiled from diplomatic files available at the Public Record Office, Kew. Wherever he is now, I wish Marine Andrew Condron the best of luck.

Patrick Dransfield, London NW3.

□ PATRICK Dransfield seems to have left his critical faculties at the front door when he visited the Public Record Office. Marine Andrew Condron was not persuaded to stay on in China because of rumours of the Americans' use of germ warfare; he was basically motivated by an admiration for the Chinese as a nation. Also present in the equation was a youthful spirit of adventure. Under the terms of the ceasefire treaty, any prisoner on either side was entitled to remain with his captors. Some 25,000 North Koreans took this opportunity, as did 22 UN personnel. Several more of his fellow British POWs wanted to stay but were dissuaded by the Chinese (who also tried to persuade Condron to return home). During his time in Peking, he applied for, and was given, all of his back-pay for the period of his incarceration and in 1961 he received an honourable discharge from the Royal Marines with the conduct rating 'very good'. This is the highest classification a Royal Marine can achieve. The British Embassy's glee at the 'scandal' they uncovered about Mr Condron's liking for a few drinks and the company of attractive members of the opposite sex makes one wonder what planet they were living on. As he was a vigorous 27-year-old, who had recently been released from three years' imprisonment under very harsh conditions, it would have been very surprising if his thoughts had turned in any other direction. It is now strange that the 'legitimacy' (a rather outmoded concept) of Mr Condron's girlfriend, who later became his wife, is called into question. Her father, Philippe Baudet, later French ambassador in Moscow, always maintained that he had married her mother in church, although perhaps the Chinese authorities did not recognise the union. It is unfortunate that this rather taste-less insinuation is made now. Mr and Mrs Condron returned to Britain in 1962 and have lived here ever since. In 1986, Mr Condron was at a reunion in the Royal Marine Commando School at Lympstone near Exeter and he has attended several other gatherings. Some of his fellow POWs recommended him for a decoration on their return from captivity in recogniton of his efforts, while a prisoner, to save lives and improve living conditions. Needless to say, these suggestions fell on deaf ears.

Michael McDermott, Abergavenny, Gwent.

☐ IN ABOUT 1963 a man came to our door selling the *Encyclopae-dia Britannica*. He was extremely nice, my parents bought the encyclopaedia and we became friends. This was Andrew Condron. The former serviceman showed us newspaper cuttings about him-self and talked about his life in China. By this time he was married to Jaqueline (who was working as a producer for the BBC World Service) and they had a son, whose name was, I think, Simon. We remained friends for a few years and I think Andrew returned to journalism. In the mid-1970s I bumped into Jaqueline on a bus. She was still working for the BBC and their son was planning to go to Cambridge. By this time Andrew and Jaqueline had di-vorced. I can confirm that Andrew liked to drink spirits but the files quoted are wrong when they say that he had lost his Glasgow accent.
David Freedman, London NW2.

QUESTION: Each plastic lid on a tube of Smarties has a letter of the alphabet embossed upon it. Does it have a purpose?

☐ DURING my prefectorial tenure as a school tuck-shop manager 20 years ago, I consumed many thousands of Smarties and built up a fine collection of Smartie tops. One or two of the chaps were slightly impressed. I wrote to Rowntrees, asking if this might en-title me to a substantial prize in recognition of my patronage of their splendid product, and whether there was any point in saving the tops. They sent no prize and seemed unsure of the purpose of the moulded letters beyond suggesting that they could perhaps be helpful for early reading skills. I ate no more Smarties.
John V. Chamberlain, Letchworth, Herts.

☐ MOST children are very acquisitive. Once they possess one of these bright, attractively coloured, durable, satisfyingly round and holdable discs they will want more – at least enough to spell their

name, if not the alphabet, or at worst (or best for Rowntree) the complete works of Roald Dahl.
S. Rogers, Ellesmere Port, South Wirral.

QUESTION: Does anyone know the whereabouts of Hancock's paintings from his film, *The Rebel*?

☐ THERE is an exhibition of Picasso's work in Antibes, France, where, in one of the gallery rooms stands Tony Hancock's Aphrodite sculpture. Either that or Picasso was greatly influenced by the school of Hancock.
Jane Noar, Chandler's Ford, Hants.

QUESTION: How are chocolate-coated sweets like Maltesers kept spherical while the chocolate sets?

☐ ONLY Mars knows the secret, but I can reveal that the sweets are continually (and cleverly) rolled in a drum as the chocolate dries, producing perfectly spherical Maltesers.
Kay Randall, Mars Confectionery, Slough.

QUESTION: Why is a dog's nose cold?

☐ SIMPLY because it's moist, therefore its surface cools – as does damp skin under certain conditions. Usually, a dog's nose is continuously kept moist (by licking) though, unlike skin, its surface does not warm up to such a degree. But it must be pointed out that a dog's nose is not always cold; quite the opposite when exposed to high temperatures, especially with low humidity, for a period of time.
M. Moody, Great Bookham, Surrey.

☐ NOAH'S ark sprang a leak, so he sent the dog to plug it with his nose. But the hole was too big, so he sent Mrs Noah to stop it with

her elbow. But it was still too big, so he sat on it and sent Shem to mend it. That's why dog's noses are cold, women have cold elbows and men lift their coat tails to warm their backsides at the fire. So my mother (born 1910) told me.
(Mrs) H. D. Maclean, Argyll.

QUESTION: The film *When Worlds Collide* ends with 43 people leaving a doomed Earth to start a new life on an uninhabited planet. With all the other circumstances being favourable, would 43 be a viable number to propagate a new race?

☐ AS LONG as they were not all men, all women or committed or practising homosexuals and/or lesbians, I don't see why not. One man and 42 women (assuming their offspring produced a mix of sexes) could do very nicely; or with more men (ergo fewer women) if the avoidance of incest were to be important. On the other hand, it takes 64 great-great-great-great-great-grandparents to produce one child.
F.G. Robinson, Glasgow.

QUESTION: Are there scientists trying to prove that astrology is true?

☐ NO, BECAUSE proof that astrology is true would, ipso facto, be proof that the whole of science is false.
B. J. Hazzard, London SE21.

☐ YES. Michel Gauquelin, a French statistical scientist (1928–1991) and his wife, Françoise, analysed the birth dates of many thousands of professional people. Their findings prove beyond doubt that certain planets do have a significant effect on personality traits and the choice of profession. Dr Percy Seymour, Principal Lecturer in Astronomy at Plymouth Polytechnic, has developed a theory which incorporates the latest advances in

astronomy, space science, solar physics, geomagnetism and biology (published in 1988 as *Astrology: The Evidence of Science*).
Kenneth Woodward, Wrexham, Clwyd.

☐ CONTRARY to what Kenneth Woodward implies, science con-
siders all kinds of astrology as thoroughly debunked. Every
double-blind study of astrology's claims to date has found them
to be useless, most notably a famous paper in the British journal,
Nature (5 December 1985, p. 419). Mr Woodward does not mention that Michel Gauquelin arrived at the same conclusion (that
'classical' astrology is nonsense) before inventing a completely
different astrological concept of his own. Unfortunately (for his
followers) the 'Mars Effect' that it rests upon has never been verified with any data set other than Gauquelin's own. Thus the
answer to the initial question is no, science isn't interested in astrology any more . . . no observable effect, no need to investigate
any 'causes'.
Daniel Fischer, editor-in-chief, Skyweek *(Astronomische
Nachrichten), Konigswinter, Germany.*

**QUESTION: Returning from the hairdressers, I noticed a
cut on the back of my neck, presumably caused by a razor.
Is it possible to catch the HIV virus in this way? Are hairdressers obliged to sterilise equipment?**

☐ THE virus is very fragile and is killed by soap and water, and
ordinary household disinfectants. It cannot survive for a significant time outside the body. *The National AIDS Manual* (published by NAM Publications) states that there is a very low theoretical
risk of being infected by 'sharing a razor or electric shaver'. This
is because 'the virus needs to get into the bloodstream in fairly
large quantities'. This would be extremely unlikely in the case
described. For further information on any health issue, including
HIV and AIDS, ring 0800 838 909. Calls are free and confidential,
and lines are open between 10a.m. and 10p.m. every day.
Dave Watkins, Healthwise Helpline, Liverpool 2.

QUESTION: Does anybody know the location of a quote which I think comes from Kingsley Amis: 'Never let a day go by without annoying someone'?

☐ THE Pan *Dictionary of Contemporary Quotations* includes the following from Kingsley Amis: 'If you can't annoy somebody, there's little point in writing' (*Radio Times*, 1971). In order to give my letter some point, I hope this will be of no help whatsoever to the questioner.
Amanda Tolworthy, Basingstoke, Hants.

QUESTION: I am told there are only two words in the English language that end in '. . . amt'. One of them is 'dreamt'; what is the other?

☐ SORRY the answer is so prosaic: the other word is 'undreamt'. This can be verified in Chambers' *Backwords for Crosswords*.
Andrew Shields, London E11.

QUESTION: Has there ever actually been a book in which 'the butler did it'?

☐ OF COURSE there has – one of Sherlock Holmes's very first cases, *The Musgrave Trial*. Investigating a suspicious light in the library at dead of night, Reginald Musgrave of Hurlstone Manor caught his butler, Brunton, red-handed, prying into confidential family papers. However, the philandering Brunton has the double distinction of being the butler who had it done to him as well. Attempting to involve her as his accomplice, he was ultimately lured into a trap and murdered by his former mistress, the passionate Celtic maid Rachel Howells.
Tim Owen, London SW19.

☐ YES – in *The Complete Steel* by Catherine Aird, published by

Corgi. A true classic detective story, written with a light touch and
well worth reading – even if you now know who did it.
Mrs A. M. Loughborough, Alton, Hants.

☐THE butler did it in *The Ivory Dagger* by Patricia Wentworth. In
another of her books, *The Benevent Treasure*, the butler and his
employer are jointly responsible for the murky goings-on. In a
third, *The Case is Closed*, the butler is a paid accomplice to the
original murder and is later only prevented from murdering his
wife by Mrs Wentworth's redoubtable spinster detective, Maud
Silver.
A. Robinson, Sheffield.

☐ I DON'T know about the butler, but in *Lady Chatterley's Lover*
it was the gamekeeper who did it.
F. G. Robinson, Glasgow.

**QUESTION: Why, of all musical instruments, has the
organ been chosen for use in churches?**

☐ HAVING a keyboard for the feet, it is the only instrument on
which you can play 'Hear My Prayer' with your hands clasped
together.
A. E. Baker, Pytchley, Northants.

☐ CHURCH services from the 1600s onward were often accompanied by local musicians, playing a variety of instruments. However, relations between these church bands and the local parson
were sometimes rather strained. Thomas Hardy, in *Absent
Mindedness in a Parish Choir*, recounts how the members of one
such band, being suddenly roused after a sermon one very dark
afternoon, forgot where they were and started playing the dance
music they had performed at a party the previous evening. The
local squire insisted on replacing them with a barrel organ that
could play 'two and twenty new psalm tunes'. With an organ one

could get a wide range of sounds and better volume from one person than from a motley band; and with less risk of personality clashes. It is interesting to note that things have gone almost full circle, since many churches now have musical groups drawn from their congregations. This is seen particularly in those churches that meet in schools or other non-church buildings.
John Webb, St Albans, Herts.

QUESTION: Why are 'inverted commas' only inverted on one side?

☐ AS THE question implies, to describe quotation marks as inverted commas is only half true. The reason is that printed characters have evolved from hand scripts. If you draw curved quotation marks by hand with an old-fashioned (thick and thin) pen nib, the opening commas will be thicker at the base and the closing ones thicker at the top, due to the different angles of the pen strokes. Printers' typefaces usually imitate this effect. Incidentally, office typewriters save a key by having neutrally orientated marks which can be used at either end of the quotation. Neither of these is inverted but nor, perhaps, are they really commas.
Trevor Denning, Birmingham.

QUESTION: Why do many people confuse left and right (when giving directions, for example) but not up and down? Is it simply because of gravity?

☐ YES. We evolved from little wormy things swimming about in the sea where a sense of up and down was important – to swim up would result in reaching the surface, to swim down would eventually mean crash-diving into the seabed. But whether to swim to the left or to the right was hugely unimportant – one encountered still more sea in either direction. As we made it on to dry land, gravity gave us a top and a bottom and locomotion gave

us a front and a back. We can easily distinguish top from bottom thanks to gravity (top is furthest from the centre of the earth) and we can determine our front from our back since our sense organs are fixed facing front where they can tell us where we're going rather than where we've been. We cannot, however, determine our left from our right without resorting to a variety of conventions unique to this planet (and not easily communicable to alien intelligences). The notion of left/right implies asymmetry and plenty of natural examples exist to establish this convention – the anticlockwise twists and helixes of certain molluscs and plants, Maxwell's Corkscrew Rule in electromagnetics, the 'handedness' of certain molecules and crystalline structures, etc. Most of us can remember the convention by virtue of our own inbuilt left or right dominance, whether we are in the dextral majority or in the sinistral minority. If one tends towards ambidextrousness it becomes more difficult and one has to resort to established asymmetric conventions such as checking the button-hole on the left side of a jacket. But for such a person, naked and without recourse to any form of asymmetric object the problem is still more difficult since our external appearance is essentially bilaterally symmetrical – apart from the male whose left testicle often hangs lower than the right. I make absolutely no correlation between this and the male's ability or otherwise in giving left/right directions.
A. Reader, London SW1.

☐ I RAISED this very question with my wife nearly 30 years ago because I am one of those 'many people'. She told me it was because I had not had the benefit of a Roman Catholic upbringing. Apparently, making the sign of the cross depends on conquering the confusion.
Professor Alan Alexander, Hellensburgh, Scotland.

QUESTION: J. E. Galliard (1687–1749) is reputed to have written a piece for 24 bassoons and four double basses. What is it called and has anyone assembled such a formidable consort to record it?

□ JOHN Ernest Galliard was born in France, the son of a Huguenot wig-maker. He came to England at the age of 19 where he made his name as, among other things, a composer of opera in English, as opposed to the customary Italian. He is well known to bassoon players for whom he wrote six sonatas. It is true that he wrote a concerto grosso for 24 bassoons and cello continuo, but unfortunately the manuscript was lost.
Andrew Morris, Alec Forshaw, Martin White (The Galliard Trio), London N1.

QUESTION: Where and when was the first one-way street introduced in Britain?

□ DURING the first 10 or 20 years of the 19th century, Italian opera was so popular at the King's Theatre in London, and the Haymarket so crowded that 'the nobility were asked to give directions to their servants to set down and take up at the theatre with their horses' heads turned towards Pall Mall'.
John Cooper, Cheam, Surrey.

QUESTION: The Danube Waves by the Romanian I. Ivanovici (1845–1902) is so much like Johann Strauss's The Blue Danube that one suspects plagiarism by one or the other. Did these two men ever meet?

□ I CAN discern no similarity between these waltzes, except perhaps in the titles. The Ivanovici is predominantly in minor keys; the Strauss in major keys throughout.
Michael Maxwell (MMus, PhD, LRAM), London W4.

QUESTION: Oxygen, ozone and water vapour are heavier than air, yet none of them sinks under gravity. Water vapour forms layers we call clouds, the ozone layer is some

15–30km high and oxygen doesn't form a layer at all. Why?

☐ THIS question really deserves the attention of a meteorologist but in case they are all too busy I offer the following: the main constituents of the (dry) atmosphere are nitrogen and oxygen at 78 per cent and 21 per cent respectively. Most of the remaining 1 per cent is argon, with carbon dioxide and other trace components making up the balance. The process which prevents these gases settling out into layers is diffusion and this arises from the random motion of the molecules. Since nitrogen and oxygen are quite close in density, diffusion is very rapid and ensures an almost perfect mixture in the atmosphere. This is just as well, otherwise these gases would separate in still air and we would need noses at about knee level to ensure that we did not encounter oxygen deficiency on entering a closed room. Contrary to the statement in the question, the density of water vapour is much less than that of dry air. Water vapour enters the atmosphere at ground level and is carried upwards in rising thermal currents of warm, moist air. At high altitude the low temperature becomes important and the water condenses, forming clouds. Under the correct circumstances, and particularly in a region of the atmosphere directly above Manchester (the *Guardian* should be ideally placed to confirm this phenomenon), the clouds further coalesce into large droplets which then fall as rain. Above the 12km lower atmosphere where the effects of weather systems predominate are regions of rarefied atmosphere with few vertical currents which form stable strata, mixing very slowly with the layers above and below. The ozone layer exists at this level and interacts with sunlight, making the stratosphere warmer than the region below. Long-lived gases such as the well-known CFCs can be effectively trapped in the static layers of the stratosphere and may tend to accumulate over periods of years with effects not fully understood but much debated .

Colin Townsend, Birkenshaw, Bradford.

□ THEY all try to sink, but a gas is not a stable fixed object. Individual atoms are stuck together into molecules, which are themselves vibrated constantly by thermal energy which stops them condensing as a liquid or cystallising out as a solid or, if you like, keeps the mud stirred. The white droplets in fresh milk do not settle out for similar reasons. Air containing water vapour is indeed denser than dry air, but if it is warmer, up it goes to become cloudy air. The atmosphere is not stable and neatly layered, or meteorologists would be out of a job and we would have no weather. The tiny droplets making up clouds are actually falling but the bigger the faster, till they become rain. Ozone is not stable at all, but has to be supplemented daily by the ultraviolet in sunlight acting on oxygen molecules, but only if there are no chlorine molecules such as CFCs to destroy the reaction. This ozone is not a stable layer like a blanket, but a zone where this process is most active. Below this 'layer,' most of the short wavelength ultraviolet has been soaked up by the process. Ozone is a rather nasty chemical best kept up high, but if we succeed in destroying this zone, the ultraviolet will continue this process at ground level, bathing our cancerous bodies in toxic gas.

Dave Brinicombe, Ealing, London W5.

INDEX